THE ESSENTIAL
MENGZI

THE ESSENTIAL
MENGZI

SELECTED PASSAGES WITH
TRADITIONAL COMMENTARY

Translated, with Introduction and Notes, by
BRYAN W. VAN NORDEN

Hackett Publishing Company, Inc.
Indianapolis/Cambridge

19 18 17 16   2 3 4 5 6

For further information, please address:

Hackett Publishing Company, Inc.
P.O. Box 44937
Indianapolis, IN 46244-0937
www.hackettpublishing.com

Cover design by Abigail Coyle
Text design by Carrie Wagner
Composition by Agnew's, Inc.

Library of Congress Cataloging-in-Publication Data

Mencius.
    [Mengzi. English]
    The essential Mengzi : selected passages with traditional commentary
/ translated, with introduction and notes, by Bryan Van Norden. —
[Abridged ed.]
        p.   cm.
    Includes bibliographical references.
    ISBN 978-0-87220-986-2 (cloth) — ISBN 978-0-87220-985-5 (pbk.)
    1. Mencius. Mengzi.   I. Van Norden, Bryan W. (Bryan William)
II. Title.
    PL2474.Z6M3613   2009
    181'.112—dc22   2009026713

CONTENTS

ORIGINAL PREFACE

I first read Mengzi (Mencius) out of a sense of intellectual obligation. I was studying Chinese philosophy, and he is historically important, so I felt that I ought to be familiar with him. I found him somewhat intriguing but uninspiring. But the influence of three of my teachers at Stanford fundamentally altered my reading of Mengzi. First, Lee H. Yearley impressed upon me the hermeneutic principle that we must read classic texts carefully and charitably. Second, the work of David S. Nivison introduced me to the grammatical and lexical complexities of Mengzi's Chinese. Third, Philip J. Ivanhoe taught me the importance of classical commentaries and how to read them. As a result, I changed not only my understanding of Mengzi but also my outlook on life. I have come to see the *Mengzi* as one of the treasures of world literature, easily in a class with Plato's *Republic*, the Qur'an, and the Bhagavad Gita.

This translation began with a series of "Comments and Corrections to D. C. Lau's *Mencius*," which I first wrote in 1991 to help my students. Much of this was cribbed from my teachers' classroom presentations as well as Nivison's "On Translating Mencius."[1] I gradually translated more and more portions of the *Mengzi* for use in my own classes. Then when Ivanhoe and I coedited *Readings in Classical Chinese Philosophy*, I finally was able to publish much of my work. However, I still hoped to produce a complete translation.

In order to provide something genuinely distinctive, I formulated the project of translating the *Mengzi* along with all of Zhu Xi's commentary on it from his *Sishu jizhu* ("Collected Commentaries on the *Four Books*"). In 2005 I was awarded a National Endowment for the Humanities grant and a Fulbright fellowship to work on completing this project while at Academia Sinica in Taiwan. Hackett Publishing gave me a contract to publish the resulting work. My editor at Hackett, Deborah Wilkes, has been immensely helpful at every stage, showing Confucian "timeliness" in knowing when to be patient and when to enforce deadlines. At my request, she has offered substantive suggestions and repeatedly solicited outside feedback on drafts of the translation.

---

[1]   David S. Nivison, "On Translating Mencius," was originally published in *Philosophy East and West* in 1980 and reprinted in Nivison, *The Ways of Confucianism* (Chicago: Open Court Press, 1996), 175–201.

Paul R. Goldin, Justin Tiwald, Stephen C. Angle, and several anonymous referees provided invaluable advice. As a result of their suggestions, I changed the project from a scholarly translation of the *Mengzi* with Zhu Xi's complete commentary to a more idiomatic rendering with a commentary that is intended to make the work accessible to the general reader. I still frequently cite Zhu Xi's commentary, but my primary aim is to elucidate the text for a contemporary audience. Harbour Hodder, my copyeditor, made suggestions that greatly improved the readability of the final draft. And, of course, I would be remiss if I failed to thank Kongzi (Confucius), Mengzi, Zhu Xi, and the countless others who have transmitted the Way down to us.

The commentary in this translation is primarily interpretive and historical. For grammatical and lexical notes on this translation, go to www.hackett publishing.com and look under "Title Information" for "Title Support Pages," which leads to a link to my detailed textual notes.

PREFACE TO THE ESSENTIAL MENGZI

I have been very gratified by the positive response to my original translation, *Mengzi: with Selections from Traditional Commentaries*.[2] However, no one version of a text can meet the needs of every audience. *The Essential Mengzi* differs from the earlier version in three major ways. First, it is a selective translation that allows students to focus on what are perhaps the most historically important and philosophically engaging passages. Provided that we use such an abridgement in the right way, Zhu Xi would approve: "In reading, don't strive for quantity. Instead become intimately familiar with what you do read. If today you are able to read a page, read half a page; read that half page over and over with all your strength."[3] Second, the format of this version differs from that of the earlier translation. The translation has been separated from the commentary, in place of the original interlineal commentary. In the body of the translation, the character 注 indicates that a passage has corresponding commentary. A handful of footnotes are used with the translation, but only at points where I judge the first-time reader is very likely to be confused or to miss an important nuance of the text without some guidance. Identifications of passages that Mengzi cites from the *Analects*, *Odes*, and *Documents* are found in the Finding List, not in footnotes. Third, I have made a handful of stylistic changes (mostly due to helpful suggestions from my copyeditor, Kate Lawn), and one significant content change (in 3A2.3).

Conventions

- Unless otherwise identified, quotations from commentary are from Zhu Xi's commentary on the relevant passage in the *Sishu jizhu* ("Collected Commentaries on the *Four Books*").

---

[2] See, e.g., Hui-chieh Loy, *Notre Dame Philosophical Reviews* (March 29, 2009), http://ndpr.nd.edu/review.cfm?id=15648, Aaron Stalnaker, *Journal of Religion* 89 (April 2009): 280–82, and Jeffrey L. Richey, *Religious Studies Review* 35:1 (March 2009): 75–6.

[3] Daniel K. Gardner, trans., *Learning to Be a Sage: Selections from the* Conversations of Master Chu (Berkeley: University of California Press, 1990), 4.24, p.132.

- The pinyin romanization system is used, except when quoting other English sources.

- Dates are identified not as B.C. or A.D., but as B.C.E. (Before the Common Era) or C.E. (Common Era), meaning the era common to Christianity and the other great world religions. This is not intended to denigrate the importance of Christianity, but merely to provide a usage that is comfortable to adherents of other religions.

- Passages in the *Mengzi* are identified by the standard divisions into "books," "parts" ("A" and "B" in English), and "chapters." I subdivide chapters into "verses" according to the places where Zhu Xi inserts commentary. Chapter and verse numbers are provided in the outside margins of the translation.

- The translation is often functional rather than literal. For example, *li*, an ancient unit of length equivalent to about a third of a mile, is rendered "league," while other units are rendered "foot," "pound," etc.

- When used in a proper name, or when referring to someone Confucians would consider a genuine monarch, "King" is capitalized. When referring to someone who merely happens to have usurped the title, "king" is in lowercase.

- When used as a translation of the Chinese term *dé*, "Virtue" is capitalized. When used in a more general sense to refer to good traits of character, "virtue" appears in lowercase.

- Quotations of Kongzi are identified by the *Analects* passage in which they occur (following the sectioning in Edward Slingerland's translation, *Analects: With Selections from Traditional Commentaries*). If no citation is given, Mengzi is attributing to Kongzi a quotation not found in the received text of the *Analects*. Passages from the *Odes* are identified by their numbering in the standard Mao edition. (On the *Odes*, see "The Confucian Way" in the Introduction.)

- In the commentary, Zhu Xi is referred to in the present tense (e.g., "Zhu Xi says . . ."), while earlier commentators whom Zhu Xi cites are referred to in the past tense (e.g., "Yin Tun commented . . .").

- There is a bibliography accompanying the Introduction. Consequently, citations of works in the commentary are abbreviated to the author's surname, the title, and the pages cited. Complete bibliographical information is supplied in footnotes for works not mentioned in the Introduction.

- A third-level quotation (a quotation within a quotation within another quotation) is generally italicized rather than put in double quotation marks (e.g., 5A1.2), unless doing so would lead to confusion.

INTRODUCTION

Why Read This Book?

Here's what is necessary: one blow with a club, one scar; one slap on the face, a handful of blood. Your reading of what other people write should be like this. Don't be lax! —Zhu Xi

When people ask me which Confucian classic to read first, I answer without hesitation: the *Mengzi*.

The *Mengzi* is one of the *Four Books* that are traditionally taken to express the essence of Confucianism: the others are the *Analects*, the *Greater Learning*, and the *Mean*. The *Analects* contains the sayings of Kongzi (better known to us by the Latinization of his name, "Confucius"). The *Greater Learning* supposedly consists of a brief statement by Kongzi, followed by an interpretive commentary on it by his immediate disciple, Zengzi. The *Mean* has been attributed to Zisi, the grandson of Kongzi. Finally, Mengzi (also known as "Mencius") was a Confucian who studied in the school of Zisi, and whose collected sayings, dialogues, and debates bears his name. The *Analects*, the *Greater Learning*, and the *Mean* are very elusive and enigmatic books. The best way to approach them is often through examining the significance they have had for people in the later tradition. Furthermore, the *Analects* presents numerous problems of textual authenticity that are sometimes hard to ignore. Of the *Four Books*, the eponymous *Mengzi* is the most cogent, coherent, and comprehensible. It is also the one most likely to speak to contemporary readers.[1]

One of the things that distinguishes this translation is that it includes a philosophical commentary. Not everyone will see this as an advantage. Contemporary Western readers frequently have a prejudice that, in order to best

---

[1] For two views on the composition of the *Analects*, see Bruce Brooks and Taeko Brooks, *The Original Analects* (New York: Columbia University Press, 1998) and Edward Slingerland, "Why Philosophy Is Not 'Extra' in Understanding the *Analects*," *Philosophy East and West* 50:1 (January 2000): 137–41, 146–47. For interpretive studies of the *Analects*, see Bryan W. Van Norden, ed., *Confucius and the Analects: New Essays* (New York: Oxford University Press, 2002) and Herrlee G. Creel, *Confucius and the Chinese Way*, reprint (New York: Harper, 1960).

understand a text, one should read it by itself, ignoring the commentarial tradition that has developed around it. Indeed, it is often a selling point for an interpretation that it gets back to the "real" meaning of the text that has been obscured (perhaps intentionally) by the orthodoxy. (The mania surrounding Dan Brown's novel *The Da Vinci Code* is just a special case of this phenomenon.) But even a text like the *Mengzi,* which often speaks in terms that a person in any era or culture could appreciate, sometimes cries out for philosophical commentary. Consider this sentence, which is central to understanding Mengzi's account of courage: "Meng Shishe's preserving his *qi* was not as good as Zengzi's preserving what is crucial" (2A2.8). It is utterly impossible for even the most brilliant and determined English reader to understand this sentence without assistance.

As a result of increased appreciation of the need for commentaries, we have begun to see more translations-with-commentaries. If someone wishes to read the *Analects,* I would heartily recommend Edward Slingerland's *Analects: with Selections from Traditional Commentaries*. In addition, Daniel K. Gardner's *The Four Books: The Basic Teachings of the Later Confucian Tradition* does an excellent job of presenting the "orthodox" interpretation of selected passages from those texts. And for a complete translation of the *Mengzi* with a contemporary, philosophical commentary, see my *Mengzi: with Selections from Traditional Commentaries*.

Many of my comments are drawn from the *Sishu jizhu* ("Collected Commentaries on the *Four Books*"), written by Zhu Xi (1130–1200 C.E.). Zhu Xi was a brilliant philosopher who made the *Four Books* central to Confucianism. In 1313 his commentary was identified as the "orthodox" interpretation for the civil service examinations and remained so for the next six hundred years. As a result, generations of Chinese scholars literally memorized Zhu Xi's interpretation. And Zhu Xi's influence lives on. For example, I have more than once heard a scholar earnestly discuss "Mengzi's claim that human nature is *originally* good," but Mengzi never says this. Mengzi says "Human nature is good" *simpliciter*. Why has this "originally" crept in? Because Zhu Xi glosses Mengzi's "Human nature is good" as "Human nature is originally good." To paraphrase Santayana: Those who do not read the commentaries are doomed to repeat them.[2]

---

[2] For a fine overview of Zhu Xi's life, social context, philosophy, and historical influence, see Daniel K. Gardner, trans., *Learning to Be a Sage* (Berkeley: University of California Press, 1990), 3–81. For an example of a misstatement of Mengzi's view on human nature, see Chad Hansen, *A Daoist Theory of Chinese Thought* (New York: Oxford University Press, 1992), 79. Ironically, Hansen describes himself as rejecting what he claims is the "orthodox" view (5–7). For an explanation of why Zhu Xi glosses Mengzi's position as he does, see "Zhu Xi's Reinterpretation" later in this Introduction. Loy Hui-chieh has noted that the *Three Character Classic* has done much to popularize the phrase "human nature is originally good" (Loy, review of *Mengzi: with Selections from Traditional Commentaries*, *Notre Dame Philosophical Reviews* [March 29, 2009]

The great historical influence of Zhu Xi's commentary is not the only reason that I frequently cite it. Zhu Xi quotes from a well-chosen selection of earlier commentaries. In addition, he himself is a very insightful interpreter. I can pay him the highest compliment we can give any philosopher: even when he is wrong, he is wrong for interesting reasons. At the same time, I have not hesitated to disagree with Zhu Xi. As I explain later in this Introduction, Zhu Xi often sees Mengzi through the distorting lens of concepts inherited from Buddhism. And my primary goal is not to present Zhu Xi's interpretation, but to empower modern English readers to understand and appreciate the *Mengzi* for themselves.

In the remainder of this Introduction, I shall provide some background to enable the general reader to appreciate the translation and commentary. First, I shall sketch "Mengzi's Historical Context," including the historical myths that informed his self-understanding. This section will help the reader to recognize the many individuals and events that Mengzi assumes his audience is familiar with. Next, I shall give an overview of some of the key claims and concepts of "Mengzi's Philosophy." This will assist the reader in seeing how the discrete dialogues, stories, and aphorisms of the *Mengzi* fit together into a systematic whole. I shall then discuss the social and intellectual evolution that occurs "From Mengzi to Zhu Xi." This section will enable the reader to understand the particular metaphysical lens through which Zhu Xi reads the *Four Books*. Finally, I shall provide some examples of how "Zhu Xi's Reinterpretation" of Confucianism was, despite his evident genius, sometimes distorted by this lens.

Mengzi's Historical Context

People have long lived in the world, sometimes with order, sometimes in chaos. —Mengzi

Mengzi accepted the Confucian view that social order is achieved when a sage comes to power and rules via Virtue rather than coercion. "Virtue" (*dé*) is a kind of charisma generated by the possession of benevolence, righteousness, and other traits that *we* would call "virtues." The masses willingly follow a ruler with Virtue. Kongzi expresses this by saying, "One who rules through the power of Virtue is analogous to the Pole Star: it simply remains in its place and receives the homage of the myriad lesser stars" (*Analects* 2.1).[3] (If this

---

http://ndpr.nd.edu/review.cfm?id=15648). This is quite correct. But we should bear in mind that the *Three Character Classic* is itself derivative of Zhu Xi's perspective.

[3] Cf. *Mengzi* 2A3. Citations in the form "2.1" identify a book and chapter in the *Analects*, according to the sectioning in Slingerland's translation. Recall that "Kongzi" is the Chinese form

seems naive, think of the extent to which the successful leadership of people like the Rev. Martin Luther King, Jr. and Mahatma Gandhi depended upon their perceived virtue.)

The first of the ancient, sagely sovereigns whom Mengzi mentions is Emperor Yao.[4] As Yao approached the end of his life, he decided to find a virtuous successor. Searching his kingdom, Yao heard about Shun, a simple farmer who was known for his great "filialilty" (*xiào*, often rendered "filial piety"). Shun had what we would describe today as a dysfunctional family, to say the least. His father, stepmother, and stepbrother repeatedly schemed to murder him in order to steal his wealth. For example, Shun's family asked him to dig a well for them. They planned to remove the ladder and cover the well while Shun was still inside. Thinking that they had succeeded in their plot, Shun's brother told his parents that they could have Shun's livestock and his storehouses of grain. "But his shields and spears—mine. His zither—mine. His bow—mine. And his two wives shall service me in my bed!" However, Shun had survived the murder attempt. (According to one account, he suspected something, so he had already dug an escape tunnel from the well; 5A2.3.) But despite all this, Shun continued to love and care for his family, until eventually they were won over by his devotion. Impressed by Shun's character and achievements, Yao made Shun his Prime Minister. Shun was so successful at this that, when Yao passed away, the people spontaneously made Shun the new emperor (5A5.7).

As ruler, Shun was concerned with the problems of flood control and irrigation, which have long been issues in China. He appointed an able minister, Yu, to handle these problems (3B9.3–4, 4B26). Yu worked tirelessly, dredging silt out of rivers and building canals. Mengzi states that "Yu spent eight years away from home. Three times he passed the gate of his home but did not enter" (3A4.7). Owing to his success, he became Shun's Prime Minister, and in a parallel with the previous succession, his abilities led the people to treat him as the new emperor upon Shun's death.

Yu was a great ruler in his own right, and he followed the pattern set by Yao and Shun of choosing the person he found most worthy as his Prime Minister. However, this time, when the emperor died, the people did not make Yu's Prime Minister the new emperor. Instead, they treated Yu's son as the emperor. Because of this event, Yu posthumously became the founder of the first Chinese dynasty, the Xia (5A6).

---

of the name that was Latinized in the West as "Confucius," and the *Analects* are the sayings attributed to him (and some of his immediate disciples).

[4]   Up until late in the Shang dynasty, we are discussing myth rather than history. For a brilliant interpretation of the role of sagely myths in Chinese thought, see Michael Puett, *The Ambivalence of Creation* (Stanford, CA: Stanford University Press, 2001). For a detailed historical account, see Michael Loewe and Edward L. Shaughnessy, eds., *The Cambridge History of Ancient China* (New York: Cambridge University Press, 1999).

The traditional Chinese view is that dynasties follow a cyclic pattern. A dynasty is founded by a sagacious ruler who possesses Virtue. He brings order and prosperity to society, but in a way that is noncoercive. As a result of his Virtue, he is given a "Mandate" (*mìng*) to rule by "Heaven" (*tiān*), a kind of semipersonal higher power. Because of this intimate relationship between Heaven and the King, he is often referred to as the "Son of Heaven" (*tiānzǐ*). The Mandate is transmitted to the founder's descendants, but over the centuries there is a gradual decline in the quality of the rulers, with a corresponding increase in social disorder, dissatisfaction, and disaffection. Eventually a dynasty will reach its nadir, and an evil last king will inspire full-fledged revolt against his atrocities, leading to the revocation of the Mandate in favor of a new sage who founds the next dynasty.[5] So Yu was the sage who founded the Xia dynasty, which was brought to an end centuries later due to the actions of the evil Tyrant Jie. Jie arrogantly proclaimed, "I have the world, like the Heavens have the Sun. When the Sun perishes, only then shall I perish!" But his rule was so cruel that, according to Mengzi, his subjects said, "When will this Sun expire? We will perish together with you" (1A2.4). So the people gladly followed sagacious King Tang when he overthrew Jie. (On Tang, see 3B5.2–4.)

Tang founded the Shang dynasty, which followed the same pattern as the Xia: beginning with sagacious Virtue but gradually losing the support of the people.[6] The evil last king of the Shang dynasty was Zhou. Unfortunately for English speakers, the name of the dynasty that succeeded the Shang is also romanized as "Zhou." In Chinese, you would never confuse the two, since they are written with different characters and pronounced with different tones: Zhòu 紂 is the tyrant and Zhōu 周 is the dynasty. But to keep them straight in English, I will always call the last ruler of the Shang dynasty "*Tyrant Zhou*"; "Zhou" without qualification will mean the dynasty.

The most important of the early Zhou rulers were King Wen, King Wu, King Cheng, and the Duke of Zhou. Wen's Virtue was so great that his own subjects eagerly served him (1A2), and good and wise people from all over the world came to live in his state. However, throughout his reign he deferred to the authority of Tyrant Zhou. His son, King Wu, found that leaders of the Central States flocked to follow him, hoping that he would lead them to overthrow Tyrant Zhou. He did so and, around 1040 B.C.E., founded the Zhou dynasty. Unfortunately, Wu died soon after the conquest. His son, King Cheng, succeeded to the throne, but he was only a child. To have a minor on the throne immediately after the founding of a new dynasty, with potentially

---

[5] Even in modern Chinese, the word for "revolution" (as in "Cultural Revolution") is *gémìng*, which is literally "stripping the Mandate."

[6] The Shang dynasty is sometimes also called the Yin dynasty, after the name of its last capital city.

rebellious subjects to govern, was a precarious situation. King Cheng's regent was his uncle, the Duke of Zhou. It must have been tempting for the Duke of Zhou to seize the throne for himself. However, the Duke of Zhou supported King Cheng with loyalty and wisdom throughout his life. Because of this, he was regarded as a paragon of Virtue among later Confucians.

The territory controlled by the Zhou was divided into states, each ruled by one of the "various lords" (*zhūhòu*), the highest ranking of whom were dukes. These rulers, often blood relatives of the royal family, were expected to provide tribute and military support to the central authority when needed. When one of the various lords died, the succession to his eldest son had to be approved by the king. This system seems to have worked well for a time, but over a few centuries, the states became essentially autonomous entities. The weakness of the Zhou court was demonstrated definitively in 771 B.C.E., when a group of disaffected nobles attacked and murdered the king. A surviving member of the royal family was installed as king in a new capital to the east, deeper in the Zhou territory, but the Zhou king would be largely a figurehead from then on. This event marks the division between the Western Zhou (c. 1040–771 B.C.E.) and the Eastern Zhou (770–221 B.C.E.) dynasties.

The Era of Kongzi

Two important subdivisions within the Eastern Zhou are the Spring and Autumn period and the Warring States period. The former is named after a historical chronicle covering the years from 722 to 481 B.C.E. Mengzi states that Kongzi wrote a work called the *Spring and Autumn Annals* as a critique of society's moral decay (3B9.8, 4B21, 7B2). However, the surviving work by that name seems like a bare historical chronicle, so it is unlikely to be the same work Mengzi refers to. Nonetheless, the *Zuo Commentary on the* Spring and Autumn Annals gives a fascinating narrative history of this period in which the "various lords" vied for supremacy by waging war, assassinating opponents, and forming and then betraying alliances.[7]

It was during the Spring and Autumn period that the institution of the "Hegemon" (*bà*) developed. The Hegemon was a leader of one of the states who was able, through his individual military strength and judicious alliances, to become de facto ruler of China. This position was intrinsically unstable, however, because any ruler who was too successful would incite the fear and envy of the others. The most famous of the Hegemons were Duke Huan of Qi and Duke Wen of Jin (1A7.1). Duke Huan's success was due in part to his brilliant minister, Guan Zhong. Many rulers and ministers wished to emu-

---

[7] A good and readable selective translation of this work is Burton Watson, trans., *The Tso Chuan* (New York: Columbia University Press, 1989). Yuri Pines presents an intriguing discussion of intellectual developments in this period in his *Foundations of Confucian Thought* (Honolulu: University of Hawaii Press, 2002).

late Duke Huan and Guan Zhong, but Confucians typically condemned them for usurping the authority of the Zhou King and ruling by force and guile rather than by Virtue.[8]

Kongzi lived during the later part of the Spring and Autumn period. He was deeply sympathetic to the suffering of the common people caused by the warfare, misrule, and social chaos of his era. One of his disciples asked, "What would you make of someone who bestowed bounty upon the people and rescued the masses? Could he be called 'humane'?" Kongzi enthusiastically replied, "What difficulty is there in his being humane? Such a person would certainly be a sage!" (6.30) Like everyone in his era, Kongzi took for granted the institutions of hereditary monarchy and dukedoms. However, he accepted anyone as a disciple, regardless of family background or wealth, and emphasized that a true "gentleman" (*jūnzǐ*) is not merely someone born into a particular social class but rather a person who has achieved virtues like "humaneness" (*rén*) and "wisdom" (*zhì*).[9] As a result, Kongzi strongly advocated the meritocratic promotion of government ministers. He believed that such gentlemen could guide hereditary rulers and inspire the people to return society to the Way (*dào*). By this he meant the right Way to live and to organize society that had already been discovered by the ancient sage Kings.

The Confucian Way

So what was the Way of Kongzi? This has been much disputed over the last two and a half millennia. However, five themes have been central to every form of Confucianism: happiness in the everyday world, tradition, the family, ritual, and ethical cultivation.

Kongzi did not advocate asceticism or transcendence of ordinary life. The best life is characterized by simple, everyday pleasures and rich personal relationships with family, friends, and members of one's community. Thus, when Kongzi's disciple Zilu asked about how to serve ghosts and spirits, Kongzi replied, "You are not yet able to serve people—how could you be able to serve ghosts and spirits?" Zilu persisted, asking about death, but Kongzi just answered, "You do not yet understand life—how could you possibly understand death?" (11.12) When asked what his own aspirations were, Kongzi mentions values manifested among humans in this world: "To bring comfort to the aged, to inspire trust in my friends, and to be cherished by the youth" (5.26; cf. 11.26).

---

[8] *Mengzi* 2A1.1–4; *Analects* 3.22. Nowadays, when the People's Republic of China condemns what it sees as U.S. "hegemony" against other nations, it is using a word derived from this ancient title for someone who rules by brute force.

[9] "Gentleman" is one of a number of terms whose primary connotation shifted from social class to ethical achievement, including "noble" (*shì*), "great person" (*dà rén*), and "worthy" (*xián*). Opposed to these is the "petty person" (*xiǎo rén*).

For Kongzi there is no higher standard of judgment than human civiliza-
tion at its best. Thus he said of himself, "I transmit rather than innovate. I am
faithful to and love the ancients" (7.1). It is possible within a Confucian
framework to modify or reject elements of one's tradition, but this must always
be done by appealing to other values, beliefs, and practices within that tradition. For example, when people switched from using ceremonial caps of linen
to using cheaper ones made of silk, Kongzi approved of the change, because
it was more frugal yet maintained the spirit of the ritual (9.3).

It is not surprising that a philosopher who emphasized the everyday world
and tradition should also place great importance on the family. The family is
important in Confucianism in two related ways. First, it is in the family that
one begins to acquire the virtues. A disciple of Kongzi was making this point
when he said that "filiality and respect for elders constitute the root of humaneness" (1.2). To put it in very modern terms, it is by loving and being
loved by others in one's family that one learns to be kind to others, and it is
by respecting the boundaries of others in one's family and having one's own
boundaries respected that one develops integrity.

The crucial role of the family in one's moral development is one of the
reasons that Confucians advocate "differentiated love" (also called "graded
love"). Differentiated love is the doctrine that one has stronger moral obligations toward, and should have stronger emotional attachment to, those who
are bound to oneself by ties such as community, friendship, and especially
kinship. For example, the duke of one state bragged to Kongzi about how "upright" his people were, saying that one son turned in his own father for stealing a sheep. Kongzi replied, "Among my people, those whom we consider
'upright' are different from this: fathers cover up for their sons, and sons cover
up for their fathers. 'Uprightness' is to be found in this" (13.18).

Perhaps the Confucian notion that is the most difficult for many of us to
understand and appreciate today is that of rituals or rites. Rituals, in their most
fundamental sense, are religious activities such as offering food and wine to
the spirits of one's ancestors or performing a funeral. Some rituals were very
lively, involving elaborate dances accompanied by music. But ritual also includes matters involving what we would describe as etiquette, such as how to
greet or say farewell to a guest, and what manner is appropriate when addressing a subordinate ("pleasant and affable"; 10.2), a superior ("formal and
proper"; 10.2), or a person in mourning ("respectful"; 10.25). Finally, Kongzi
sometimes speaks as if ritual encompasses all of ethics (12.1).

Some of the most famous (and controversial) of the Confucian rituals have
to do with funerals and mourning. A Confucian funeral is often elaborate,
with inner and outer coffins, special garments for the corpse, and other goods
buried in the grave. After the funeral, there is a long period of ritualized
mourning. Opponents of Confucianism like Mozi criticized these practices
as wasteful. (For more on Mozi, see "Mengzi's Philosophy," later in this Introduction.) It is interesting to note, however, that Kongzi himself emphasized
having appropriate feelings over ostentatious display. "When it comes to rit-

ual, it is better to be spare than extravagant. When it comes to mourning, it is better to be excessively sorrowful than fastidious" (3.4). This suggests that the real point of the rituals is expressing and reinforcing emotions that are conducive to communal life.[10]

Ritual is one tool for cultivating virtue. Education is another. Kongzi pioneered educational techniques for making people not just more skillful or more knowledgeable, but more benevolent, wise, and reverent. Kongzi used the *Odes*, an already ancient anthology of poems, as his primary educational classic. In addition to the *Odes*, Mengzi frequently cites the *Documents*, a collection of primary historical texts.[11] Kongzi's general philosophy of education is summed up in a pithy quotation: "If you learn without reflecting upon what you have learned, you will be lost. If you reflect without learning, however, you will fall into danger" (2.15). Much of the lively debate among later Confucians during the last 2,500 years is over the comparative emphasis one should give to "reflecting" and "learning" in ethical cultivation, and over what human nature must be like to justify this emphasis. Mengzi, because of his belief in the goodness of human nature, tended to emphasize our ability to "reflect" upon what we know innately. But the later Confucian Xunzi stressed "learning" as a tool for overcoming the badness of human nature.[12]

Kongzi attracted many disciples who were inspired by the preceding five themes: happiness in the everyday world, tradition, the family, ritual, and ethical cultivation. However, within a century of Kongzi's death, Confucianism was under attack from powerful philosophical alternatives. Part of Mengzi's historical importance is that he brilliantly defended Confucianism against these competing philosophies.

The Era of Mengzi

Mengzi lived in the fourth century B.C.E., near the beginning of the Warring States period (403–221 B.C.E.). The military and political situation had

---

[10] This account of ritual was developed explicitly by the later Confucian Xunzi (fl. third century B.C.E.) (see *Xunzi* 19, "Discourse on Ritual," in *Readings in Classical Chinese Philosophy*, 2d ed., ed. Philip J. Ivanhoe and Bryan W. Van Norden (Indianapolis: Hackett Publishing, 2005), 272, 274–85; hereafter simply *Readings*. As A. R. Radcliff-Brown observed, this anticipates the anthropological "functionalist" account of ritual by over two millennia (see "Religion and Society," in *Structure and Function in Primitive Society* [New York: The Free Press, 1968], 153–77).

[11] See, e.g., *Mengzi* 5A4.4, 7B3. On the *Odes*, see Paul Goldin, "The Reception of the *Odes* in the Warring States Era" in *After Confucius* (Honolulu: University of Hawaii Press, 2005), 19–35. For a translation, see Arthur Waley, *The Book of Songs*, rev. ed. (New York: Grove Press, 1996). For a translation of the *Documents* (also known as the *Book of History*), see James Legge, *The Shoo King*, vol. 3 of *The Chinese Classics*, reprint (Taipei: SMC Publishing, 1991).

[12] Philip J. Ivanhoe explores the historical dialectic of reflecting and learning in his *Confucian Moral Self Cultivation*, 2d ed. (Indianapolis: Hackett Publishing, 2000).

deteriorated since the Spring and Autumn period: not even a Hegemon could maintain interstate order. The larger states frequently annexed the smaller ones, and some of the more powerful rulers usurped the title of "King," which was the prerogative of the Zhou monarch. (For example, Mengzi visited "King" Hui of Liang and "King" Xuan of Qi.) Because of the deaths and social disruption due to warfare and misrule, farmland frequently lay fallow, resulting in famine. Consequently, China was severely underpopulated during this era, and rulers sought to draw peasants to their own states. Rulers also invited wise people from all over China to come to their courts to offer advice on governing well (which for them meant gaining a strategic advantage over other states). But sometimes the rulers merely wanted the prestige that comes from having a famous "Master" in their state. Mengzi's dialogues with rulers must be understood in this context. (See 1A3 for a paradigmatic example.)[13]

We have few details about Mengzi's life, other than those contained in his eponymous text. His full name was Meng Ke (the suffix -*zi* simply means Master). He was born in Zou, a small state near Kongzi's home state of Lu, both of which were in what is now Shandong Province. His father died when he was young.[14] In Meng's patriarchal society, this must have left him and his mother in precarious circumstances. However, his mother still managed to send him to study in the Confucian school of Zisi, Kongzi's grandson.

There are several famous stories about Mengzi's mother that are charmingly edifying, whether or not they are true.[15] One is that "Meng's mother moved thrice" (*Mèng mǔ sān qiān* 孟母三遷) to find a suitable environment in which to raise her son. After the death of her husband, she first moved with her son next to a cemetery, and the young sage played at performing funerals. Judging this inappropriate for a child, Mengzi's mother moved to a house near a marketplace. But now Meng Ke took to imitating someone hawking goods. Still dissatisfied, his mother moved to a home beside a school. Meng began playing at being a teacher, which finally pleased his mother.

After Meng Ke started to actually attend school, his mother would ask him every day what he had learned. But one day he answered with casual indifference toward his studies. In response, "Meng's mother cut the weft" (*Mèng mǔ duàn jī* 孟母斷機) of the fabric that she had been weaving, thereby ruining it. Her weaving was probably one of their few sources of income, so Meng was startled that she would waste a piece of it. But his mother explained that if he wasted a day of learning it was as bad as her wasting a day of work. Thereafter, Meng always applied himself fully in his schoolwork.

---

[13]   Mark Edward Lewis, *Sanctioned Violence in Early China* (Albany: State University of New York Press, 1990) is an excellent discussion of many aspects of Spring and Autumn and Warring States society and thought.

[14]   But contrast 1B16, which suggests Mengzi was old enough to arrange his father's funeral.

[15]   Liu Xiang, *Lie nü zhuan jiaozhu* 1.11, reprint (Taibei: Zhonghua shuju, 1983).

Beyond this, "the first forty years of his life are little more than a blank to us. . . . How he supported himself in [Zou] we cannot tell. Perhaps he was possessed of some patrimony; but when he first comes forth from his native State, we find him accompanied by his most eminent disciples."[16] Like Kongzi, Mengzi traveled from state to state, hoping to find a ruler who would put the Way into practice. He depended for his support on gifts from students and grants from rulers. Like a contemporary politician, his need placed him in the position of having to defend his decisions about which donations to accept (2B3, 5B4). But it is clear that he would turn down a salary if he felt it would violate his integrity to accept it. He did eventually accept a position as High Minister in the state of Qi, but he resigned when it became clear that the king was ignoring his advice (2B10). Mengzi eventually retired from public service and, with the help of some of his disciples, edited his collected sayings and dialogues.[17]

The *Mengzi* gives the impression of someone brilliant and quick-witted who, like Aristotle's "great-souled" man, expects to be treated with deference, but only because he genuinely deserves it.[18] And, like Plato, Mengzi is one of those rare philosophers who is equally adept at precise argumentation and moving rhetoric. He is, in fact, a contemporary of Plato and Aristotle, and "when we place Mencius among them, he can look them in the face. He does not need to hide a diminished head."[19] Like Kongzi, Gandhi, or Martin Luther King, Jr., he was actively engaged in the struggle for positive social change. Unfortunately, he never saw the social transformation he worked for. This left him saddened, but he assured his disciples that he was not bitter: he had faith that Heaven would, in its own time, raise up a sage to bring peace to the world (2B13).

Mengzi's Philosophy

The doctrines of Yang Zhu and Mozi fill the world. —Mengzi

The centerpiece of Mengzi's political philosophy was "benevolent government," by which he meant rule by virtuous "gentlemen" who would aim at

---

[16] James Legge, trans., *The Works of Mencius*, 1895, reprint (New York: Dover Books, 1970), 19–20.

[17] For more detailed discussions of Mengzi's biography and the text of the *Mengzi*, see D. C. Lau, "The Dating of Events in the Life of Mencius," "Early Traditions about Mencius," and "The Text of the *Mencius*," Appendices 1–3 in D. C. Lau, trans., *Mencius* (New York: Penguin Books, 1970), 205–22.

[18] Aristotle, *Nicomachean Ethics*, IV.3. Cf. *Mengzi* 3B1, 5B7, 7A43.

[19] Legge, *Mencius*, 16.

the well-being of the people as a whole. Mengzi stressed that most people will engage in crime if they are poor and hungry:

> Only a noble is capable of having a constant heart while lacking a constant livelihood. As for the people, if they lack a constant liveli-hood, it follows that they will lack a constant heart. No one who lacks a constant heart will avoid dissipation and evil. When they there-upon sink into crime, to go and punish the people is to trap them. When there are benevolent persons in positions of authority, how is it possible for them to trap the people? (1A7.20)

Consequently, it is the obligation of government to ensure that the basic needs of the people are met. Mengzi offered much more specific advice than had Kongzi about how to secure the livelihood of the people, including rec-ommendations about everything from tax rates to farm management to the pay scale for government employees (e.g., 3A3). However, as the reference to "nobles" with "constant hearts" suggests, Mengzi agreed with Kongzi that ethical cultivation is crucial for both individual and social well-being. Thus, Mengzi advocated an educational system that instructs people in how to live up to the "human roles," such as being a good parent, child, ruler, minister, spouse, and friend (3A4.8).

We find in Mengzi an emphasis on the themes that we saw are character-istic of all Confucians: achieving happiness in the everyday world, tradition, familial relations (as the basis of other ethical obligations and "differentiated love"), ritual, and ethical cultivation. In addition, Mengzi agreed with Kongzi in regarding war as, at best, a regrettable last resort. In what has become a Chi-nese proverb, he stated that to try to rule via brute force is as ineffectual as "climbing a tree in search of a fish."[20]

However, Mengzi could not simply repeat what Kongzi had said. Confu-cianism was now under attack by a variety of alternative philosophies. Mengzi saw two positions as the primary competitors to the Way: "If a doctrine does not lean toward Yang Zhu, then it leans toward Mozi. Yang Zhu is 'for one-self.' This is to not have a ruler. Mozi is 'impartial caring.' This is to not have a father. To not have a father and to not have a ruler is to be an animal" (3B9.9).

Against the Mohists and Yang Zhu

Mozi (fifth century B.C.E.) was the first systematic critic of Confucianism. In place of cultivating Virtue in individuals, he advocated a kind of consequen-tialism: policies and institutions were to be judged by how much "benefit" (or

---

[20]   1A7.16; cf. 4A14, 7B4, and Analects 15.1.

"profit," *lì*) they produced. These judgments were to be totally impartial, granting no favoritism to one's family, friends, or community. The Mohists thus rejected the differentiated love that was central to Confucianism in favor of "impartial caring." Mozi had great optimism that human motivations are highly malleable. He claimed that, through proper rewards and punishments, previous rulers had gotten their soldiers to march onto burning ships to their certain deaths, or induced their subjects to eat so little food that they could barely walk. How much easier, he claimed, to turn the people to something as beneficial as impartial caring.[21] The Mohists, therefore, had no patience for ethical cultivation, and also rejected most Confucian ritual (including elaborate funerals and musical performances) as a pointless waste of resources.

The opening passage of the *Mengzi* is probably an implicit criticism of Mohism. King Hui politely asks Mengzi what teachings he has that would bring "profit" (*lì*) to his state (1A1). But Mengzi immediately rebukes the king, asking "Why must Your Majesty speak of 'profit'?" Mengzi goes on to argue that if people aim at profit, whether it is the profit of their state, their family, or themselves, the ultimate result will be that "superiors and subordinates will seize profit from each other" so that "the state will be endangered." Instead, the ruler should encourage his subjects to emphasize benevolence and righteousness: "Never have the benevolent left their parents behind. Never have the righteous put their ruler last." Mengzi might seem to be objecting to profit itself. But on what grounds does Mengzi instruct King Hui to avoid emphasizing profit? It turns out that emphasizing profit is itself unprofitable. So when the Mohists claim that "the business of a benevolent person is to promote what is beneficial (*lì*) to the world and eliminate what is harmful," Mengzi replies that emphasizing profit or benefit is self-undermining.[22]

But Mengzi's most fundamental objection to Mohism is that the impartiality it demands is impractical and perverse because it is contrary to human nature. In order to fully understand Mengzi's view on human nature, we must see how it is a reaction to the position of Yang Zhu. Yang Zhu (fourth century B.C.E.) made the phrase "human nature" central to philosophical debate in China, and he used it in a way that presented a challenge to both Confucians and Mohists. The latter two movements agreed that Heaven is on the side of the Way. (They just disagreed over what the Heaven-sanctioned Way was.) But if there is such a thing as human nature, it must be implanted in us by Heaven. Now, Kongzi's own pronouncements on the rarity of Virtue as he understood it suggest that it is something very difficult and artificial for humans to obtain. And the Mohist claim that people can be converted to impartial caring "as easily as" soldiers can be taught to march onto burning

---

[21] See *Mozi* 16, "Impartial Caring," in *Readings*, 75–76.

[22] For the phrase from the Mohists, see *Readings*, 68. Mengzi gives a similar line of argument in 6B4.

ships seems to simply ignore the existence and resilience of innate human motivations. In contrast to both the Confucian and Mohist Ways, what could be more "natural" for a human than to be self-interested? So why not follow the nature that Heaven has given us by simply acting in a purely self-interested manner? Thus, in Western terms, Yang Zhu's position was a kind of ethical egoism based on a conception of humans as naturally self-interested.[23]

As you can see, "nature" (*xìng* 性) is etymologically related to the word *shēng* 生, whose senses include "to be born," "to grow," and "to live." Some thinkers emphasize the first sense. So for Mengzi's later Confucian critic Xunzi, "that which is so by birth is called 'human nature.'"[24] However, Mengzi thinks of the nature of something as the manner in which it will live, grow, and develop if given a healthy environment for the kind of thing it is. For example, it is the nature of a pear tree to bear fruit, but the sprout of a pear tree will not yet be able to do so. Indeed, most pear tree sprouts never mature into full-grown trees, because they get insufficient soil, water, and light. But it is still their "nature" to produce pears. Similarly, a Chinese juniper tree will, if given a healthy environment, grow to be as much as sixty feet tall. However, a bonsai artist can warp the growth of the tree to produce one that is eight inches tall. So Yang Zhu's claim is that a human who acts in a supposedly benevolent or righteous manner is analogous to a warped bonsai version of a Chinese juniper.

Mengzi responded to both Yang Zhu and the Mohists with his doctrine that humans have innate tendencies toward virtue. The existence of these tendencies falsifies Yang Zhu's claim that human nature is purely self-interested. In addition, Mengzi argues that the way in which these tendencies naturally develop invalidates Mohist impartiality. It is via loving others in the family that humans learn to have compassion for others, and it is by respecting others in the family that humans develop a sense of ethical shame (7A15). Because of this psychological mechanism, it is natural for humans to care more for their family than for strangers (5A3). So it would require extensive warping of human nature to achieve Mohist impartial caring.[25]

This objection comes out particularly clearly in Mengzi's debate with the Mohist Yi Zhi (3A5). Mengzi begins by pointing out that Yi Zhi had himself

---

[23] For a dialogue that may represent something like Yang Zhu's position, see "Robber Zhi," in *Readings*, 369–75.

[24] *Xunzi* 22, "On Correct Naming," in *Readings*, 292. See also *Xunzi* 23, "Human Nature Is Bad," in *Readings*, 298–306.

[25] Philosophers continue to debate the relative merits of the Mohist and Mengzian positions. See, for example, David Wong, "Universalism vs. Love with Distinctions," *Journal of Chinese Philosophy* 16:3/4 (September/December 1989): 251–72, Qingping Liu, "Confucianism and Corruption," *Dao* 6:1 (Spring 2007): 1–19, Qiyong Guo, "Is Confucian Ethics a 'Consanguinism'?" *Dao* 6:1 (Spring 2007): 21–37, and Bryan W. Van Norden, "On 'Humane Love' and 'Kinship Love,'" *Dao* 7:2 (Summer 2008): 125–29.

given his parents elaborate funerals. Yi Zhi's natural attachment to his parents was thus so strong that it led him to ignore his abstract commitment to the Mohist principle of frugal burials.

Now, an implausible aspect of early Mohism was that it regarded human motivations as almost infinitely malleable. It turns out that Yi Zhi holds what seems to be a modified version of Mohism, designed to make it more psychologically plausible. He suggests that "love is without differentiations, but it is bestowed beginning with one's parents." Yi Zhi thus seems to be agreeing with the Confucian claim that children first learn to love and have compassion for others in the family (1.2), but arguing that this natural compassion should be redirected until it reaches everyone equally, thereby achieving the Mohist goal of "impartial caring."

Mengzi suggests that Yi Zhi's revisionist Mohism still ends up with a position that is psychologically impractical: "Does Yi Zhi truly hold that one's affection for one's own nephew is like one's affection for a neighbor's baby?" Mengzi sums up his objection with the aphorism, "Heaven, in giving birth to things, causes them to have one source, but Yi Zhi gives them two sources." The first source is our innate love for our family members (which is naturally greater for them than for strangers), while the second source is the Mohist doctrine of impartiality. The problem is that, for the Mohists as much as for the Confucians, the will of Heaven and the Way coincide. So once the Mohists acknowledge that our greater love for family members is part of the nature implanted in us by Heaven, they cannot consistently claim that it is part of the Way to override these motivations in order to achieve impartiality.[26]

The Goodness of Human Nature

Mengzi describes his position with the slogan, "human nature is good," by which he means that humans have innate but incipient tendencies toward virtue that will develop given a healthy environment and ethical cultivation.[27] He argues for this in several ways. First, individuals can experience these incipient tendencies themselves, as Yi Zhi did when he was moved to give his

---

[26] On 3A5, see also David S. Nivison, "Two Roots or One?" in *The Ways of Confucianism*, 133–48, Kwong-loi Shun, "Mencius' Criticism of Mohism," *Philosophy East and West* 41 (April 1991): 203–14, and Bryan W. Van Norden, *Virtue Ethics and Consequentialism in Early Chinese Philosophy* (New York: Cambridge University Press, 2007), 305–12.

[27] On the goodness of human nature, see 3A1 and 6A6. On "nature" in general, see 3A1, 4B26, 6A1–4, 6A6–8, 7A1, 7A30, 7B24, and 7B33. Mengzi shares the common view of his era that other things besides humans have a "nature," including nonhuman animals, plants, and even water and mountains (6A1–3, 6A8). See also A. C. Graham, "The Background of the Mencian Theory of Human Nature," in *Studies in Chinese Philosophy and Philosophical Literature* (Albany: State University of New York Press, 1990), 7–66, and Paul Goldin, "Xunzi in the Light of the Guodian Manuscripts," in *After Confucius*, 36–57.

parents elaborate funerals (3A5), or King Xuan did when he spontaneously spared an ox being led to slaughter (1A7). In addition, Mengzi appeals to thought experiments, the most famous of which is the following:

> The reason that I say that all humans have hearts that are not unfeeling toward others is this. Suppose someone suddenly saw a child about to fall into a well: anyone in such a situation would have a feeling of alarm and compassion — not because one sought to get in good with the child's parents, not because one wanted fame among one's neighbors and friends, and not because one would dislike the sound of the child's cries. From this we can see that if one is without the feeling of compassion, one is not human. (2A6.3–4)

Mengzi hopes we will share his intuition that any human would have this feeling (literally, "heart") of compassion and that "if one is without the feeling of compassion, one is not human."

Mengzi uses an analogous thought experiment to illustrate the virtue of righteousness:

> Life is something I desire; righteousness is also something I desire. If I cannot have both, I will forsake life and select righteousness. . . . It is not the case that only the worthy person has this heart. All humans have it. The worthy person simply never loses it.
>
> A basket of food and a bowl of soup — if one gets them, then one will live; if one doesn't get them, then one will die. But if they're given with contempt, then even a homeless person will not accept them. If they're trampled upon, then even a beggar won't take them. (6A10)

The previous passage argued for an innate "heart of compassion," which is the basis of benevolence; this second passage argues that all humans disdain to do certain shameful things that would otherwise benefit them, and this "heart" is the basis of righteousness. So whereas Yang Zhu claimed that human nature consists only of self-interested desires for food, sex, physical comfort, and survival, Mengzi uses these thought experiments to argue that human nature also includes distinctively ethical motivations.

But aren't Mengzi's claims falsified by the simple fact of human wrongdoing? If we are all innately benevolent and righteous, why does anyone ever hurt another person or compromise his integrity? This objection misinterprets Mengzi's position, though. Mengzi does not claim that *humans* are innately good; he claims that *human nature* is innately good. Recall our earlier discussion of the concept of the "nature" of a thing. It is the nature of a pear tree to bear fruit, but it will fail to realize this nature if denied a healthy environment (with water, sunlight, etc.). Mengzi uses a carefully chosen agricultural metaphor to explain how this applies to human nature. He says that the "heart of compassion" (manifested when one sees the child about to fall into a well) is "the *sprout* of benevolence," while the "heart of disdain" (illustrated by the starving beggar who refuses a handout given with contempt) is the "*sprout* of righteousness" (2A6, 6A10). Just as the sprout of a pear tree is not yet a tree, but does have an active potential to develop into a mature tree, so are our "sprout of benevolence" and "sprout of righteousness" potentials for full benevolence and righteousness. But we must develop this potential in order to become fully virtuous. As Mengzi explains when asked to clarify his position, "As for what they are inherently, they can become good. This is what I mean by calling their natures good. As for their becoming not good, this is not the fault of their potential" (6A6.5–6). Until our potential for virtue is fully developed, the reactions of the sprouts will be haphazard and inconsistent. This is why humans can show great kindness and even self-sacrifice in one situation but stunning indifference to the suffering of others in a slightly different situation.

So Mengzi's doctrine that human nature is good is perfectly consistent with the fact that humans often (perhaps usually) fail to do good. But is Mengzi even right in claiming that all humans have at least the *sprouts* of benevolence and righteousness? We are all too familiar with the chilling example of the psychopath: a "human" (such as a serial killer) who lacks anything like ordinary compassion or sympathy. Although he would not phrase it in our terms, Mengzi's metaphor of Ox Mountain is his explanation for the rare cases of people who seem to lack the sprouts of virtue:

> The trees of Ox Mountain were once beautiful. But because it bordered on a large state, hatchets and axes besieged it. Could it remain verdant? Due to the respite it got during the day or night, and the moisture of rain and dew, there were sprouts and shoots growing there. But oxen and sheep came and grazed on them. Hence, it was as if it were barren. Seeing it barren, people believed that there had never been any timber there. But could this be the nature of the mountain?
>
> When we consider what is present in people, could they truly lack the hearts of benevolence and righteousness? The way that they discard their genuine hearts is like the hatchets and axes in relation to the trees. With them besieging it day by day, can it remain beautiful? . . . Others see that he is an animal, and think that there was never any capacity there. But is this what a human is like inherently? (6A8.1–2)

So Mengzi acknowledges that some people seem to lack the sprouts of virtue. However, this is not what a human is "inherently" (6A6.5, 6A8.2). "Humans" who fail to manifest the sprouts have been destroyed by a bad environment (such as physical deprivation, lack of ethical guidance, or even abusive parenting).[28]

The Virtues

Mengzi identifies four cardinal virtues, each of which is grounded in our innate emotional reactions:

> Humans all have the feeling of compassion. Humans all have the feeling of disdain. Humans all have the feeling of respect. Humans all have the feeling of approval and disapproval. The feeling of compassion is benevolence. The feeling of disdain is righteousness. The feeling of respect is propriety. The feeling of approval and disapproval is wisdom. Benevolence, righteousness, propriety, and wisdom are not welded to us externally. We inherently have them. It is simply that we do not reflect upon them. Hence, it is said, "Seek it and you will get it. Abandon it and you will lose it." (6A6.7)

Benevolence (*rén*) is compassion or sympathy for others. The benevolent person is pained by the suffering of others and takes joy in their happiness. The Mohists also emphasized this term, but for them it is ideally a purely impartial concern for others. For a Confucian like Mengzi, though, compassion should extend to everyone but be stronger for those tied to one by bonds such as kinship and friendship. Confucian benevolence acts like the ripples emanating from a stone dropped into a pond, proceeding out from the center but gradually decreasing in strength as they move out. This is related to the Confucian hypothesis that it is loving and being loved in the family that first germinates our capacity for compassion.

Righteousness (*yì*) is the integrity of a person who disdains to demean himself by doing what is base or shameful, even if doing so would reap benefits. So, for example, a righteous person will not accept a gift given with contempt (6A10), beg in order to obtain luxuries (4B33), or cheat at a game (3B1). As with benevolence, the capacity for righteousness is innate, but its growth is first stimulated in the family, where respect for the opinions of one's elders is internalized as an ethical sense of shame. To simplify, benevolence is a virtue

---

28 Although Mengzi was unaware of modern science, it provides support for some of his conclusions. Charles Darwin argued that evolution would encourage altruistic motivations in pack animals like humans. See *The Descent of Man*, 2d ed., reprint (New York: Prometheus Books, 1998), Part 1, Chapters 4–5, 100–138. For a sampling of contemporary views, see Leonard D. Katz, ed., *Evolutionary Origins of Morality* (Bowling Green, OH: Imprint Academic, 2000). Contemporary developmental psychology also provides evidence of innate compassion in humans. See Martin Hoffman, *Empathy and Moral Development* (New York: Cambridge University Press, 2000).

involving our *obligations* to help others, while righteousness emphasizes *prohibitions* against our performance of certain actions.

Wisdom (*zhì*) has many aspects, each of which is illustrated by the story of the sage Boli Xi (5A9). When the ruler of Yu made foolish concessions to the state of Jin, Boli Xi knew that these policies would result in the destruction of Yu. Recognizing that this ruler was too stubborn to listen to his advice, Boli Xi fled to the state of Qin, whose ruler showed great promise. Boli Xi waited until he was approached respectfully by the ruler of Qin (refusing to violate righteousness or propriety in order to obtain an audience), but then served so ably as his minister that the ruler became illustrious. So Boli Xi showed great wisdom in judging the characters of the rulers of Yu and Qin. He manifested great skill at "instrumental reasoning" (i.e., finding the best means to achieve a given end) in the fine advice he gave when he was minister to the ruler of Qin. He revealed his commitment to righteousness by insisting that the ruler of Qin show him respect in requesting an audience. And he demonstrated prudence in fleeing Yu when the situation was hopeless.[29] Boli Xi thus manifests four aspects of wisdom: being a good judge of the character of others, skill at means-end reasoning, an understanding of and commitment to the other virtues, and prudence.

The word rendered "propriety" (*lǐ*) is the same as the word for "rites" or "rituals." This is appropriate since propriety is the virtue that consists in performing the rites with the proper motivations. In comparison with some other Confucians, Mengzi has relatively little to say about the rites (hence little to say about propriety as a virtue). But one way of conceptualizing propriety is that it is manifested when we express deference or respect to others through ritualized actions (such as bowing, letting someone else walk first through a door, etc.).

Ethical Cultivation

Why do the sprouts develop into the full virtues in some people but not in others? In addition to a bad environment (hunger, cold, homelessness, violence), Mengzi emphasizes two other impediments to the growth of virtue: pernicious doctrines and lack of individual ethical effort.

In Mengzi's era as in our own, many people either denied that they were capable of virtue or opposed virtue as naive. Mengzi categorizes "those who say 'I myself am unable to dwell in benevolence and follow righteousness'" as "those who throw themselves away" and "those whose words slander propriety and righteousness" as "those who are destroying themselves" (4A10.1).

---

[29] It surprises some readers that running away was virtuous in this situation, but keep in mind that a good person does care about her own well-being; she just doesn't care about herself excessively; see also 4B31.

Both attitudes are roadblocks to moral growth. So a significant part of Mengzian moral self-cultivation is simply being aware of and delighting in the manifestations of the sprouts when we do have them. In other words, we reinforce and strengthen our benevolent and righteous motivations when we act out of them with awareness and approval. As Mengzi puts it, "If one delights in them, then they grow. If they grow, then how can they be stopped? If they cannot be stopped, then one does not notice one's feet dancing to them, one's hands swaying to them" (4A27).

Mengzi more than once says that people fail to develop morally simply because they do not engage in "reflection" (*sī*). The Chinese term can also mean "to concentrate upon" or "to long for," as when someone longs for an absent loved one (19.6). As Arthur Waley explained, "reflection" refers to:

> a process that is only at a short remove from concrete observation. Never is there any suggestion of a long interior process of cogitation or ratiocination, in which a whole series of thoughts are evolved one out of another, producing on the physical plane a headache and on the intellectual, an abstract theory. We must think of [reflection] rather as a fixing of the attention . . . on an impression recently imbibed from without and destined to be immediately re-exteriorized in action.[30]

Reflection is thus a mental activity whose focus is both internal and external. One reflects upon one's own virtuous feelings, but one also reflects upon the aspects of situations that call forth those feelings.

The stages of moral development are illustrated by a much-discussed dialogue between Mengzi and King Xuan of Qi. Mengzi asks the king about how he had spared an ox being led to slaughter because, as the king put it, "I cannot bear its frightened appearance, like an innocent going to the execution ground" (1A7.4). Mengzi explains to the king that the kindness he showed to the ox is the same feeling he needs to exercise to be a great king. King Xuan is pleased and replies, "I examined myself and sought to find my heart but failed to understand it. But when you discussed it, my heart was moved" (1A7.9). So Mengzi has helped the king to "reflect upon" and appreciate his own innate kindness. This is an important first step in stimulating the growth of the king's sprouts of virtue. But then Mengzi challenges the king:

> In the present case your kindness is sufficient to reach animals, but the effects do not reach the commoners. . . . Hence, one fails to lift a feather only because one does not use one's strength. One fails to

---

[30] Arthur Waley, trans., *The Analects of Confucius*, 1938, reprint (New York: Vintage Books, 1989), 45. For more on reflection, see 4A1.5, 4B20.5, 6A6.7, 6A9, 6A15.2, and 6A17; see also *Analects* 2.15 and 15.31.

see a wagon of firewood only because one does not use one's eyesight. The commoners fail to receive care only because one does not
use one's kindness. Hence, Your Majesty fails to become King because you do not act, not because you are unable to act. (1A7.10)

This dialogue raises many intriguing and complicated questions. Is Mengzi
presenting some sort of *argument* to the king about why he ought to care for
the commoners? Perhaps Mengzi is effectively saying to the king: you agree
that it is right to show compassion for the suffering ox (Case A), but your
people are also suffering due to your exorbitant taxes, wars of conquest, corrupt government, etc. (Case B). Case B is similar to Case A in all relevant respects. Therefore, in order to be consistent, you ought to show compassion
for your people. Alternatively, perhaps Mengzi merely wishes to convince the
king that he is *capable* of ruling with benevolence: you can show compassion
for a simple animal, so certainly you can also show compassion for a suffering human.

My own view is that neither of these analyses is completely correct. I think
Mengzi is leading the king to "reflect upon" relevant similarities between the
suffering of the ox and the suffering of his subjects. But this is not an argument for simple consistency. (After all, Mengzi also makes clear in the passage that slaughtering animals is ethically permissible, even if a "gentleman"
is too kind-hearted to do it himself. So Mengzi is asking the king to treat his
subjects better than he normally treats animals, not the same.) And Mengzi
does want the king to recognize his own demonstrated capacity for compassion. But it is not merely the capacity that Mengzi is getting at. He wants
to frame the comparison between the ox and the commoners in a way that
encourages the king's compassion to flow from one case to the other. For example, Mengzi reminds the king that he spared the ox because of its "frightened appearance, like an innocent going to the execution ground." He hopes
the king will be led from this to reflect upon, and sympathize with, the suffering of his own innocent subjects. In other words, Mengzi is helping the
king to achieve cognitive ethical growth as a means to achieving affective ethical growth.

Mengzi describes this process of ethical growth as "extending" or "filling
out" the manifestations of the sprouts. In other words, all of us will have righteous or benevolent reactions to certain paradigmatic situations. We feel love
for our parents, which is a manifestation of benevolence, or we disdain to allow ourselves to be addressed disrespectfully, which is a manifestation of righteousness. However, there are other situations where we do not have these
reactions, even though they are in the same "category" (3B3.5, 3B10.6, 5B4.5,
7B31.4). For example, a person who would find it shameful to have an illicit
affair might think nothing of lying to his ruler to achieve some political benefit. However, these are both in the category of base, unrighteous actions, so
we ought to disdain to do either. "Reflection" is the process by which we identify the relevant similarities between those cases where we already have the

appropriate reactions and other cases where we do not yet react appropriately. This guides our emotions so that we come to feel similarly about the cases. Or, as Mengzi succinctly put it: "People all have things that they will not bear. To extend this reaction to that which they will bear is benevolence. People all have things that they will not do. To extend this reaction to that which they will do is righteousness" (7B31.1).

Extension is not a matter of learning to apply a set of explicit rules. Mengzi is similar to Kongzi in having a comparatively particularistic conception of wisdom.[31] For example, a rival philosopher once attempted to trap Mengzi with an ethical dilemma. He began by asking, "Does ritual require that men and women not touch when handing something to one another?" When Mengzi acknowledged that it does, his opponent asked, "If your sister-in-law were drowning, would you pull her out with your hand?" His opponent thinks that he has Mengzi trapped, but Mengzi easily replies,

> Only a beast would not pull out his sister-in-law if she were drowning. It is the ritual that men and women should not touch when handing something to one another, but if your sister-in-law is drowning, to pull her out with your hand is a matter of discretion. (4A17.1)

But this particularism is not relativism. Mengzi thinks that there is a best way to respond in any given situation, and it is not a matter of personal or cultural opinion. So after describing how differently sages of the past have acted, Mengzi insists that if they "had exchanged places, they all would have done as the others did" (4B29.5; cf. 4B1, 4B31). In addition, Mengzi does recognize some absolute ethical prohibitions. When asked if there is anything that all sages have in common, he explains that there is: "if any could obtain the world by performing one unrighteous deed, or killing one innocent person, he would not do it" (2A2.24). However, there is much more to the Confucian Way than can be captured in any set of rules.[32]

Mengzi thinks that we generally have the capacity to "extend" to what is ethically required of us. So once when someone gave him excuses for not immediately doing what is right, Mengzi replied,

---

[31] Mengzi is not, in other words, a "rule-deontologist." On the distinction between "particularism" and rule-deontology, see Van Norden, *Virtue Ethics and Consequentialism in Early Chinese Philosophy*, 35–37.

[32] On Mengzian "extension" as it is developed in 1A7 and other passages, see David S. Nivison, "Motivation and Moral Action in Mencius," in *The Ways of Confucianism*, 91–119, Kwong-loi Shun, "Moral Reasons in Confucian Ethics," *Journal of Chinese Philosophy* 16:3/4 (September/ December 1989): 317–43, Eric Hutton, "Moral Connoisseurship in Mengzi," in *Essays on the Moral Philosophy of Mengzi*, ed. Xiusheng Liu and Philip J. Ivanhoe (Indianapolis: Hackett Publishing, 2002), 163–86, and David Wong, "Reasons and Analogical Reasoning in Mengzi," in *Essays on the Moral Philosophy of Mengzi*, 187–220.

Suppose there is a person who every day appropriates one of his neighbor's chickens. Someone tells him, "This is not the Way of a gentleman." He says, "May I reduce it to appropriating one chicken every month and wait until next year to stop?" If one knows that it is not righteous, then one should quickly stop. (3B8)

However, Mengzi stresses the importance of acting with appropriate feelings and motivations. Thus, Mengzi praises the sagely sovereign Shun by saying that "he acted out of benevolence and righteousness; he did not act out benevolence and righteousness" (4B19). To force oneself to do what one abstractly believes is right is to treat virtue as "external" (6A4–5). This not only fails to be genuinely virtuous, it is ethically damaging. Mengzi illustrates this using another agricultural metaphor: the story of the farmer from Song.

One must work at it, but do not assume success. One should not forget the heart, but neither should one "help" it grow. Do not be like the man from Song. Among the people of the state of Song there was a farmer who, concerned lest his sprouts not grow, pulled on them. Obliviously, he returned home and said to his family, "Today I am worn out. I helped the sprouts to grow." His son rushed out and looked at them. The sprouts were withered. Those in the world who do not "help" the sprouts to grow are few. Those who abandon them, thinking it will not help, are those who do not weed their sprouts. Those who "help" them grow are those who pull on the sprouts. Not only does this not help, but it even harms them. (2A2.16a)

To use a modern illustration, I cannot simply decide today that I will be the next Mother Teresa and expect to suddenly have the unwavering compassion to save the world. If I tried to do so, I would fail, and probably end up being a bitter cynic. Instead, I should begin by showing more consistent kindness to my family and friends and then gradually grow into a better person.

Cosmology

Mengzi situates his philosophical anthropology in a broader worldview: "To fully fathom one's heart is to understand one's nature. To understand one's nature is to understand Heaven" (7A1.1). For Mengzi, Heaven (*tiān*) is not as anthropomorphic as it was for the Mohists (whose Heaven is as personal as the God of the Jewish, Christian, and Islamic traditions), but neither is it as naturalized as it would be for some later Confucians (such as Xunzi).[33] On

---

[33] See, respectively, *Mozi* 26, "Heaven's Will," and 31, "On Ghosts," in *Readings*, 90–94, 94–104, and *Xunzi* 17, "Discourse on Heaven," in *Readings*, 269–74.

the one hand, Mengzi sometimes treats Heaven as almost identical with the natural (and amoral) course of events (4A7). But, on the other hand, Heaven provides a moral standard. Thus, Mengzi approvingly quotes one of the *Odes*, which says: "Heaven gives birth to the teeming people. / If there is a thing, there is a norm." (6A6.8).

Mengzi illustrates both the naturalistic and the moral aspects of Heaven in his discussion of the problem of diplomacy between powerful and weak states: "Those who serve the small with the big delight in Heaven; those who serve the big with the small are in awe of Heaven" (1B3.2). In other words, it should be the case (normatively) that the powerful are generous enough to serve the weak. But it is the case (descriptively) that antagonizing powerful states has dangerous consequences. The complexity of Mengzi's view is also evident in his comments about political justification. He stresses that Heaven is the ultimate source of political legitimacy (5A5.2). However, Heaven primarily manifests itself in the reactions of the common people, rather than in any supernatural agency: "Hence, I say that Heaven does not speak but simply reveals the Mandate through actions and affairs" (5A5.5). Heaven is a causal agent that affects the course of human history: "When no one does it, yet it is done—this is due to Heaven. When no one extends to it, yet it is reached—this is fate" (5A6.2). Nonetheless, when "gentlemen" find themselves unable to restore order to the world, they must not be "bitter toward Heaven" (2B13.1). Rather, they must accept Heaven's will while still striving to make the world a better place (7A1).

In order to persevere in the face of adversity without becoming bitter, one must cultivate one's *qi*. This is one of the most intriguing yet difficult-to-understand aspects of Mengzi's thought. *Qi* has been rendered various ways, including "ether," "material force," and "psychophysical stuff." But there is really no adequate translation, since this is a concept that we do not have a precise analogue for. For Mengzi and his contemporaries, *qi* is a kind of fluid, found in the atmosphere and in the human body, closely connected to the kind and intensity of one's emotional reactions. *Qi* therefore straddles the dualism between "mind" and "body" that has become a fixture of post-Cartesian philosophy in the West: *qi* is physically embodied emotion. Here are two examples to give an intuitive understanding of it.

> (1) You are with a group of people in someone's living room, having a pleasant, casual conversation. Someone tries to make an offhand joke, but it ends up sounding like a cutting personal criticism of another guest. It suddenly seems as if the atmosphere in the room has literally changed. It feels like there is something palpably heavy in the air, making further conversation difficult and awkward. That "something" is a kind of negative *qi*, which is both an expression and reinforcement of the feelings of those present. (Compare this to Mengzi's example in 7A36 of the effect of an august person's *qi* on how one feels in his presence.)

(2) Imagine a beautiful April morning. The sun is already bright when you arise. The air smells crisp and fresh. You feel energized for the day ahead. You laugh off any minor problems and annoyances. Your positive mood is partially a product of absorbing some of the vibrant *qi* that circulates on this spring day. (Compare this to Mengzi's example in 6A8.2 of the effects of morning and evening *qi* on restoring one's ethical feelings.)

These examples should not lead us to assume that we are purely passive to the influence of *qi*. Our hearts can resist the effects of negative *qi*, as when I refuse to allow my fear to dissuade me from doing what I know is right. (Mengzi describes this as "maintaining one's will.") But for success in the long run I cannot continue to force myself to act against the promptings of my *qi*. To do so would be to "injure one's *qi*," eventually producing a person who is dispirited —whose *qi* is "starved." Instead, one must cultivate an ethically informed *qi* ("a *qi* that harmonizes with righteousness and the Way"). This *qi* gives one the moral stamina to persevere in the face of dangers, challenges, and setbacks. Among the highly cultivated, this reservoir of fortitude is so deep that it is essentially inexhaustible (or "floodlike," as Mengzi puts it). The way to develop this *qi* is simply through the gradual cultivation of the sprouts of virtue.[34]

From Mengzi to Zhu Xi

In my opinion, after the immediate disciples of Kongzi passed away, the only one who really venerated the sages was Mengzi. —Han Yu

Centuries after Mengzi's death, China achieved long-term unity and stability during the Han dynasty (202 B.C.E.–220 C.E.). In this era, Confucianism became the orthodox philosophy of government. However, it was a form of Confucianism mixed together with elements from other systems of thought that were alien to the worldviews of Mengzi and Kongzi.[35] In addition, after Buddhism arrived from India (bringing novel and subtle metaphysical views), it gradually became intellectually dominant, even among many who were nominally Confucian. By the middle of the Tang dynasty (618–906 C.E.), Empress Wu was routinely hosting and honoring leading Buddhists, especially of the Huayan and Chan (Zen) schools. But toward the end of the same dynasty, Han Yu spearheaded a movement that traced China's social

---

[34] On the concepts discussed in this paragraph, see 2A2.8–9 and 12–15.

[35] See Mark Csikszentmihalyi, trans., *Readings in Han Chinese Thought* (Indianapolis: Hackett Publishing, 2006), and Csikszentmihalyi, "Confucius and the *Analects* in the Han," in *Confucius and the* Analects, ed. Van Norden, 134–62.

and political problems to the supposedly pernicious influence of the "barbarian" Buddhist teaching. Han Yu sought to reawaken China to the lost Confucian Way and stated that Mengzi had an especially pure understanding of it. This "School of the Way" (*Dào xué*, also called "Neo-Confucianism") came to philosophical maturity during the Song dynasty (960–1279 C.E.), with the brilliant theorizing of Zhou Dunyi, Zhang Zai, Cheng Yi, Cheng Hao, and Zhu Xi.[36] Although these thinkers conceived of themselves as simply explicating the same Way as the ancient sages, they could not help but interpret the texts they read in terms of the concepts they had at their disposal. In particular, their two primary metaphysical concepts—*qì* and *lǐ*—meant something very different for them than they had for Kongzi or Mengzi.

Originally, in the Warring States period, *qi* was conceived of as just one entity among others in the world. This is suggested by the expressions "clouds and *qi*" and "blood and *qi*"—pairings in which neither term is metaphysically fundamental.[37] Within a few centuries, however, Chinese philosophers began to think of *qi* as the underlying "stuff" out of which everything else condenses, analogous to the manner in which water condenses as dew or crystallizes into ice.[38] Entities are distinguished by the degree to which their *qi* is "turbid" or "clear."

Li originally referred to any "pattern" that distinguishes one thing from another. It was a term of only peripheral importance to early Confucians, occurring precisely zero times in all of the *Analects*. (But Zhu Xi first mentions it in his commentary on the second passage of the *Analects* and countless times thereafter.) In the *Mengzi*, *li* describes the "harmonious patterns" with which an orchestral performance begins and ends (5B1.6), the "order" that is pleasing to one's mind (6A7.8), and whether or not someone's speech is "articulate" (7B19). Furthermore, the contemporaneous Daoist work, *Zhuangzi*, refers to the "Heavenly pattern" (*tiān lǐ*) of the bones, muscles, and joints that a skilled butcher intuitively follows as he carves up an ox carcass. None of these uses entails any elaborate metaphysical commitments.[39]

---

[36]   Among the seminal essays of the School of the Way are Han Yu, "Memorial on a Bone of the Buddha," "On the Origin of the Way," and "On Reading Xunzi"; Zhou Dunyi, "An Explanation of the Diagram of the Supreme Ultimate"; Zhang Zai, "The Western Inscription"; Cheng Yi, "Letter in Reply to Yang Shi's Letter on the 'Western Inscription.'"

[37]   "When a gentleman reaches old age, and his blood and *qi* have begun to decline, he guards against being acquisitive" (*Analects* 16.7). "[The bird Breeze] spirals upward ninety thousand leagues, bursts through the clouds and *qi*, carrying the blue sky" (*Zhuangzi* 1; cf. *Readings*, 210).

[38]   Benjamin Schwartz, in his nuanced discussion of this concept, notes that *qi* in this sense is analogous to the *apeiron* of Anaximander (*The World of Thought in Ancient China* [Cambridge, MA: Harvard/Belknap, 1985], 183). Another helpful discussion of *qi*, focusing on the ancient use of the concept, may be found in Lewis, *Sanctioned Violence in Early China*, 213–41.

[39]   On the "Heavenly pattern," see *Zhuangzi* 3, "The Key to Nourishing Life," in *Readings*, 225. See also Dai Zhen, *Mengzi ziyi shuzheng* (in Hu Shih, *Dai Dongyuan de zhexue*, 1927, reprint

Now, a key claim in some kinds of Chinese Buddhism is that, because of the causal interrelatedness of all entities, "one is all and all is one." For example, this book would not exist without the tree pulp used in its paper, which would not exist without the sunlight and soil that helped the trees to grow, which would not exist without the Sun and the Earth, which would not exist without the Big Bang (and so on). This concept is symbolized by the metaphor of Indra's Net, a web with a jewel at the intersection of every two strands that is so brilliant it reflects every other jewel. Huayan and Chan (Zen) Buddhists adopted the earlier term "*li*" ("Pattern" or "Principle") to refer to this cosmic web of interrelations. The metaphysical consequence of this view is that things lack individual natures but share a transpersonal "Buddha nature." The ethical implication is that wrongdoing is fundamentally due to "selfishness," a failure to recognize how we are connected with and dependent upon everything else. "Enlightenment" about the true nature of reality produces universal compassion (a virtue reminiscent of the "impartial caring" of the Mohists).

Although the School of the Way opposed Buddhism, it saw Confucianism through Buddhist lenses. Thus, Song dynasty Confucians adopted the term "Pattern" to refer to the structure of the universe, fully present in everything that exists, from a mote of dust, to a cat, to Tyrant Jie, to Kongzi himself. This Pattern is simultaneously descriptive and prescriptive. Because of the Pattern, it *is* the case that everyone will feel alarm and compassion at the sight of a child about to fall into a well. But the Pattern also dictates that we *ought* to extend this compassion to everyone. Although the Pattern is the same in everything, entities are individuated and speciated by having distinct allotments of *qi*. Thus, rocks differ from plants because the *qi* of the latter is more "clear" than the "turbid" *qi* of the former, resulting in a more full manifestation of the Pattern (as shown in the greater responsiveness of plants to their environments). Furthermore, I am different from Kongzi because our *qi* is spatially and temporally distinct, but also (and more importantly) because his clear *qi* manifests the Pattern fully, while my turbid *qi* does not. This view is moderately monistic, in that everything is part of a potentially harmonious whole. However, unlike the Buddhist position, there genuinely are distinct individuals, such as *this* son who owes filial piety to *his* father, and *this* mother who loves *her* children more than those of her neighbor. This justifies the differentiated love so central to Confucianism.

[Tabei: Shangwu yinshuguan, 1996]), Chapter 1, for a general discussion of the early meaning of *li*.

Zhu Xi's Reinterpretation

Generally, in reading a text, you should examine most closely those
passages for which there are differing explanations. Supposing expla-
nation A puts it one way; take firm hold of it, and probe its words
through and through. Supposing explanation B puts it another way;
take firm hold of it, and probe its words through and through. Once
you have probed each of the explanations fully, compare them criti-
cally, analyzing them inside and out. Invariably, the truth will become
clear. —Zhu Xi

One of Zhu Xi's greatest achievements was to show how the metaphysical
framework he inherited could be used to give a unified, systematic interpretation of the *Four Books* and their technical vocabulary.

On his view, human nature in itself ("originally") is simply the Pattern.
However, the Pattern has to be embodied in particular "endowments" of *qi*.
The Pattern is "obscured" in people whose *qi* is turbid, leading them to act
out of "human desires" that are "selfish." In contrast, sages have clear *qi*, so
they are "enlightened." They clearly understand the "Heavenly Pattern" and
therefore act in accordance with it. Although each of us is born with a particular allotment of *qi*, which determines our initial level of understanding
and virtue, education and individual moral effort can clarify the *qi*, while suc-
cumbing to selfish desires can further obscure it.

We can learn a great deal from Zhu Xi's interpretations of the *Four Books*,
but his Buddhist-influenced metaphysics sometimes leads him astray. For example, Mengzi describes our compassion for a child about to fall into a well
as the "sprout" (*duān*) of benevolence. But Zhu Xi glosses the passage as follows: "'Tip' (*duān*) is an end point. By following the expression of the feelings,
one can see what the nature is like originally (*běn*). It is like when there is a
thing inside a box and the end point of it is visible outside" (*Sishu jizhu*, Commentary on 2A6.5). Zhu Xi would thus have us envision our innate virtuous
reactions as the "tips" (manifestations) of a completely formed virtuous nature that is obscured by selfish desires. But for Mengzi, we innately have only
incipient virtues that must be gradually cultivated, like the sprouts of plants,
until they grow to maturity. In other words, Zhu Xi has substituted a spatial
metaphor for Mengzi's agricultural metaphor. For Zhu Xi, becoming virtuous is a process of stripping away selfishness to *discover* one's true nature; for
Mengzi, becoming virtuous is a process of *developing* an incipient potential
for virtue.[40]

---

[40] Philip Ivanhoe was the first to note how Zhu Xi's interpretation alters Mengzi's key metaphor
(*Confucian Moral Self Cultivation*, 46, 56n15). For a defense of interpreting *duān* in 2A6 as
"sprout," see Van Norden, *Virtue Ethics and Consequentialism in Early Chinese Philosophy*,
217–18. For an insightful discussion of the importance of metaphors in early Chinese thought,
see Edward Slingerland, *Effortless Action* (New York: Oxford University Press, 2003).

Consider also *Analects* 17.2, in which Kongzi states, "Natures are close to one another. It is by practice that they become far apart." The claim that our natures are merely "close to one another" seems to be in tension with Mengzi's claim that human nature is the same in everyone. But Zhu Xi is committed to the view that the *Four Books* express an identical Confucian Way. Consequently, he approvingly cites Cheng Yi's view that *Analects* 17.2

> is discussing natures as embodied in *qi*. It is not discussing the origin (*běn*) of the nature. If one discusses its origin, then the nature is simply the Pattern. The Pattern never fails to be good. This is what Mengzi meant by "the nature is good." How could they be (merely) "close to one another"?[41]

We see here why Zhu Xi feels compelled to gloss Mengzi's teaching as "Human nature is originally (*běn*) good."[42] I will try to identify in my commentary other places where Zhu Xi's metaphysics derails his otherwise keen textual insight.

In this Introduction I have stressed how textual commentary, properly used, enables and encourages independent thinking rather than frustrating it. Thus, it seems appropriate to end with a quotation in which Zhu Xi, supposed defender of narrow orthodoxy, shows us the complexity of his own thinking on this topic:

> There's a kind of talk going around these days that makes the younger students lax. People say things like, "I wouldn't dare criticize my elders," or "I wouldn't dare engage in pointless speculation"—all of which suits the fancy of those who are lazy. To be sure, we wouldn't dare criticize our elders recklessly, but what harm is there in discussing the rights and wrongs of what they did? And to be sure, we mustn't engage in idle speculation, but some parts of our reading pose problems while some others are clear, so we have to discuss it. Those who don't discuss it are reading without dealing with the problems.[43]

So turn the page and let the discussion continue.

---

[41] *Sishu jizhu,* Commentary on *Analects* 17.2.

[42] See my commentary on 3A1.2–3.

[43] Translation slightly modified from Gardner, trans., *Learning to Be a Sage,* 5.46, 154.

TIMELINE

Yao becomes Emperor and chooses Shun as his Prime Minister.

Yao dies. The people spontaneously choose Shun as the new Emperor. Shun puts Yu in charge of flood control. Yu's success in this leads Shun to choose him as his Prime Minister.

Shun dies. The people spontaneously choose Yu as the new Emperor.

Yu dies. The people spontaneously choose his son as the new Emperor, thereby creating the first Chinese dynasty: the Xia.

Over many generations, the Virtue of the Xia kings declines, culminating in the vicious rule of Tyrant Jie.

Tyrant Jie is overthrown by the sage Tang, who becomes King of the second Chinese dynasty: the Shang.

Over many generations, the Virtue of the Shang kings declines, culminating in the vicious rule of Tyrant Zhou.

King Wen patiently endures Tyrant Zhou, but his Virtue increasingly draws the support of the people and other nobles.

CIRCA 1040–771 B.C.E.: Western Zhou Dynasty.

King Wen's son, King Wu, leads the rebellion that overthrows Tyrant Zhou and founds the third Chinese dynasty: the Zhou.

A few years after the conquest, King Wu dies of natural causes, leaving his young son, King Cheng, on the throne. King Cheng's regent is his uncle, the Duke of Zhou, who loyally advises and defends King Cheng, solidifying Zhou rule.

Over many generations, the Virtue of the Zhou kings declines.

771 B.C.E.: A group of disaffected nobles and "barbarians" attacks and murders King You.

770–221 B.C.E.: Eastern Zhou Dynasty.

A *surviving member* of the Zhou royal family is established as king in a new capital to the east, deeper in the Zhou territory.

722–481 B.C.E.: Spring and Autumn period.

680 B.C.E.: Duke Huan of Qi, with the assistance of his Prime Minister Guan Zhong, becomes the first Hegemon.

551–479 B.C.E.: Lifetime of Kongzi (Confucius).

Fifth century B.C.E.: Lifetime of Mozi, anti-Confucian philosopher who advocated "impartial caring."

403–221 B.C.E.: Warring States period.

Fourth century B.C.E.:

Birth of Yang Zhu, egoist philosopher.

Birth of Mengzi (Mencius), Confucian who argued that "human nature is good."

Birth of Zhuangzi, Daoist philosopher who advocated emptying rather than cultivating one's heart.

Birth of Xunzi, Confucian who argued that "human nature is bad."

Third century B.C.E.:

Possible date of composition of the Daodejing, attributed to Laozi.

Birth of Hanfeizi, Legalist philosopher.

221–207 B.C.E.: The Qin Dynasty, founded by the self-proclaimed "First Emperor."

202 B.C.E.–220 C.E.: Han Dynasty.

156–87 B.C.E.: Reign of Emperor Wu, under whom Confucianism is made state orthodoxy.

First century C.E.: Buddhism arrives from India.

Over a period of several centuries, spanning several dynasties, Buddhism flourishes and develops in China.

618–906 c.e.: Tang Dynasty.

> *684–705 c.e.:* Reign of Empress Wu, under whom patronage of Huayan and Chan (Zen) Buddhism reached new heights.

> *819 c.e.:* Han Yu writes "Memorial on a Bone of the Buddha" to the Emperor, harshly criticizing Buddhism.

960–1279 c.e.: Song Dynasty.

> *Birth of Zhou Dunyi,* author of "Explanation of the Diagram of the Supreme Ultimate," a seminal metaphysical text of the School of the Way.

> *Birth of Zhang Zai,* author of "The Western Inscription," an ethical manifesto of the School of the Way.

> *Births of Cheng Hao and Cheng Yi,* brothers responsible for developing the mature School of the Way metaphysics.

> *Birth of Lu Xiangshan,* who criticized Zhu Xi for what he saw as dualisms in his interpretation of Confucianism.

> *1130–1200 c.e.:* Lifetime of Zhu Xi, who placed the Four Books at the center of the Confucian curriculum and interpreted them in the light of the new metaphysics.

1313 c.e. (Yuan Dynasty): Zhu Xi's Collected Commentaries on the Four Books becomes the basis of the civil service examinations.

1472–1529 c.e. (Ming Dynasty): Lifetime of Wang Yangming, whose criticisms of Zhu Xi are similar to those of Lu Xiangshan.

1905 c.e. (Qing Dynasty): Civil services examinations are eliminated.

SELECTED BIBLIOGRAPHY
OF WORKS ON MENGZI
AND ZHU XI

Chan, Alan K. L., ed. *Mencius: Contexts and Interpretations*. Honolulu: University of Hawaii Press, 2002.

Chan, Wing-tsit, ed. *Chu Hsi and Neo-Confucianism*. Honolulu: University of Hawaii Press, 1986.

Dobson, W. A. C. H., trans. *Mencius*. Toronto: University of Toronto Press, 1963.

Gardner, Daniel K., trans. *The Four Books: The Basic Teachings of the Later Confucian Tradition*. Indianapolis, IN: Hackett Publishing, 2007.

———, trans. *Learning to Be a Sage: Selections from the* Conversations of Master Chu. Berkeley: University of California Press, 1990.

Giles, Lionel, trans. *The Book of Mencius*. 1942. Reprint. Rutland, VT: Charles E. Tuttle Company, 1993.

Graham, Angus C. "The Background of the Mencian Theory of Human Nature." 1967. Reprinted in Angus C. Graham, *Studies in Chinese Philosophy and Philosophical Literature*, 7–66. Albany: State University of New York Press, 1990.

Hinton, David, trans. *Mencius*. Washington, DC: Counterpoint, 1998.

Ivanhoe, Philip J. *Confucian Moral Self-Cultivation*. 2d ed. Indianapolis, IN: Hackett Publishing, 2000.

———. *Ethics in the Confucian Tradition: The Thought of Mengzi and Wang Yangming*. 2d ed. Indianapolis, IN: Hackett Publishing, 2002.

Jiao Xun. *Mengzi zhengyi* ("The Correct Meaning of the *Mengzi*"). Reprinted in *Zhuzi jicheng*, edited by Cai Shangsi. Shanghai: Shanghai shudian, 1996.

Lau, D. C., trans. *Mencius*. New York: Penguin Books, 1970.

———. trans. *Mencius*. Rev. ed. Hong Kong: Chinese University Press, 2003.

———. "Some Notes on the *Mencius*." 1969. Reprinted in Lau, *Mencius* (1970). Appendix 6, 391–415.

Legge, James, trans. *The Works of Mencius*. 1895. Reprint. New York: Dover Books, 1970.

Liu, Xiusheng. *Mencius, Hume, and the Foundations of Ethics*. Burlington, VT: Ashgate Publishing, 2003.

———, and Philip J. Ivanhoe, eds. *Essays on the Moral Philosophy of Mengzi*. Indianapolis, IN: Hackett Publishing, 2002.

Nivison, David S. *The Ways of Confucianism*. Chicago: Open Court Press, 1996.

———. "Protest against Conventions and Conventions of Protest." In *The Confucian Persuasion*, edited by Arthur Wright, 177–201. Stanford, CA: Stanford University Press, 1960.

Richards, I. A. *Mencius on the Mind: Experiments in Multiple Definition*. 1932. Reprint. Whitefish, MT: Kessinger Publications, 2005.

Shun, Kwong-loi. *Mencius and Early Chinese Thought*. Stanford, CA: Stanford University Press, 2000.

Tsai, Chih Chung, and Brian Bruya. *Mencius Speaks*. Modern Publishing House, 2005.

Van Norden, Bryan W. *Virtue Ethics and Consequentialism in Early Chinese Philosophy*. New York: Cambridge University Press, 2007.

———. "What Is Living and What Is Dead in the Philosophy of Zhu Xi?" In *Chinese Ethics in an Age of Globalization*, edited by Robin R. Wang, 99–120. Albany: State University of New York Press, 2004.

Waley, Arthur. "Notes on *Mencius*." 1949. Reprinted in *The Chinese Classics*, translated by James Legge, vol. 2, vii–xiv. Taipei, Taiwan: SMC Publishing, 1991.

Yearley, Lee H. *Mencius and Aquinas: Theories of Virtue and Conceptions of Courage*. Albany: State University of New York Press, 1990.

Zhao Qi. *Mengzi zhu* ("Commentary on the *Mengzi*"). Reprinted in *Zhuzi jicheng*, edited by Cai Shangsi. Shanghai: Shanghai shudian, 1996.

Zhu Xi. *Sishu jizhu* ("Collected Commentaries on the *Four Books*"). Sibu beiyao ed.

———. *Zhuzi yulei* ("Classified Conversations of Master Zhu"). Reprint. Beijing: Zhonghua shuju, 1986.

SELECTED BIBLIOGRAPHY OF OTHER WORKS

Brooks, Bruce, and Taeko Brooks, trans. *The Original Analects*. New York: Columbia University Press, 1998.

Csikszentmihalyi, Mark, trans. *Readings in Han Chinese Thought*. Indianapolis, IN: Hackett Publishing, 2006.

Goldin, Paul. *After Confucius: Studies in Early Chinese Philosophy*. Honolulu: University of Hawaii Press, 2005.

Graham, Angus C. *Disputers of the Tao*. Chicago: Open Court Press, 1989.

———. *Two Chinese Philosophers*. 1958. Reprint. Chicago: Open Court Press, 1992.

Henderson, John B. *Scripture, Canon, and Commentary*. Princeton, NJ: Princeton University Press, 1991.

Ivanhoe, Philip J., trans. *Readings from the Lu-Wang School of Neo-Confucianism*. Indianapolis, IN: Hackett Publishing, 2009.

———, and Bryan W. Van Norden, eds. *Readings in Classical Chinese Philosophy*. 2d ed. Indianapolis, IN: Hackett Publishing, 2005.

Legge, James, trans. *The Chinese Classics*, 5 vols. 1895. Reprint. Taipei, Taiwan: SMC Publishing, 1991.

Lewis, Mark Edward. *Sanctioned Violence in Early China*. Albany: State University of New York Press, 1990.

Loewe, Michael, and Edward L. Shaughnessy, eds. *The Cambridge History of Ancient China*. New York: Cambridge University Press, 1999.

Pines, Yuri. *Foundations of Confucian Thought*. Honolulu: University of Hawaii Press, 2002.

Puett, Michael. *The Ambivalence of Creation*. Stanford, CA: Stanford University Press, 2001.

————. "The Ethics of Responding Properly: The Notion of Qíng 情 in Early Chinese Thought." In *Love and Emotions in Traditional Chinese Literature*, edited by Halvor Eifring, 37–68. Leiden, the Netherlands: Brill, 2004.

Radcliff-Brown, A. R. "Religion and Society." In *Structure and Function in Primitive Society*, 153–77. New York: The Free Press, 1968.

Sawyer, Ralph D., trans. *Sun Tzu: Art of War*. Boulder, CO: Westview Press, 1994.

Schwartz, Benjamin. *The World of Thought in Ancient China*. Cambridge, MA: Harvard/Belknap, 1985.

Slingerland, Edward, trans. *Analects: with Selections from Traditional Commentaries*. Indianapolis, IN: Hackett Publishing, 2003.

————. *Effortless Action*. New York: Oxford University Press, 2003.

————, trans. *The Essential Analects: Selected Passages with Traditional Commentary*. Indianapolis, IN: Hackett Publishing, 2006.

————. "Why Philosophy Is Not 'Extra' in Understanding the *Analects*." *Philosophy East and West* 50:1 (January 2000): 137–41, 146–47.

Ssu-ma, Ch'ien. *The Grand Scribe's Records*, vol. 1, trans. Tsai-fa Cheng et al. Indianapolis: University of Indiana Press, 1994.

Van Norden, Bryan W., ed. *Confucius and the Analects: New Essays*. New York: Oxford University Press, 2002.

Waley, Arthur, trans. *The Analects of Confucius*. 1938. Reprint. New York: Vintage Books, 1989.

————, trans. *The Book of Songs*. Rev. ed. New York: Grove Press, 1996.

Watson, Burton, trans. *The Tso Chuan*. New York: Columbia University Press, 1989.

Wong, David. *Natural Moralities*. New York: Oxford University Press, 2006.

————. "Universalism vs. Love with Distinctions: An Ancient Debate Revived." *Journal of Chinese Philosophy* 16:3/4 (September/December 1989): 251–72.

BOOK 1A

This book consists of dialogues between Mengzi and the rulers of the power-
ful states of Wei (here referred to as "Liang," after its capital city) and Qi.
Mengzi tries to convert them to ruling benevolently, and he provides specific
policy advice when they seem receptive. (The first dialogue probably took
place in 319 B.C.E.) Among the most interesting and often-discussed passages
in this book are 1A1 and 1A7.

Mengzi had an audience with King Hui of Liang. The king said, "Vener-   *1.1–1.2*
able sir, you have not regarded hundreds of leagues too far to come, so you
must have a way of profiting my state."

Mengzi replied, "Why must Your Majesty speak of 'profit'? Let there   *1.3*
simply be benevolence and righteousness. If Your Majesty says, 'How can I   *1.4*
profit my state?' the Chief Counselors will say, 'How can I profit my clan?'
and the nobles and commoners will say, 'How can I profit my self?' Superiors and subordinates will seize profit from each other, and the state will
be endangered. When the ruler in a state that can field ten thousand chariots is assassinated, it will invariably be by a clan that can field a thousand
chariots. When the ruler in a state that can field a thousand chariots is assassinated, it will invariably be by a clan that can field a hundred chariots.
To have a thousand out of ten thousand or a hundred out of a thousand is
plenty. But when people put profit before righteousness, they cannot be satisfied without grasping for more.[1]

Never have the benevolent left their parents behind. Never have the right-   *1.5*
eous put their ruler last. Let Your Majesty speak only of benevolence and   *1.6*
righteousness. Why must one speak of 'profit'?" 注

Mengzi had an audience with King Hui of Liang. The king was standing by   *2.1*
the pond, gazing at the geese and deer, and said, "Do the worthy also delight in these things?"

---

[1] The size of states and the strength of powerful families were typically measured in terms of
how many war chariots they could field in battle.

1

2.2
2.3   Mengzi replied, "Only the worthy delight in these things. Those who
are not worthy, even if they have these things, do not delight in them. The
Odes say,

> He laid out and began the Spirit Tower.
> He laid it out and planned it.
> The common people worked on it,
> And in less than a day completed it.
> He laid it out and began it: "Hurry not!"
> But the common people like children came.
> The King was in the Spirit Park.
> The doe rested,
> The doe so sleek and plump,
> The white birds so pure.
> The King was at the Spirit Pond
> Oh, it was full of jumping fish.

King Wen, with the strength of the people, made the Tower and made the
Pond, but the people welcomed and were delighted by them: they called his
tower the 'Spirit Tower'; they called his pond the 'Spirit Pond'; they delighted in its having deer, fish, and turtles. The ancients were happy together
with the people, hence they were able to be happy. 注

2.4   "According to 'The Declaration of Tang' from the *Documents,* the subjects
of Jie said, 'When will this Sun expire? We will perish together with you.'
The people desired to perish together with him. Although he had a tower,
pond, birds, and beasts, was he able to enjoy them alone?" 注

3.1   King Hui of Liang said, "We use our heart to the utmost for our state. When
the region within the river has a famine, we move some of the people to
the region to the east of the river and move grain to the region within the
river. When there is a famine in the region to the east of the river, we do
likewise. When we examine the governments of neighboring states, there
are none that use their hearts to the utmost like we do. Why is it that the
people of neighboring states do not grow fewer and our people do not grow
more numerous?" 注

3.2   Mengzi replied, "Your Majesty is fond of war, so allow me to use war as
an illustration. Thunderingly, the drums spur the soldiers on. Blades clash
together. Casting aside their armor and weapons, they run. Some stop after
running a hundred paces; some stop after running only fifty paces. How
would it be if those who ran fifty paces were to laugh at those who ran a
hundred paces?"

The king said, "That is not acceptable. They simply did not run a hundred paces. But this too is running."

Mengzi replied, "If Your Majesty understands this, then you will not expect your people to be more numerous than those of neighboring states. 注

"If one does not disrupt the farming seasons with building projects, but only waits until after the crops have been harvested, the grain will be inexhaustible. If overly fine nets are not used in the ponds, so that sufficient fish and turtles are left to reproduce, they will be inexhaustible. If people bring their axes into the mountain forests only in the proper season, the wood will be inexhaustible. When grain, fish, turtles, and wood are inexhaustible, this will make the people have no regrets in caring for the living or mourning the dead. When the people have no regrets about caring for the living or mourning the dead, it is the beginning of the Kingly Way. If each household with a five-acre plot of land is planted with mulberry trees to raise silkworms, fifty-year-olds can wear silk. If the care of chickens, pigs, dogs, and sows does not miss its season, seventy-year-olds can eat meat. If one does not steal the labor during the farming seasons of each hundred-acre field, a clan with many mouths can go without hunger. If one is careful about providing instruction in the village schools, emphasizing the righteousness of filiality and brotherliness, those whose hair has turned gray will not carry loads on the roadways. It has never happened that someone fails to become King when, among his subjects, seventy-year-olds are wearing silk and eating meat, and the black-haired people are neither hungry nor cold. 注

"Currently, no one knows to limit how much of the food is consumed by dogs and sows. Then no one knows to disburse food from the granary when there are bodies in the streets dead of starvation. When someone dies, you say, 'It wasn't me. It was due to the harvest.' How is this different from killing someone by stabbing him and saying, 'It wasn't me. It was due to the weapon'? If Your Majesty does not blame the harvest, then the people of the world will come to you."

King Hui of Liang said, "We are willing to calmly accept your instruction."

Mengzi replied, "Is there any difference between killing a person with a club and killing him with a blade?"

The king said, "There is no difference."

Mengzi continued, "Is there a difference between using a blade and government?"

The king said, "There is no difference."

Mengzi said, "In your kitchens there is fat meat, and in your stables there are fat horses. Yet the people appear starved, and there are corpses of the starved in the wilds. This is to lead animals to devour people. People are appalled even when animals eat others of their kind. Now, one who governs is the people's parent. But in what respect is one a parent to the people if one leads animals to devour them? Kongzi said, 'May the one who first created tomb figurines have no posterity!' That was merely because that person buried *images* of people. What about someone who causes the people to die from starvation?"

4.6

6.1–6.2 Mengzi had an audience with King Xiang of Liang.[2] When Mengzi left, he said to some others, "When I looked up at him, he did not seem like a ruler of people. When I approached him, I did not see anything awe-inspiring in him. He simply blurted out, 'How can the world be pacified?' 注

"I responded, 'It can be pacified by being unified.'

6.3   "The king asked, 'Who can unify it?'

6.4   "I replied, 'One who does not have a taste for killing people can unify it.'

6.5   "The king asked, 'Who can give it to him?'

6.6   "I replied, 'No one in the world will fail to give it to him. Does Your Majesty know about sprouts? During the dry period of the summer months, the sprouts shrivel. But when Heaven abundantly makes clouds, and copiously sends down rain, then the sprouts vigorously rise up. If it is like this, who can forbid it? But nowadays, there are none, among those who shepherd the people, who do not have a taste for killing people. If there were one who did not have a taste for killing people, the people of the world would crane their necks to look for him. If it were genuinely like this, the people would turn to him like water flowing down, copiously. Who would be able to forbid it?'" 注

7.1   King Xuan of Qi asked, "May I hear from you of the actions of Huan of Qi and Wen of Jin?"[3]

7.2   Mengzi replied, "The followers of Kongzi did not give accounts of the actions of Huan and Wen. Because of this, they were not passed on to later generations, and I have not heard of them. But, if you insist, then may we talk about being King?" 注

7.3   The king said, "What must one's Virtue be like so that one can become King?"[4]

---

[2] While Mengzi was in Liang, King Hui died and was succeeded by his son, King Xiang. This passage probably describes Mengzi's first meeting with the new ruler.

[3] Duke Huan of Qi and Duke Wen of Jin were famous "Hegemons," rulers who dominated other states with their military power.

[4] "Virtue" is a sort of ethical charisma that induces others to submit without the need for coercion.

Mengzi said, "One cares for the people and becomes King. This is something no one can stop."

The king said, "Can one such as ourselves care for the people?"   7.4

Mengzi said, "You can."

The king said, "How do you know that we can?"

Mengzi said, "I heard your attendant Hu He say,

> While the king was sitting up in his hall, an ox was led past below. The king saw it and said, 'Where is the ox going?' Hu He replied, 'We are about to ritually anoint a bell with its blood.' The king said, 'Spare it. I cannot bear its frightened appearance, like an innocent going to the execution ground.' Hu He replied, 'So should we dispense with the anointing of the bell?' The king said, 'How can that be dispensed with? Exchange it for a sheep.'

Mengzi continued, "I do not know if this happened."[5]

The king said, "It happened."   7.5

Mengzi said, "This heart is sufficient to become King. The commoners all thought Your Majesty was being stingy. But I knew that Your Majesty simply could not bear the suffering of the ox." 注

The king said, "That is so. There were indeed commoners who said that.   7.6
But although Qi is a small state, how could I be stingy about one ox? It was just that I could not bear its frightened appearance, like an innocent going to the execution ground. Hence, I exchanged it for a sheep."

Mengzi said, "Let Your Majesty not be surprised at the commoners taking   7.7
you to be stingy. You took a small thing and exchanged it for a big thing. How could they understand it? If Your Majesty were pained at its being innocent and going to the execution ground, then what is there to choose between an ox and a sheep?"

The king laughed, saying, "What was this feeling, actually? It's not the case that I grudged its value and exchanged it for a sheep. But it makes sense that the commoners would say I was stingy." 注

Mengzi said, "There is no harm. What you did was just a technique for   7.8
(cultivating your) benevolence. You saw the ox but had not seen the sheep. Gentlemen cannot bear to see animals die if they have seen them living. If

---

they hear their cries of suffering, they cannot bear to eat their flesh. Hence, gentlemen keep their distance from the kitchen." 注

7.9   The king was pleased and said, "The *Odes* say,

> Another person had the heart,
> I measured it.

This describes you, Master. I was the one who did it. I examined myself and sought to find my heart but failed to understand it. But when you discussed it, my heart was moved. So in what way does this heart accord with becoming King?" 注

7.10   Mengzi said, "Suppose there were someone who reported to Your Majesty, 'My strength is sufficient to lift five hundred pounds, but not sufficient to lift one feather. My eyesight is sufficient to examine the tip of an autumn hair, but I cannot see a wagon of firewood.' Would Your Majesty accept that?"

The king said, "No."

Mengzi said, "In the present case your kindness is sufficient to reach animals, but the effects do not reach the commoners. How is this different from the examples I just gave? Hence, one fails to lift a feather only because one does not use one's strength. One fails to see a wagon of firewood only because one does not use one's eyesight. The commoners fail to receive care only because one does not use one's kindness. Hence, Your Majesty fails to become King because you do not act, not because you are unable to act." 注

7.11   The king said, "How does one distinguish between concrete cases of not acting and not being able?"

Mengzi said, "'Tuck Mount Tai under your arm and leap over the North Sea.' If you tell others, 'I am unable,' you are genuinely unable. 'Collect kindling for an elderly person.' If you tell others, 'I am unable,' you are simply not acting, not genuinely unable. Hence Your Majesty's failure to become King is not in the category of tucking Mount Tai under your arm and leaping over the North Sea. Your Majesty's failure to become King is in the category of collecting kindling. 注

7.12   "Treat your elders as elders, and extend it to the elders of others; treat your young ones as young ones, and extend it to the young ones of others, and you can turn the world in the palm of your hand. The *Odes* say,

> He set an example for his little woman,
> It extended to his brothers,
> And so he controlled his clan and state.

This means that he simply took this feeling and applied it to that. Hence, if one extends one's kindness, it will be sufficient to care for all within the Four Seas. If one does not extend one's kindness, one will lack the wherewithal to care for one's wife and children. That in which the ancients greatly exceeded others was no other than this. They were simply good at extending what they did. In the present case your kindness is sufficient to reach animals, but the effects do not reach the commoners. Why is this case alone different? 注

"Weigh it, and then you will distinguish the light and the heavy. Measure it, and then you will distinguish the long and the short. Things are all like this, the heart most of all. Let Your Majesty measure it. 7.13

"Perhaps Your Majesty can only be happy in your heart by rallying soldiers, endangering your military officers, and building up the resentment of the various lords?" 注 7.14

The king said, "No. How could I be made happy by these things? It is that I am seeking my greatest desire." 注 7.15

Mengzi said, "Could I hear your Majesty's greatest desire?" The king smiled and did not speak. 7.16

Mengzi said, "Do you do these things because you don't have enough savory and sweet foods for your mouth? Because you don't have enough summer or winter clothes for you body? Because you don't have enough beautiful and charming sights for your eyes to look at? Because you don't have enough music for your ears to listen to? Because you don't have enough personal attendants to order about in front of you? Your Majesty's various ministers certainly are enough to serve you. So how could Your Majesty actually do what you do for any of these things?"

The king said, "No. I do not do it for the sake of these things."

Mengzi said, "Then Your Majesty's greatest desire can be known. You desire to open up new lands for cultivation, bring to your court the states of Qin and Chu, oversee the Central States, and dominate the border tribes. But to seek what you desire by the means that you employ is like climbing a tree in search of a fish." 注

The king said, "Could it really be as extreme as that?" 7.17

Mengzi said, "It is worse than that! If one climbs a tree in search of a fish, although one will not get a fish, there will be no disaster afterward. If you fully apply yourself to seeking what you desire by the means that you employ, it can only lead to disaster."

The king said, "Could I hear more about this?"

Mengzi said, "If the people of the small state of Zou and the large state of Chu fought, who does your Majesty think would win?"

The king said, "The people of Chu would win."

Mengzi said, "So the small certainly cannot match the big, the few certainly cannot match a multitude, the weak inherently cannot match the strong. The region within the seas is nine thousand leagues square. Qi amounts to one thousand. To take on eight with one, how is this different from Zou matching up against Chu?

7.18   "Instead, simply return to the root. Suppose Your Majesty were to bestow benevolence in governing. This would cause all those under Heaven who serve to want to take their place in Your Majesty's court, all those who plow to want to plow in Your Majesty's uncultivated fields, all traveling merchants and shopkeepers to want to place their goods in Your Majesty's markets, all those who travel to wish to use Your Majesty's roads. All those under Heaven who wish to complain of their rulers would all desire to report to Your Majesty. If it were like this, who could stop it?" 注

7.19   The king said, "I am unable to undertake this because of my ignorance. But I am willing for you, Master, to redirect my will, enlighten, and instruct me. Although I am not clever, please let me try."

7.20   Mengzi said, "Only a noble is capable of having a constant heart while lacking a constant livelihood. As for the people, if they lack a constant livelihood, it follows that they will lack a constant heart. No one who lacks a constant heart will avoid dissipation and evil. When they thereupon sink into crime, to go and punish the people is to trap them. When there are benevolent persons in positions of authority, how is it possible for them to

7.21   trap the people? 注 For this reason, an enlightened ruler must regulate the people's livelihood to ensure that it is sufficient, on the one hand, to serve their fathers and mothers, and on the other hand, to nurture their wives and children. In good years, they are always full. In years of famine, they escape death. Only then do they rush toward the good, and thus the people follow the ruler easily. 注

7.22   "Nowadays, the people's livelihood is regulated so that it is neither sufficient to serve their fathers and mothers, nor is it sufficient to nurture their wives and children. Even in good years, they are always bitter. In years of famine, they cannot escape death. This is a case in which one fears not having the means to escape death. How could they have leisure for cultivating ritual and righteousness? 注

7.23   "If Your Majesty wishes to put the Way into effect, then why not return
7.24   to the root? Plant every household of five acres with mulberry trees to cultivate silkworms, and fifty-year-olds can wear silk. Let the nurturing of chickens, pigs, and dogs not be neglected, and seventy-year-olds can eat meat. If you do not disturb the seasonal work in each field of one hundred acres, a clan with eight mouths need not go hungry. If you are careful that the schools engage in instruction, explaining the righteousness of filiality and brotherliness, then those with gray hair will not carry loads on the roads. It has never happened that a person fails to become the King when his old people wear silk and eat meat, and the black-haired people are neither hungry nor cold." 注

BOOK 1B

This book consists of dialogues between Mengzi and the rulers of various states, mostly King Xuan of Qi; he gives them specific political advice but also tries to convert them to ruling benevolently. Among the most interesting and often-discussed passages in this book are 1B5, 1B6, and 1B8.

King Xuan of Qi asked, "Is there a Way for interacting with neighboring states?"

Mengzi replied, "There is. Only the benevolent are able to serve the small with the big. Hence Tang served the Ge tribe, and King Wen served the Kun Yi tribe. Only the wise are able to serve the large with the small. Hence, King Tai served the Xun Yu, and Gou Jian served the Wu. 注 Those who serve the small with the big delight in Heaven; those who serve the big with the small are in awe of Heaven. Those who delight in Heaven care for the world; those who are in awe of Heaven care for their state. 注 The *Odes* say,

> In awe of august Heaven
> Thus we care for the state.

The king said, "Great are your teachings! But we have a weakness: we are fond of courage."

Mengzi replied, "I ask Your Majesty to not be fond of small courage. Wielding a sword, angrily staring, and saying, 'How dare he face me?!'—this is the courage of a common fellow. It is for opposing a single person. I ask Your Majesty to enlarge it. 注 The *Odes* say,

> Frightful was his anger
> So he assembled his units
> To stop the army invading Ju,
> To increase the fortunes of the Zhou,
> In answer to the hopes of the world.

Such was the courage of King Wen. King Wen brought peace to the people of the world with one burst of anger. The *Documents* say, 'Heaven sent down the people, and made for them rulers, made for them teachers, saying simply, *They are helpers to the Lord on High!* It distinguished them throughout the four quarters. *The guilty and the innocent only rest in me!* How dare the world overstep Heaven's intentions?' Similarly, if one person in the world made trouble, King Wu was ashamed of it. Such was the courage of King Wu. And King Wu also brought peace to the people of the world with one

3.8 burst of anger. In the present case, if Your Majesty also brought peace to the
people of the world with one burst of anger, the people would only fear lest
Your Majesty were not fond of courage."

5.1 King Xuan of Qi asked, "People all tell me to destroy the Bright Tower. Should
I destroy it or leave it?" 注

5.2 Mengzi replied, "The Bright Tower is the tower of a King. If Your Majesty
desires to put into effect Kingly government, do not destroy it."

5.3 The king said, "May I hear more about Kingly government?"
Mengzi replied, "In former times, King Wen ruled his state like this. For farming, there was the nine-one system. For those in positions of responsibility, there
were stipends for their descendants. The customs officers of the roads and markets made inspections but levied no duties. The people were not prohibited from
fishing in the ponds and weirs. Guilt for crime did not extend to the criminals'
wives. The old without wives were called 'widowers,' the old without husbands
were 'widows,' the old without children were 'bereft,' the young without fathers
were 'orphans.' These four were the poorest among the people and had none to
bring their cares to. King Wen, in applying benevolent government, put these
four first. The *Odes* say,

> Fitting it is for those with funds
> To be sad for these wretched, lonely ones." 注

5.4 The king exclaimed, "What excellent teachings!"
Mengzi responded, "If Your Majesty regards them as excellent, then why do
you not put them into effect?"
The king said, "We have a weakness. We are fond of wealth."
Mengzi responded, "In former times, Duke Liu of Zhou was fond of wealth.
The *Odes* say,

> They stacked, they stored,
> Bundled up dried goods,
> In bags, in sacks,
> Thinking to gather together and bring glory.
> His bows and arrows were displayed,
> With shields, spears, and battle-axes,
> He commenced the march against Bin.

Hence, those who stayed at home had loaded granaries, and those who marched
had full provisions. Only then could they 'commence the march.' If Your Majesty
is fond of wealth but treats the commoners the same, what difficulty is there in
becoming King?" 注

The king said, "We have a weakness. We are fond of sex."   5.5

Mengzi responded, "In former times, King Tai of Zhou was fond of sex, and loved his wife. The *Odes* say,

> The Ancient Duke Danfu
> Came riding his horse in the morning,
> Along the banks of the Western waters.
> He came to the foot of Mount Qi,
> With his Lady Jiang.
> They came and both settled there.

At that time, there were no bitter women in private, or any unmarried men in public. If Your Majesty is fond of sex but treats the commoners the same, what difficulty is there in becoming King?" 注

Mengzi spoke to King Xuan of Qi, saying, "If, among Your Majesty's ministers,   6.1
there were one who entrusted his wife and children to his friend, and traveled to the distant state of Chu, and when he returned, his friend had let his wife and children become cold and hungry—how should he handle this?"

The king said, "Abandon his friend."

Mengzi said, "If the Chief Warden is not able to keep order among the no-   6.2
bles, how should one handle this?"

The king said, "Discharge him."

Mengzi said, "If the region within the four borders is not well ruled, then   6.3
how should one handle this?" The king turned toward his attendants and changed the topic. 注

King Xuan of Qi asked, "Is it the case that, Tang banished Jie and Wu struck   8.1
down Tyrant Zhou when Tang and Wu were their subjects?"

Mengzi replied, "That is what has been passed down in ancient texts."

The king said, "Is it acceptable for subjects to assassinate their rulers?"   8.2

Mengzi said, "One who mutilates benevolence should be called a 'mutilator.'   8.3
One who mutilates righteousness should be called a 'crippler.' A crippler and mutilator is called a mere 'fellow.' I have indeed heard of the execution of this one fellow Zhou, but I have not heard of it as the assassination of one's ruler." 注

The people of Qi invaded Yan and were victorious.[1] King Xuan asked, "Some   10.1–10.2
say that we should not annex Yan; others say that we should annex it. For a state of ten thousand chariots to have invaded another state of ten thousand chariots

---

[1]   Zhu Xi recommends that one read 2B8, 1B10, 1B11, and 2B9 in that order.

and to have taken it in fifty days is something that human power alone could not have achieved. So if we do not annex it, there will certainly be some Heavenly retribution. How would it be if I were to annex it?"[2]

10.3   Mengzi said, "If annexing it would please the people of Yan, then annex it. Among the ancients there were those who did such things. King Wu was one. If annexing it would not please the people of Yan, then do not annex it. Among

10.4   the ancients there were those who did such things. King Wen was one. 注 For a state of ten thousand chariots to invade another state of ten thousand chariots, whose people then welcome that King with baskets of food and pots of soup— what other leader could they have? But if they flee you like fleeing water and fire, as if you were deeper than water and hotter than fire, then they will simply reject you." 注

11.1   The people of Qi invaded Yan and annexed it. The various lords were planning to rescue Yan from Qi. King Xuan said, "Most of the various lords are planning to invade us. How should we deal with this?"

Mengzi replied, "I have heard of one with a territory of as little as seventy leagues square coming to govern the world. Such was Tang. But I have not heard of anyone with even a territory of a thousand leagues intimidating people suc-

11.2   cessfully. The *Documents* say of Tang, 'When he first attacked, he began with the state of Ge.' The world had faith in his intentions. 'When he attacked in the east, the tribes of the west were bitter. When he attacked in the south, the tribes of the north were bitter. They said, *Why does he make us last?*' The people looked forward to him like a drought looking forward to a rainbow amid the clouds. Those who came to the city did not stop, and farmers did not move away. He punished the rulers of these tribes and consoled the people. He was like the coming of timely rain. The people were very pleased. The *Documents* say, 'We treat him as our ruler. When our ruler comes we are revived!'

11.3   "In the current case, Yan was ferocious to its people. Your Majesty went out and attacked it. The people thought that you were going to deliver them as from flood and fire. They welcomed Your Majesty with baskets of food and pots of soup. But if you kill their fathers and older brothers, put burdens on their sons and younger brothers, destroy their shrines and temples, plundering their valuable goods—how could that be acceptable? The world is definitely intimidated by the size of Qi. But if you double its land with this annexation and do not put into effect benevolent government, you will mobilize the soldiers of the

11.4   world against you. If Your Majesty quickly issues orders to return the young and

---

[2] Qi's invasion of Yan was swift and decisive, because the people put up no resistance. They were presumably happy to have someone put an end to the chaos and internal strife of their state (see 2B8). But Xuan suggests that the ease of conquest is a sign that Heaven wants him to annex Yan.

old who have been captured or taken hostage, to stop the plundering of their valuable goods, to plan with the masses of Yan to establish rulers and then leave, then you can stop it before it occurs." 注

Duke Ping of Lu was about to go out. One of his favorites, a certain Zang Cang, asked him, "On other days when your lordship goes out you always announce to those who hold office where you are going. Today, although the horses are already harnessed to your carriage, those who hold office do not know where you are going. May I ask where you are going?"

16.1

The duke replied, "I am going to have an audience with Mengzi."

Zang Cang said, "What?! You are demeaning yourself by going to see a mere fellow. Do you regard him as worthy? Propriety and righteousness come from those who are worthy. But Mengzi's mourning rituals for his mother's death were more lavish than for his father's death. Let your lordship not have an audience with him."

The duke answered, "Alright then."

Yuezhengzi, an official in Lu who was a disciple of Mengzi, went in to have an audience with the duke and said, "Why did your lordship not see Mengzi?"

16.2

The duke said, "Someone reported to us, 'Mengzi's mourning rituals for his mother's death were more lavish than for his father's death.' Consequently, I did not go to have an audience with him."

Yuezhengzi said, "What?! What are you describing as lavish? Is it the fact that formerly he was a noble, and later he was Chief Counselor, so for his father's ritual he used three *ding* tripods, but for his mother's ritual he used five *ding* tripods?"

The duke said, "No. What I am speaking of is how fine the inner and outer coffins and funeral garments were."

Yuezhengzi said, "This is not what is called 'lavish.' This is due to the difference between being poor and being wealthy."

Yuezhengzi had an audience with Mengzi and said, "I told the ruler about you, and he was coming to meet with you. Among the ruler's favorites there was a certain Zang Cang who prevented it. Because of this the ruler, in the end, did not come to meet with you."

16.3

Mengzi said, "If a person acts, something causes it; if a person stops, something hinders it. Whether someone else acts or stops is not something a human controls. My not meeting the Duke of Lu is due to Heaven. How could this fellow of the Zang clan be capable of preventing me from meeting him?" 注

BOOK 2A

This book includes some of the most important expositions of Mengzi's philosophical psychology and political philosophy. Among the most interesting and often-discussed passages in this book are 2A2 and 2A6.

1.1 Mengzi's disciple Gongsun Chou asked, "If you, Master, were to occupy an important position in Qi, could we expect that the achievements of Guan Zhong or Yanzi would be repeated?"[1]

1.2 Mengzi said, "You are genuinely a man of Qi. All you know about are

1.3 Guan Zhong and Yanzi, and not the actions of sages and worthies. Someone once asked Zeng Xi, grandson of Kongzi's disciple Zengzi, 'Who is more worthy: you or Kongzi's disciple Zilu?' Zeng Xi replied diffidently, 'Zilu, of whom my grandfather stood in awe, is more worthy.' The questioner then said, 'So who is more worthy: you or Guan Zhong?' Zeng Xi was unhappy and angrily said, 'How dare you compare me to Guan Zhong? For Guan Zhong to have had a ruler's complete confidence like he did, and for him to have governed for as long as he did, and then for the height of his achievement to be so base—how dare you compare me to him?'" 注

1.4 Mengzi concluded, "Guan Zhong was someone whom Zeng Xi would not emulate. And you hope for me to become like him?"

1.5 Gongsun Chou then asked, "Guan Zhong made his ruler Hegemon.[2] Yanzi made his ruler illustrious. Are Guan Zhong and Yanzi not worth emulating?"

1.6 Mengzi said, "Making the ruler of Qi into a King is as easy as turning over one's hand."

1.7 Gongsun Chou said, "In that case, I have been terribly mistaken. I thought that when King Wen died after a hundred years, his Virtue had not yet spread throughout the world, and that King Wu and the Duke of Zhou perpetuated it, and only then was it broadly put into effect.[3] Now what you say makes it seem easy to become King. So was King Wen not worth modeling oneself on?"

1.8 Mengzi said, "How could anyone match King Wen? From Tang, founder of the Shang dynasty, to Wu Ding, who revived the Virtue of that dynasty, six or seven rulers who were worthies or sages arose. The world had turned

---

[1] These were ministers in Qi who helped their rulers become powerful. (Mengzi did eventually become High Minister of Qi. See 2B1ff.)

[2] A Hegemon is a ruler who dominates other states via military power and skillful strategy, rather than leading by Virtue.

[3] "Virtue" is a sort of ethical charisma that induces others to submit without the need for coercion.

toward the Shang for a long time. Because it had been a long time, it was difficult to change. Wu Ding brought the various lords to his court, and had the world as if it were in the palm of his hand. It was not long in between Wu Ding and Tyrant Zhou. Traces of the venerable families, surviving customs, prevailing trends, and good government of the earlier times persisted. There were also Tyrant Zhou's minister Jiao Ge, his uncles Prince Bigan and Jizi, and his brothers Weizi and Wei Zhong. These were all worthies who assisted him in government.[4] Hence, it was a long time before he lost it all. Before King Wen there was not a foot of ground that did not belong to Tyrant Zhou. There was not a single group of people that was not subject to him. Yet King Wen arose from a territory of just a hundred leagues square. This was very difficult.

"The people of Qi have a saying: 'Being clever isn't as good as taking an opportunity. Even if you have a hoe, that isn't as important as awaiting the right season.' In the present time it is easy to become King. At the apex of the Xia, Shang, and Zhou, their territory did not exceed a thousand leagues. But Qi now has that size territory. And you can hear roosters crow and dogs bark from one side of the state to the other. Qi has that many people. Without needing to open any more land, and without needing to gather any more people, if he puts into effect benevolent government, nothing will be able to stop Qi's ruler from becoming King.   1.9   1.10

"Moreover, never has the time without a King arising been longer than this time. Never has the people's suffering under ferocious government been greater than it is in this time. The hungry can easily be fed; the thirsty can easily be quenched. Kongzi said, 'Virtue spreads faster than couriers carrying commands.' At the current time, if a state of ten thousand chariots puts benevolent government into effect, the people would be as happy as if they had been saved from hanging upside down. Hence, only in a time like this can one exert half the effort of the ancients and be assured twice the achievement."   1.11   1.12   1.13

Mengzi's disciple Gongsun Chou asked, "Suppose that you, Master, were to be appointed Prime Minister in Qi and were able to put the Way into practice there. It would not be surprising even if the ruler of Qi were to become Hegemon or King. Would having such a great responsibility perturb your heart or not?"   2.1

---

[4]   Prince Bigan pleaded again and again with Tyrant Zhou to govern virtuously. Finally, Tyrant Zhou remarked that sages supposedly have bigger hearts than others, and that he wanted to see if Bigan had a heart to match his words. So he ordered his guards to rip the heart out of Bigan's chest (cf. 6A6.3).

2.2   Mengzi replied, "It would not. My heart has been unperturbed since I was forty."[5] Gongsun Chou continued, "In that case, you, Master, have far surpassed Meng Ben."

Mengzi replied, "This is not difficult. Even Gaozi had an unperturbed heart before I."[6] 注

2.3   Gongsun Chou then asked, "Is there a Way of having an unperturbed heart?" 注

2.4   Mengzi replied, "There is. As for Bogong You's cultivation of courage, his body would not shrink, his eyes would not blink. He regarded the least slight from someone like being beaten in the marketplace. Insults he would not accept from a man in baggy rags he also would not accept from a ruler who could field ten thousand chariots. He looked upon running a sword through a ruler who could field ten thousand chariots like running through a man in rags. He was not in awe of the various lords. If an insult came his way he had to return it. 注

2.5   "As for Meng Shishe's cultivation of courage, he said, 'I look upon defeat the same as victory. To advance only after sizing up one's enemy, to ponder whether one will achieve victory and only then join battle, this is to be in awe of the opposing armies. How can I be certain of victory? I can only be without fear.' 注

2.6   "Meng Shishe was similar to Kongzi's disciple Zengzi. Bogong You was similar to Kongzi's disciple Zixia.[7] Now, I do not really know whose courage was preferable. Nonetheless, Meng Shishe preserved something crucial. 注

2.7   "Formerly, Zengzi said to his disciple Zixiang, 'Are you fond of courage? I once heard about great courage from Kongzi:

> If I examine myself and am not upright, even if opposed by a man in baggy rags, I would not try to intimidate him. If I examine myself and am upright, even if it is thousands or tens of thousands of people who oppose me, I shall go forward.' 注

2.8   Meng Shishe's preserving his *qi* was not as good as Zengzi's preserving what is crucial."[8] 注

---

[5] Kongzi said, "at forty, I became free of doubts" (*Analects* 2.4).

[6] Meng Ben was a warrior who "when traveling by water, did not avoid serpents, and when traveling by land, did not avoid rhinoceroses or tigers" (Jiao Xun, *Mengzi zhengyi*, commentary on 2A2). Gaozi is a rival Master who is also discussed in 6A1–6.

[7] Zixia had a reputation for being intelligent and learned, but he was cold and perhaps lacking in personal commitment to the Way (see *Analects* 3.8 and 6.13). Zengzi is quoted in the next verse.

[8] *Qi* is an energetic fluid that flows between us and our environment. "Preserving his *qi*" means controlling his emotions. (See also the commentary.)

Gongsun Chou next asked, "May I hear about your unperturbed heart,   2.9a
Master, and Gaozi's unperturbed heart?"

Mengzi replied, "Gaozi said, 'What you do not get from doctrines, do not
seek for in your heart. What you do not get from your heart, do not seek
for in the *qi*.' 'What you do not get from your heart, do not seek for in the
qi,' is acceptable. 'What you do not get from doctrines, do not seek for in
your heart,' is unacceptable. 注

"Your will is the commander of the *qi*. *Qi* fills the body. When your will   2.9b
is fixed somewhere, the *qi* sets up camp there. Hence, it is said, 'Maintain
your will. Do not injure the *qi*.'"⁹

Gongsun Chou continued, "Since you have already said, 'When your will   2.10
is fixed somewhere, the *qi* sets up camp there,' why do you add, 'Maintain
your will. Do not injure the *qi*'?"

Mengzi replied, "When your will is unified, it moves the *qi*. When the *qi*
is unified, it moves your will. Now, running and stumbling have to do with
the *qi*, but nonetheless they perturb one's heart." 注

Gongsun Chou next asked, "May I ask wherein you excel, Master?"   2.11

Mengzi replied, "I understand doctrines. I am good at cultivating my
floodlike *qi*." 注

Gongsun Chou continued, "May I ask what is meant by 'floodlike *qi*'?"   2.12

Mengzi replied, "It is difficult to explain. It is a *qi* that is supremely great   2.13
and supremely unyielding. If one cultivates it with uprightness and does
not harm it, it will fill up the space between Heaven and Earth. It is a *qi* that   2.14
harmonizes with righteousness and the Way. Without these, it starves. It is   2.15
produced by accumulated righteousness. It cannot be obtained by a seizure
of righteousness. If some of one's actions leave one's heart unsatisfied, it will
starve. Consequently, I say that Gaozi never understood righteousness, because he regarded it as external. 注

"One must work at it, but do not assume success. One should not forget   2.16a
the heart, but neither should one 'help' it grow. Do not be like the man from
Song.¹⁰ Among the people of the state of Song there was a farmer who,
concerned lest his sprouts not grow, pulled on them. Obliviously, he returned
home and said to his family, 'Today I am worn out. I helped the sprouts to
grow.' His son rushed out and looked at them. The sprouts were withered.
Those in the world who do not 'help' the sprouts to grow are few. Those   2.16b
who abandon them, thinking it will not help, are those who do not weed
their sprouts. Those who 'help' them grow are those who pull on the sprouts.
Not only does this not actually help, but it even harms them." 注

---

⁹ The "will" is simply the heart when it is focused on some goal.

¹⁰ The people of the state of Song were the butt of many jokes because of their supposed
stupidity.

2.17   Gongsun Chou next asked, "What do you mean by 'understanding doctrines'?"

Mengzi replied, "If someone's expressions are one-sided, I know that by which they are obscured. If someone's expressions are excessive, I know what they have sunk into. If someone's expressions are heretical, I know that by which they are separated from the Way. If someone's expressions are evasive, I know that by which they are overwhelmed. When these faults grow in the heart, they are harmful in governing. When they are manifested in governing, they are harmful in one's activities. When sages arise again, they will surely follow what I have said." 注

2.18   Gongsun Chou continued, "Among Kongzi's disciples, Zai Wo and Zigong were good at rhetoric, while Ran Niu, Minzi, and Yan Yuan were good at discussing Virtuous actions. Kongzi combined all these, but he said, 'When it comes to rhetoric, I am incapable.' In that case, are you, Master, already a sage?" 注

2.19   Mengzi replied, "Oh, how could you ask me this?

"Formerly, Kongzi's disciple Zigong asked him, 'Are you, Master, really a sage?' Kongzi replied, 'One cannot consider me a sage. I simply learn without tiring and instruct without wearying.' Zigong said, 'To learn without tiring is wisdom; to instruct without wearying is benevolence. Being benevolent and wise, the Master is certainly already a sage!' So, even Kongzi was not comfortable with being regarded as a sage. How could you ask *me* this?"

2.20   Gongsun Chou continued, "Formerly, I heard the following: Kongzi's disciples Zixia, Ziyou, and Zizhang all had one part of the substance of a sage, while Ran Niu, Minzi, and Yan Yuan had the complete substance of a sage but in miniature. I venture to ask in which group you would be comfortable?"

2.21   Mengzi replied, "Let's talk about something else."[11]

2.22   Gongsun Chou then asked, "What about Bo Yi and Yi Yin?"

Mengzi said, "They had different Ways. If he was not his ruler, he would not serve him; if they were not his subjects, he would not direct them; if things were orderly, he would take office; if they were chaotic, he would leave office. This was Bo Yi.

"'Whom do I serve who is not my ruler? Whom do I direct who are not my subjects?' If things were orderly, he would take office, and if they were chaotic, he would also take office. This was Yi Yin.

"When one should take office, he would take office; when one should stop, he would stop; when one should take a long time, he would take a long time; when one should hurry, he would hurry. This was Kongzi. All were

---

[11] Mengzi does not want to include himself in such a distinguished group, so he changes the topic.

sages of ancient times. I have never been able to act like them, but my wish is to learn from Kongzi."[12]

Gongsun Chou continued, "Were Bo Yi and Yi Yin at the same level as Kongzi?"

2.23

Mengzi replied, "No. Since humans were first born there has never been another Kongzi."

Gongsun Chou continued, "In that case, were there any similarities?"

2.24

Mengzi replied, "There were. If any became ruler of a territory of a hundred leagues, he would be able to possess the world by bringing the various lords to his court. And if any could obtain the world by performing one unrighteous deed, or killing one innocent person, he would not do it. In these things they are the same." 注

Gongsun Chou continued, "I venture to ask wherein they differed?"

2.25

Mengzi replied, "Consider what was said by Kongzi's disciples Zai Wo, Zigong, and You Ruo. They had wisdom sufficient to appreciate the Way of Kongzi, and would not stoop to showing favoritism to someone simply because they were fond of him. Zai Wo said, 'In my view, Kongzi is far more worthy than Yao and Shun!' 注 Zigong said, 'If you see their rituals, you understand their government; if you hear their music, you understand their Virtue; from a hundred generations later, through the succession of a hundred kings, nothing can get away: from this perspective, I can see that, since humans were first born, there has never been another like Kongzi.' You Ruo said, 'There is something that is the case not only with people: the unicorn among beasts, the phoenix among birds, Mount Tai among mounds and anthills, and the Yellow River and the seas among flowing waters are all of the same kind. The sage is also of the same kind as other people. But some stand out from their kind; some stand out from the pack: since humans were first born, there has never been one who has reached a greater summit than Kongzi.'" 注

2.26
2.27

2.28

Mengzi said, "One who uses power to feign benevolence is a Hegemon. A Hegemon must have a large state. One who uses Virtue to put benevolence into effect is a King. A King does not depend on size. Tang had a territory of seventy leagues square. King Wen had a hundred leagues square. If one makes others submit with power, their hearts do not submit. Power is inadequate to make their hearts submit. If one makes others submit with Virtue, they are pleased in their hearts and genuinely submit, like the seventy disciples who served Kongzi. The *Odes* say,

3.1

3.2

---

12 Mengzi frequently cites Bo Yi and Yi Yin as examples of individuals who attain one aspect of sagehood but fall short of the complete sageliness of Kongzi. For sketches of their lives and actions, see 5B1.

                    From west, from east
                    From south, from north
                    None do not long to submit.[13]

This expresses it."

5.1   Mengzi said, "If one respects the worthy, employs the capable, and puts the
      outstanding in office, then the nobles of the world will be pleased and will
5.2   wish to take their place in your court. If one taxes the shops in one's markets,
      but not their goods, or regulates them but does not tax either the shops or
      their goods, then the merchants of the world will all be pleased and will wish
5.3   to store goods in one's markets. If one's customs officers inspect but do not
      tax, then the travelers of the world will be pleased and will wish to go out on
5.4   your roads. If those who plow must provide assistance but are not taxed, then
      the farmers of the world will be pleased and will wish to plow your fields.[14]
5.5   If shopholders need not pay the personal or village surtax, then the people
5.6   of the world will be pleased and willing to be one's subjects. If one is truly
      capable of putting into effect these five things, then the people of neighbor-
      ing states will welcome one like a father or mother. To lead sons and younger
      brothers to attack a father and mother is something that has never succeeded
      since the birth of humans. If it is like this, one will have no enemies in the
      world. One who has no enemies in the world is the agent of Heaven. It has
      never happened that someone is like this yet fails to become King." 注

6.1   Mengzi said, "All humans have hearts that are not unfeeling toward others. 注
6.2   The Former Kings had hearts that were not unfeeling toward others, so they
      had governments that were not unfeeling toward others. If one puts into
      practice a government that is not unfeeling toward others by means of a
      heart that is not unfeeling toward others, bringing order to the whole world
      is in the palm of your hand. 注
6.3   "The reason why I say that all humans have hearts that are not unfeeling
      toward others is this. Suppose someone suddenly saw a child about to fall
      into a well: anyone in such a situation would have a feeling of alarm and
      compassion—not because one sought to get in good with the child's par-
      ents, not because one wanted fame among one's neighbors and friends, and
      not because one would dislike the sound of the child's cries.[15] 注

---

[13]   This ode describes the reign of King Wen.

[14]   Providing assistance is the same as the "nine-one" (or "well-field") system, described in the
commentary to 1B5.3.

[15]   Zhu Xi understands the last clause as meaning, ". . . and not because one would dislike having a bad reputation."

"From this we can see that if one is without the feeling of compassion,   6.4
one is not human. If one is without the feeling of disdain, one is not human.
If one is without the feeling of deference, one is not human. If one is without the feeling of approval and disapproval, one is not human. The feeling   6.5
of compassion is the sprout of benevolence. The feeling of disdain is the sprout
of righteousness. The feeling of deference is the sprout of propriety. The feeling of approval and disapproval is the sprout of wisdom.[16] 注

"People's having these four sprouts is like their having four limbs. To have   6.6
these four sprouts, yet to claim that one is incapable (of Virtue), is to steal
from oneself. To say that one's ruler is incapable is to steal from one's ruler.
In general, having these four sprouts within oneself, if one knows to fill them   6.7
all out, it will be like a fire starting up, a spring breaking through! If one can
merely fill them out, they will be sufficient to care for all within the Four
Seas. If one merely fails to fill them out, they will be insufficient to serve
one's parents." 注

Mengzi said, "Is the arrow-maker less benevolent than the armor-maker? Yet   7.1
the arrow-maker only fears that he may not harm people; the armor-maker
only fears that he may harm people. The shaman-healer and the coffin-
maker are the same way, respectively. Hence, one may not fail to be careful
about one's choice of craft. 注

"Kongzi said, 'To dwell in benevolence is beautiful; if one chooses to not   7.2
dwell in benevolence, how can one be wise?' Now, benevolence is Heaven's
rank of respect and people's abode of peace. If one is not benevolent though
nothing prevents it, this is to fail to be wise. If one fails to be benevolent and   7.3
fails to be wise, then one lacks propriety and righteousness. This is to be the
lackey of other people. To be the lackey of other people yet to be ashamed
of being a lackey is like being a bow-maker yet to be ashamed of making
bows, or to be an arrow-maker yet to be ashamed of making arrows. 注

"If you are ashamed of it, there is nothing as good as becoming benevo-   7.4
lent. Benevolence is like archery. An archer corrects himself and only then   7.5
shoots. If he shoots but does not hit the mark, he does not resent the one
who defeats him but simply turns and seeks for it in himself." 注

Mengzi said, "Kongzi's disciple Zilu was pleased if someone informed him   8.1
of his faults. When King Yu heard good teachings he bowed down in thanks.   8.2
The Great Shun was even greater than they. He was good at unifying himself   8.3

---

[16]   The Daoist Zhuangzi is criticizing this passage when he argues that "the sprouts of benevolence and righteousness and the pathways of right and wrong are all snarled and jumbled"
(*Zhuangzi* 2, "On Equalizing Things," in *Readings*, 222).

with others. He put himself aside and joined with others. He delighted in
copying from others in order to do good. From plowing, planting, making
8.4
8.5
pottery, and fishing on up to being Emperor—he never failed to copy from
others. To copy others when they do good is to do good with others. Hence,
for a gentleman, nothing is greater than to do good with others." 注

9.1 Mengzi said, "If someone was not Bo Yi's ruler, he would not serve him. If
someone was not his friend, he would not treat him as his friend. He would
not take a position at the court of a bad person, nor would he have a discussion with a bad person. He looked upon taking a position at the court
of a bad person or having a discussion with a bad person like wearing one's
court cap and gown and sitting down in filth. He extended his heart of disdain for evil to the point that, if he stood with an ordinary villager whose
cap was not on correctly, he would leave without meeting his eyes, as if he
thought he was about to be defiled. For this reason, when the assorted lords
came with fine rhetoric, he would not accept them. He did not accept them
because he was adamant that going to serve them was not pure. 注

9.2 "Liuxia Hui was not ashamed of a corrupt lord, and did not consider a
petty office unworthy. In taking office, he did not conceal what was worthy but would necessarily act in accordance with the Way. When he was discharged, he was not bitter. In difficult and impoverished circumstances, he
was not anxious. Hence, he said, 'You are you, and I am I. Even if you are
stark naked beside me, how can you defile me?' Hence, contentedly, he was
with others without losing himself. If constrained to remain, he would remain. He remained when constrained to remain because he was adamant
that leaving was not pure." 注

9.3 Mengzi observed, "Bo Yi was too constrained; Liuxia Hui was not digni-
fied. A gentleman is neither too constrained nor lacking in dignity." 注

BOOK 2B

*Zhu Xi comments, "Beginning with Chapter 2, this book records in detail
Mengzi's travels and actions." In particular, it covers Mengzi's controversial
service as a minister and adviser to King Xuan of Qi. Among the most interesting and often-discussed passages in this book are 2B8, 2B9, and 2B13.*

2.1 Mengzi was about to go to the court of King Xuan of Qi. The king sent
people with the message, "We were about to come to see you, but we have
a chill and cannot be exposed to drafts. If this morning we hold court, I
wonder whether you would allow us to see you?"

Mengzi replied, "Unfortunately, I am ill and am incapable of getting to court."

The next day, Mengzi went out to offer condolences to the Dongguo clan. 2.2 His disciple Gongsun Chou said, "Yesterday, you excused yourself due to illness. Today, you offer condolences. Isn't this unseemly?" 注

Mengzi said, "Yesterday I was ill; today I have improved. How could I not offer condolences?"

The king sent someone to ask about his illness, and a doctor arrived. 2.3 Mengzi's younger brother Zhongzi replied, "Yesterday, when the king issued his command, he was under the weather and was incapable of getting to court. Today, he has gotten a little better, and he has hurried to get to court. I don't know whether he has been able to get there or not." He then sent several people to seek for Mengzi on the road, telling him, "Please definitely do not return here but get to court!" 注 Mengzi could only go to the 2.4 family of Jingzi and spend the night there.

Jingzi said, "Within the family, there is father and son; outside the family, there is ruler and minister. These are the greatest human relations. Father and son emphasize generosity; ruler and minister emphasize reverence. I have seen the king revere you, but I have not yet seen how you revere the king."

Mengzi said, "How can you say that? The people of Qi do not discuss benevolence and righteousness with the king. Could this be because they do not regard benevolence and righteousness as something fine? No, their hearts say, 'How could he be up to discussing benevolence and righteousness?' No irreverence is greater than this! I dare not present anything to the king other than the Way of Yao and Shun. Hence, none of the people of Qi revere the king as I do." 注

Jingzi said, "No, that is not what I mean. The *Rites* say, 'When one's father 2.5 calls, one says *Yes!* not *Oh, alright*. When one's ruler commands one to attend, one does not wait to harness the horses.' You were, on your own, about to go to court, but when you heard the king's command, you did not end up doing it. Considering the rituals, this does not seem appropriate."

Mengzi said, "How can you say that? Kongzi's disciple Zengzi said, 'The 2.6 wealth of Jin and Chu cannot be equaled. They have their wealth, I have my benevolence. They have their official ranks, I have my righteousness. What should I be dissatisfied about?' How could Zengzi state this if it were not righteous? It is certainly one aspect of the Way.

"Three things are universally respected in the world. One is rank, one is age, and one is Virtue. At court, nothing is better than rank. In the village, nothing is better than age. In assisting the world and nurturing the people, nothing is better than Virtue. How could one who has one of these three be disrespectful to the other two? 注

2.7   "Hence, a ruler who will have great effectiveness must have ministers
          whom he does not summon. If he wishes to consult with them, then he
          goes to them. If his respect for Virtue and delight in the Way is not like this,
2.8   then he is not worth taking action with. 注 Therefore, King Tang learned
          from Yi Yin and only then made him a minister. Hence, he could become
          King without much effort. Duke Huan learned from Guan Zhong and only
          then made him a minister. Hence, he could become Hegemon without much
2.9   effort. 注 Nowadays, among the states in the world, the territories are com-
          parable, and their Virtue is equal. None can surpass another. This is simply
          because they are fond of making ministers of those whom they instruct, but
          they are not fond of making ministers of those from whom they receive in-
2.10   struction. 注 Tang did not dare to summon Yi Yin, and Duke Huan did not
          dare to summon Guan Zhong. Even Guan Zhong could not be summoned.
          What of someone who, like me, would rather not be a Guan Zhong?" 注

3.1   Mengzi's disciple Chen Zhen asked, "The other day in the state of Qi, the
          king offered you a grant of one hundred ounces of fine gold and you would
          not accept it. But in Song, they offered you a grant of seventy ounces and
          you accepted, and in Xue they offered you a grant of fifty ounces and you
          accepted. If not accepting on the former day is right, then accepting on the
          latter days is wrong. If accepting on the latter days is right, then not ac-
          cepting on the former day is wrong. One of these two must apply to you,
          Master."
3.2–3.3   Mengzi said, "Both were right. When I was in Song, I was about to go on
          a long journey. Such traveling must be done with a farewell grant. The ex-
          pression the ruler used was, 'I am giving you a farewell grant.' Why should
3.4   I not accept it? When I was in Xue, I was concerned about precautions.
          The expression the ruler used was, 'I heard of your precautions.' Hence, he
3.5   gave me a grant for guards. Why should I not accept it? When I was in Qi,
          there was never anything to deal with. To give a grant without anything
          to deal with is to bribe someone. How could a gentleman go as low as to be
          bribed?" 注

4.1   Mengzi went to the city of Ping Lu in Qi and said to Kong Juxin, its Chief
          Counselor, "If one of your spearmen broke ranks three times in one day,
          would you execute him or not?"
          He replied, "I would not wait for the third time."
4.2   Mengzi said, "But you have 'broken ranks' many times already. In bad years
          with poor harvests, the old and weak who are tossed into the gutters and
          the strong who scatter to the four directions are numbered in the thousands
          among your people."
          He replied, "This is not something that I could do anything about." 注

Mengzi said, "Suppose someone gets another person's oxen and sheep to   4.3
shepherd. He must seek to find pastures and grass for them. If he is unable
to get pastures and grass for them, then should he return them to the man,
or should he stand and watch while they die?"

Kong Juxin acknowledged, "What you refer to *is* my fault."

On a later day, Mengzi appeared before the king and said, "Of those who   4.4
rule Your Majesty's ancestral cities, I know five. The only one who knows
his faults is Kong Juxin." He repeated the conversation for the king.

The king said, "What you refer to is *our* fault." 注

Mengzi left Qi for the funeral of his mother in Lu. When he was returning,   7.1
he stopped in Ying. His disciple Chong Yu asked permission to speak, saying, "The other day, ignoring the fact that I am unworthy, you directed me
to oversee the activities of the coffin-makers. This was such a serious thing
that I did not dare to ask to speak to you then. But today I humbly ask to
speak: it seems as if the wood used was of excessively high quality."

Mengzi said, "In high antiquity, inner and outer coffins had no standard   7.2
measure. But in middle antiquity, inner coffins were seven inches, and outer
coffins matched them, for everyone from the Son of Heaven on down to
commoners. This was not just for the beauty of their appearance, but because in this manner people's hearts were fathomed. They would not be   7.3
pleased if they could not get such coffins. They would not be pleased if
they did not have such materials. If they could get such coffins because they
had such materials, the ancients would all use them. Why should I alone not
be like this? Furthermore, does it not make the hearts of people happy to   7.4
prevent the earth from touching the flesh of those who are transforming? I   7.5
have heard that a gentleman will not, for the world, economize in regard to
his parents."[1]

Shen Tong asked on his own behalf, "Is it permissible to invade Yan?"   8.1

Mengzi said, "It is. Zikuai may not give Yan to others. Zizhi may not receive Yan from Zikuai. Suppose there is someone here with an office, and
you are pleased with him. You do not inform the king but on your own behalf give him your salary and rank. And this official also accepts it on his
own behalf without the king's mandate. Would this be acceptable? How is
that different from this?" 注

The Qi people invaded Yan. Someone asked, "Is it the case that you en-   8.2
couraged Qi to invade Yan?"

---

[1] For further discussion of the psychology of funeral practices, see 3A5. For more on the controversy surrounding Mengzi's burial of his mother, see 1B16.

Mengzi replied, "I never did. Shen Tong asked whether it was permissible to invade Yan. I answered, 'It is.' They then invaded it. If they had asked me, 'Who may invade it?' then I would have answered, 'One who is the agent of Heaven may invade it.' Suppose there is someone who murders another. Someone asks, 'May this person be executed?' then I would answer, 'He may.' If then asked, 'Who may execute him?' then I would answer, 'The Chief Warden may execute him.' In the current case, why would I encourage a Yan to invade a Yan?"[2] 注

9.1 The Yan people rebelled against Qi. The king said, "I am quite ashamed to face Mengzi."[3]

9.2 Chief Counselor Chen Jia said, "Let Your Majesty not be anxious about this. Whom does Your Majesty regard as more benevolent and wise—yourself or the Duke of Zhou?"

The king said, "Oh, how can you even ask?"

Chen Jia said, "The Duke of Zhou assigned his older brother Guan Shu to be supervisor of the conquered Shang people, and Guan Shu revolted with the Shang. If he knew this yet still assigned him, that was not benevolent. If he did not know and assigned him, that was not wise. So benevolence and wisdom were things the Duke of Zhou had not fully fathomed. Could we expect more of Your Majesty? I ask to see Mengzi so that I may explain this to him." 注

9.3 When he saw Mengzi, Chen Jia asked, "What sort of person was the Duke of Zhou?"

Mengzi said, "He was an ancient sage."

Chen Jia asked, "Is it the case that he appointed Guan Shu to oversee the Shang, and Guan Shu revolted with them?"

Mengzi said, "That is so."

Chen Jia asked, "Did the Duke of Zhou know that he was going to revolt when he appointed him?"

Mengzi said, "He did not know."

Chen Jia said, "In that case, can even a sage have faults?"

Mengzi said, "The Duke of Zhou was the younger brother to his older brother Guan Shu. Was the Duke of Zhou's mistake not, after all, appropri-

9.4 ate? 注 Furthermore, when the gentlemen of ancient times made a mistake, they corrected it. When the gentlemen of today make a mistake, they stick to it. The mistakes of ancient gentlemen were like eclipses of the Sun

---

[2] Zhu Xi recommends that, after 2B8, one read 1B10 and 1B11, before proceeding to 2B9.

[3] The king is ashamed both because he used a comment by Mengzi as a pretext to justify his invasion and then ruled Yan in a manner opposed to the benevolent government advocated by Mengzi.

or Moon. The people all saw them. When they fixed their mistakes, the people all looked up to them. The gentlemen of today do not only stick to their mistakes, they even rationalize them." 注

Mengzi resigned his post as minister to return home. 注 The king came to see Mengzi and said, "Previously, we wished to see you, but we could not. But your visit and being part of our court has pleased us greatly. Now you are going to cast us aside and return home. We wonder whether you could continue your stay so that we may see you?"   *10.1–10.2*

Mengzi replied, "I dared not ask for this. But it is certainly what I wish."

A later day, the king said to his minister Shizi, "I want to give Mengzi a dwelling in the center of the state, give him a salary of ten thousand bushels of grain for training disciples, in order that the various Counselors and people of the state should have a model to respect. Why don't you discuss this with him for me?"[4]   *10.3*

Shizi entrusted Mengzi's disciple Chen Zhen to inform Mengzi about this.   *10.4*
Chen Zhen informed Mengzi about what Shizi had said. Mengzi said, "Ah,   *10.5* yes. Someone like Shizi could not understand that I may not do this, could he? Suppose it were the case that I desired wealth. Would declining one hundred thousand and accepting ten thousand be because I desired wealth? 注

"Ji Sun once said, 'How strange is Zishu Yi! He got himself into govern-   *10.6* ment, but when his advice was not used, he quit. But then he made his sons and younger brothers High Ministers. What person does not want wealth and prestige? But to be solely concerned with wealth and prestige is to take a selfish *vantage point*.' 注

"When the ancients had markets, they were for exchanging what they had   *10.7* for what they lacked. The officials merely kept order. But there were some base fellows there who would seek for a 'vantage point' and climb up on it. They would gaze left and right, monopolizing the profit from the market. Everyone thought they were base, so they followed up by fining them. Tax- ing merchants had its origin in dealing with these base fellows." 注

Mengzi left the state of Qi. While on the road, his disciple Chong Yu asked,   *13.1* "It seems that you have an unhappy countenance, Master. Yet, the other day I heard it from you that 'The gentleman is not bitter toward Heaven and does not blame others.'"

Mengzi said, "The situation has not changed from when I said that. Every   *13.2–13.3* five hundred years, a King must arise. Between them, there must be those

---

[4] The king wants the prestige of having Mengzi in his state, without having to listen to his ad- vice about how to govern.

13.4   illustrious in their time. Since the founding of the Zhou, it has already been more than seven hundred years. This is more than enough time. And if one examines the situation in our era, it seems an appropriate time. 注

13.5   "Nonetheless, Heaven does not yet desire to pacify the world. If it desired to pacify the world, who besides me in the present time is there? Why would I be unhappy?" 注

BOOK 3A

This book consists of a series of dialogues that occurred immediately prior to and during Mengzi's visit to the small state of Teng. The discussions range over topics including funeral and mourning rituals and sociopolitical philosophy. Among the most interesting and often-discussed passages in this book are 3A4 and 3A5.

1.1   When Duke Wen of Teng was still only Heir Apparent, he had to go to Chu.
1.2   Passing through Song, he met Mengzi. Mengzi told him the Way of the goodness of the nature, and in his discussions always praised Yao and Shun.
1.3   The Heir Apparent returned from Chu, and again met with Mengzi. Mengzi said, "Do you doubt my teachings, your lordship? The Way is one, and only one. 注

1.4   "Cheng Jian said to Duke Jing of Qi, 'If they are men and I am a man, why should I be intimidated by their achievements?' Kongzi's disciple Yan Yuan said, 'What sort of person was Shun? What sort of person am I? Those who achieve something are simply like this.' Gongming Yi said, 'King Wen is my teacher. How could the Duke of Zhou mislead me about following

1.5   him?' Now, Teng is approximately fifty leagues square. But it still can become a good state. As the *Documents* say, 'If the medicine does not make you dizzy, it will not cure your illness.'" 注

2.1   Duke Ding of Teng passed away. The Heir Apparent said to his tutor, Ran You, "Formerly, Mengzi had some discussions with me in Song. My heart has never forgotten them. Now, unfortunately, I arrive at the momentous event of the mourning ritual. I wish you to go and make inquiries of Mengzi, and only then will I carry out this affair."

2.2   Ran You went to the state of Zou and made inquiries of Mengzi. Mengzi said, "How good of him! The mourning for one's parents is something that one must definitely do to the utmost. Kongzi's disciple Zengzi said, 'When they are alive, serve them according to the rites. When they die, bury them according to the rites, and then sacrifice to them according to the rites. Then one may be called filial.' I have not made a study of the rituals of the assorted lords. Nonetheless, I have heard of them. For the three years of mourning, one wears hemmed clothes of coarse cloth and eats thin broth and gruel. From the Son of Heaven down to the commoners, this has been the same in the Xia, Shang, and Zhou dynasties."

Ran You returned and reported this. The Heir decided to do three years of mourning. His elder relatives and ministers were all displeased, saying, "None of the former rulers of Lu, our ancestral state, practiced this. None of our own former rulers practiced this either. For the son to take it upon himself to turn his back on this is not acceptable. Moreover, the *Records* say, 'In mourning and sacrifice follow the ancestors.'" 注   2.3

But the Heir replied, "There is a precedent for what I do." The Heir then said to Ran You, "In other times I did not learn and inquire. I was fond of racing horses and practicing swordsmanship. Now, my elder relatives and officials are not satisfied with me. I fear that they will not do their utmost in this great affair. Ask Mengzi for his advice about this."   2.4

Ran You returned to Zou and inquired of Mengzi. Mengzi said, "So that is how it is. But he cannot seek for it in anyone else. Kongzi said, 'When a ruler passes away, one listens to the Master of the Stewards, eats only gruel, lets one's complexion become ashen, takes one's ceremonial place, and cries. The officials have their duties; none dare not grieve. Lead them. When superiors are fond of something, subordinates must be even more so. The Virtue of the gentleman is the wind. The Virtue of the petty person is the grass. When wind is upon the grass, it must bend.' This lies with the Heir."

Ran You returned and reported this. The Heir said, "That is so. It genuinely lies with me."   2.5

He dwelled in a thatched hut for five months, issuing no commands or prohibitions. The officials and travelers passing through the state said, "He can be said to have understanding." When it came to the time of the funeral, people came from the four directions to observe. Those who gave condolences were impressed with the grief of his expression and the sadness of his crying.[1]

Duke Wen of Teng sent his minister Bi Zhan to ask Mengzi about the well fields and to put them into effect. Mengzi said, "Your ruler is going to put into effect benevolent government and has chosen to send you. You must put your effort into it. Now, benevolent government must begin with setting the field boundaries. If the field boundaries are not straightly set, the well fields will not be equal, and the grain income will not be even. For this reason, cruel rulers and corrupt officials are necessarily lax about setting the field boundaries. When the field boundaries are straightly set, one can sit   3.13

---

[1] On the ethics and psychology of mourning, see also 3A5.

down and fix the allotments of fields and the regulations about income.
3.14 Now, the area of Teng is small. But there will be both gentlemen and the uncultivated there. Without the gentlemen, no one will rule over the un-
3.15 cultivated. Without the uncultivated, no one will support the gentlemen. I ask that, in the countryside, you use the well-field method, while in the cap-
3.16 ital you make them pay taxes of ten percent individually. Those of the rank of High Minister and below must also have a pure field of fifty acres to pro-
3.17 vide ritual offerings to their ancestors. A householder with a brother who is not yet of age gets twenty-five additional acres.

3.18 Whether burying the dead or moving one's household, the uncultivated do not leave their village. The fields of the village share the same well. They go out and return from the fields together. They keep watch against thieves and assist each other. When ill, they support each other. In this way, com-
3.19 moners are affectionate toward each other. A square league is divided into a pattern like the character *jǐng* 井 (well). The well fields are nine hundred acres. In their middle is the public field. Eight families each have a private one hundred acres and cultivate the public field in common. Only after the public work is completed do they dare to manage their private work. This is
3.20 the manner in which one manages the uncultivated people. This is the general outline. As for filling it in, this lies with your ruler and yourself." 注

4.1 There was a certain Xu Xing who, supporting the teachings of Shen Nong, went from the state of Chu to Teng. Going on foot to the gate, he told Duke Wen, "People from distant parts have heard that you, my lord, practice benevolent government. I wish to receive a homestead and become one of your subjects." Duke Wen gave him a place. His followers were a few dozen people, all of whom wore animal pelts and made sandals and mats in exchange for food.[2] 注

4.2 Chen Liang was a Confucian whose disciple Chen Xiang and his younger brother Xin carried their plows on their backs and went from Song to Teng, saying, "We have heard that you, my lord, practice the government of a sage. This is to be a sage. I wish to become the subject of a sage."

4.3 Chen Xiang met Xu Xing and was greatly pleased. He completely abandoned his former learning and learned from him instead. Chen Xiang met Mengzi and discoursed on the doctrines of Xu Xing, saying, "The ruler of Teng is genuinely a worthy ruler. Nonetheless, he has not yet heard the Way. The worthy plow with their subjects and then eat, having breakfast and din-

---

[2] Shen Nong was a legendary emperor to whom was attributed the development of agriculture. Those who claimed to follow his teachings advocated a return to a primitive agrarian society with minimal government.

ner with them, and then ruling. In the present case, Teng has granaries and treasuries; this is to harm the people in order to nurture oneself. How can this be worthy?" 注

Mengzi said, "Xu Xing must plant his grain first and only then eat?"   4.4
Chen said, "That is so."
Mengzi said, "Xu Xing must weave his cloth and only then wear clothes?"
Chen said, "No. Xu Xing wears animal pelts."
Mengzi said, "Does Xu Xing wear a cap?"
Chen said, "He does."
Mengzi said, "What sort does he wear?"
Chen said, "He wears plain silk."
Mengzi said, "Does he weave it himself?"
Chen said, "No. He exchanges millet for it."
Mengzi said, "Why does Xu Xing not weave it himself?"
Chen said, "That would interfere with farming."
Mengzi said, "Does Xu Xing use kettles and pots for cooking, and an iron plow?"
Chen said, "That is so."
Mengzi said, "Does he make them himself?"
Chen said, "No. He exchanges millet for them."
Mengzi said, "Exchanging millet for tools does not harm the potter or   4.5
blacksmith. And when the blacksmith exchanges tools for millet, does this hurt the farmer? Why does Xu Xing not become a potter and blacksmith, and only get everything from his own household to use? Why does he exchange things in such confusion with the various artisans? Why does Xu Xing not avoid all this trouble?"

Chen said, "The activities of the various artisans inherently cannot be done along with farming."

Mengzi said, "In that case, can ruling the world alone be done along with   4.6
farming? There are the activities of the great people and the affairs of the petty people. Furthermore, the products of the various artisans are available to each person. If one can make use of them only after one has made them oneself, this will lead the whole world to run around to the point of exhaustion. Hence it is said, 'Some labor with their hearts; some labor with their strength. Those who labor with their hearts rule others; those who labor with their strength are governed by others.' Those who are governed by others feed others; those who govern others are fed by others. This is the righteousness common to the world. 注

"In the time of Yao, the world was still unsettled. Great waters overflowed   4.7
their banks, spreading throughout the world. Plants and trees overgrew everything, and animals multiplied in great numbers. The five types of grain did not ripen. Animals harried people. Paths made by the tracks of animals crossed

the Central States. Yao alone was anxious about this, so he promoted Shun to rule over it. Shun directed his minister Yi to take charge of fire clearing. Yi burned the overgrown mountain fields. Only after the animals fled did Yu channel the Nine Rivers, clear the Ji and the Ta rivers to guide them into the sea, dredge the Ru and Han rivers, dredge the Huai and Si and guide them into the Yangtze. Only then were the Central States able to eat. During this time, Yu spent eight years away from home. Three times he passed the gate of his home but did not enter. Even if he wanted to farm, would he have been able to?

4.8   "Also under Shun's rule, Hou Ji taught the people planting, harvesting, and cultivating the five types of grain. When the five types of grain ripened, the people were nourished. The Way of the people is this: if they are full of food, have warm clothes, and live in comfort but are without instruction, then they come close to being animals. The sage Shun was anxious about this too, so he appointed Xie to be Minister of Instruction and to instruct them about human roles: between father and children there is affection; between ruler and ministers there is righteousness; between husband and wife there is distinction; between elder and younger there is precedence; and between friends there is faithfulness. The Distinguished Sovereign Yao advised, 'Work them, draw them, straighten them, rectify them, help them, make them practice, assist them, make them get it themselves, and thus benefit them.' Since the sage's anxiety for his subjects was like this, could he have the leisure to farm?

4.9   "Yao's personal concern was that he must not fail to employ Shun. Shun's personal concern was that he must not fail to employ Yu to control the floods and Gao Yao to be Minister of Crime. But one whose personal concern is
4.10   only that he must not fail to manage his hundred acres is a farmer. To distinguish people according to their talents is called 'kindness.' To instruct them about goodness is called 'devotion.' But to employ people for the sake of the world is called 'benevolence.' Hence, to give the world to someone is easy. To employ people for the sake of the world is difficult. 注

4.11   "Kongzi said, 'How magnificent was Yao's manner of ruling! It is only Heaven that is magnificent, and only Yao who modeled himself after Heaven. So vast was he that the people were unable to put a name to it. How consummate a ruler was Shun! So lofty was he that he had the world, yet did not get tied up in it.' Could it be that Yao and Shun, in ruling the world, had nothing to which they applied their hearts? It was simply that they did not apply them to farming.

4.12   "I have heard of using our culture to transform the uncivilized, but I have not heard of being transformed by the uncivilized. Chen Liang was born in Chu, but he was pleased by the Way of the Duke of Zhou and Kongzi, so he went north to study in the Central States. Among the scholars of the north, there was never anyone who surpassed him. He was what is called a genius. You and your brothers served him for decades, but when your teacher died, you turned your back on him. 注

"Formerly, after their three years of mourning following the death of Kongzi, his disciples packed up and were about to return to their homes. They came in and bowed to the disciple Zigong, then looked at each other and cried until they lost their voices. Only then did they return to their homes. Zigong turned around and built a hut on the burial grounds, and dwelt there alone for three more years, and only then returned home. Later, the disciples Zixia, Zizhang, and Ziyou thought You Ruo was like the Sage, and desired to serve him as they had served Kongzi. They pressed Zengzi to do likewise, but he said, 'That is unacceptable. Though you may wash something with the Jiang and Han rivers, bleach it in the autumn sun—his gleaming purity simply cannot be surpassed!'   4.13

"In the current case, some twittering southern uncivilized person opposes the Way of the Former Kings, and you turn your back on your teacher and learn from him. This is indeed different from Zengzi! I have heard of 'out of a dark valley, moving into the stately trees,' but I have never heard of descending from the stately trees and going into the dark valley. In the *Hymns of Lu* it says, 'The uncivilized west and north, he chastised. / Chu and nearby Shu, he punished.' The Duke of Zhou faced these people and chastised them. You approve of learning from them. This is a bad transformation indeed!"   4.14   4.15   4.16

Chen replied, "If we follow the Way of Xu Xing, market prices will never vary, and there will be no artifice in the state. Even if one sends a child to go to the market, no one will cheat him. Cotton cloth or silk cloth of the same length would be of equal price. Bundles of hemp or silk of the same weight would be of equal price. The same amount of any of the five grains would be the same price. Shoes of the same size would be of equal price." 注   4.17

Mengzi said, "Things are inherently unequal. One thing is twice or five times more than another, another ten or a hundred times more, another a thousand or ten thousand times more. If you line them up and treat them as identical, this will bring chaos to the world. If a fine shoe and a shoddy shoe are the same price, will anyone make the former? If we follow the Way of Xu Xing, we will lead each other into artifice. How can this bring order to the state?" 注   4.18

The Mohist Yi Zhi sought to see Mengzi through Mengzi's disciple Xu Bi. Mengzi said, "I am definitely willing to see him. But today I am ill. When my illness improves, I will go and see him. Yi Zhi does not have to come." Another day, he again sought to see Mengzi. Mengzi said, "I cannot see him today. But if I do not set him straight, the Way will not be manifest. I will straighten him out.   5.1   5.2

"I have heard that Yi Zhi is a Mohist. In dealing with funerals, Mozi took frugality as the Way. Yi Zhi surely does not long to change the world to something that he thinks is wrong and base! Nonetheless, Yi Zhi buried his parents lavishly, so he served his parents by means of what he demeans."³ 注

5.3a   Xu Bi told Yi Zhi this. Yi Zhi said, "According to the Way of the Confucians, the ancients treated the people 'like caring for a baby.' What does this saying mean? I take it to mean that love is without differentiations, but it is bestowed beginning with one's parents."

5.3b   Xu Bi told Mengzi this. Mengzi said, "Does Yi Zhi truly hold that one's affection for one's own nephew is like one's affection for a neighbor's baby? The passage from the *Documents* is only using that as a metaphor. When a
5.3c   crawling baby is about to fall into a well, it is not the baby's fault. Furthermore, Heaven, in giving birth to things, causes them to have one source, but Yi Zhi gives them two sources. 注

5.4   "Now, in past ages, there were those who did not bury their parents. When their parents died, they took them and abandoned them in a gully. The next day they passed by them, and foxes were eating them, bugs were sucking on them. Sweat broke out on the survivors' foreheads. They turned away and did not look. It was not for the sake of others that they sweated. What was inside their hearts broke through to their countenances. So they went home and, returning with baskets and shovels, covered them. If covering them was really right, then the manner in which filial children and benevolent people cover their parents must also be part of the Way." 注

5.5   Xu Bi told Yi Zhi this. Yi Zhi looked at a loss for a moment and then said, "He has convinced me."

BOOK 3B

Many passages in this book discuss the righteousness of certain actions; we see Mengzi trying to explain the mean between sanctimonious purity and moral laxity. This book also contains Mengzi's most elaborate account of his view of history. Among the most interesting and often-discussed passages in this book are 3B8 and 3B9.

---

³ Mozi criticized Confucians for their lavish funerals and extended mourning periods, and also for their doctrine of "differentiated love": that one should care more for relatives than for strangers. (See 5A3 and *Analects* 13.18 for more on differentiated love, also called "graded love" or "love with distinctions." See 3A2 and *Analects* 17.21 on Confucian mourning practices.) Mozi advocated frugal funerals, short mourning periods, and "impartial caring." Mengzi is pointing out that, although Yi Zhi is a Mohist, he gave his parents a lavish funeral, more fitting for a Confucian. (For more on Mozi, see 3B9.9–10. Impartial caring is also known as "universal love.")

Mengzi's disciple Chen Dai said, "Your not seeing the various lords seems   1.1
petty. Supposing you were to see one, a great one would thereby become
King, and a petty one would thereby become Hegemon. Furthermore, the
Records say, 'Bend the foot to straighten the yard.' This seems like something
you could do."[1]

Mengzi said, "Formerly, Duke Jing of Qi was hunting and he summoned   1.2
a gamekeeper with a plumed staff. The gamekeeper did not come, so the
duke was about to have him killed. Kongzi commented, 'An intent noble
does not forget he may end up in a ditch; a courageous noble does not forget he may lose his head.' What did Kongzi find commendable in the gamekeeper? He found commendable the fact that he did not respond to what
was not his summons. What if he had come without awaiting any summons?[2]
Furthermore, 'Bending the foot to straighten the yard' is to talk in terms of   1.3
profit. If we approach it in terms of profit, then can we also bend the yard
to straighten the foot for profit? 注

"Formerly, Viscount Jian of Zhao sent Wang Liang to drive the chariot   1.4
for his favorite, Xi. At the end of the day, they had not caught a single bird.
Xi reported back that Wang Liang was the worst at his craft in the world.
Someone told this to Wang Liang. Liang asked, 'May I try again?' Only af-
ter some pressing was he allowed to do so. In one day, they caught ten birds.
Xi reported back, 'He is the best at his craft in the world.' Viscount Jian said,
'I will have him take charge of driving for you.' When he told Wang Liang,
Liang disapproved, saying, 'I drove my horses in the prescribed manner for
him, and by the end of the day we did not catch one thing. I violated the
rules for him, and in one day we caught ten. The *Odes* say,

> They did not err in racing them
> They let loose their arrows on the mark.

I am not accustomed to driving for a petty person. I ask to decline.'[3]

"Even the charioteer was ashamed to collude with the archer. Colluding   1.5
with him to get game, although it be piled as high as a hill, is something he
would not do. So how would it be if I were to bend the Way to follow those

---

[1]   Mengzi refused to meet with a ruler who did not approach him in accordance with the rituals appropriate to greeting a learned noble. This frustrated disciples like Chen Dai, who asked
Mengzi to compromise his principles in order to get the opportunity to meet and influence rulers
who demanded that Mengzi defer to them.

[2]   See the commentary on 5B7.5–6.

[3]   Hunting was a pastime but also a ritual activity with rules governing how one should drive
the chariot. To violate these rules was comparable to cheating at a sport.

others? Besides, you are quite wrong: those who bend themselves have never been able to make others upright." 注

2.1	A certain Jing Chun said, "Were not the statesmen Gongsun Yan and Zhang Yi genuinely great men? As soon as they were angry, the various lords were afraid. When they were at peace the world rested."

2.2	Mengzi said, "How does this make them great men? Have you not studied ritual? Just as a father instructs a man when he comes of age, so does a mother instruct a daughter when she gets married. Sending her off at the threshold, she warns her, 'When you join your new family, you must be respectful and circumspect. Do not disobey your husband.' Making obedience one's standard is merely the Way of a wife or concubine.

2.3	"In contrast, to dwell in the broadest place on earth; to stand in one's proper place in the world; to put into effect the great Way of the world; to follow it with the people when one obtains one's goal; to practice the Way by oneself when one does not obtain one's goal; wealth and prestige are incapable of seducing him; poverty and low status are incapable of moving him; awe and military might cannot bend him—it is this that is called being a great man." 注

3.1	Zhou Xiao, a man from Liang, asked, "Did ancient gentlemen take office?"

	Mengzi replied, "They did. The *Commentary* says, 'When Kongzi had no ruler to serve for three months he became wistful. Leaving a state, he would always carry with him a gift for introductions to prospective rulers. Gongming Yi said, 'If the ancients went three months without a ruler to serve, they mourned.'" 注

3.2	Zhong Xiao said, "Isn't it overly anxious to mourn after only three months without serving a ruler?"

3.3	Mengzi said, "For a noble to lose his position is like one of the various lords losing his state. The *Rites* say, 'The various lords assist in plowing to supply the grain for the rituals. Their wives cultivate the silk to make the garments for the rituals.' If the sacrificial animals are not ready, if the grain is not clean, if the garments are not prepared, they dare not sacrifice. Similarly, 'If a noble lacks a field, he does not sacrifice. If the sacrificial animals, utensils, and garments are not ready so that he does not dare to sacrifice, then neither does he dare to feel at ease.' Is this not sufficient to mourn?"[4]

3.4	Zhong Xiao said, "Why is it that Kongzi would always carry a gift for introductions when he left a state?"

---

[4] When employed, a noble is given a "pure field" for sacrificial purposes as part of his salary (3A3.16). So when he is out of office, he cannot perform the required ritual sacrifices to his ancestors.

Mengzi said, "A noble being in office is like a farmer plowing. How could   3.5
a farmer leave a state and leave behind his plow?"

Zhong Xiao said, "Liang is a state where one could serve. I had never
heard of such anxiousness to take office. But if that is so, what difficulty will
a gentleman have in taking office?"

Mengzi said, "When a man is born, his parents hope he will find a wife;
when a woman is born, her parents hope she will find a husband. All parents feel like this. But those who do not wait for the command of their parents or the words of a matchmaker and instead bore holes through walls to
peep at one another and jump over fences to run off together are despised
by parents and everyone else in their state. The ancients always desired to take
office. But they also disdained failing to follow the Way. To advance through
not following the Way is in the same category as boring peepholes." 注

Mengzi's disciple Peng Geng asked, "To have dozens of carts behind us, sev-   4.1
eral hundred attendants, and be provided with provisions on our stops by
the various lords—is this not excessive?"

Mengzi said, "If it is contrary to the Way, one may not accept even a single bowl of food. If it is in accordance with the Way, then Shun accepting
the world from Yao cannot be considered excessive."

Peng Geng said, "That's not what I mean. What is unacceptable is a noble   4.2
eating food provided by others without performing a service."

Mengzi said, "If you do not exchange goods for raw materials so as to make   4.3
up for what people lack with what people have a surplus of, then the farmer
will have an excess of grain, and the women will have an excess of cloth. If
you do exchange them, then the wheelwright and carpenter will all get food
from you. So suppose there is a person who is 'filial when at home and respectful of his elders when in public,' and maintains the Way of the Former
Kings, to await the instruction of those who come later. Yet he does not receive food from you. How is it that you respect carpenters and wheelwrights,
yet regard lightly those who practice benevolence and righteousness?"

Peng Geng said, "The intention of carpenters and wheelwrights is to get   4.4
food. Is the intention of the gentleman in practicing the Way also to get food?"

Mengzi said, "Why bring up their intentions? If they benefit you, and you
can feed them, then you do. Furthermore, do you feed them for their intentions or for their benefits?"

Peng Geng, "One feeds them for their intentions."

Mengzi said, "Suppose there is a worker who breaks your roofing tiles or   4.5
tears your tapestries, but his intention was to obtain food. Will you feed him?"

Peng Geng said, "No."

Mengzi said, "In that case, you do not feed them for their intentions, you
feed them for the benefits they give."

5.1   Mengzi's disciple Wan Zhang asked, "Song is a small state. Suppose it were to put into effect Kingly government, and Qi and Chu were to attack it. How should it deal with this?" 注

5.2   Mengzi said, "Before he founded the Shang dynasty, Tang dwelled in Bo, and his neighbors were the Ge. The Count of Ge was heedless and did not perform the ritual sacrifices to his ancestors, so Tang sent people to inquire, 'Why do you not perform the ritual sacrifices?' He replied, 'We cannot supply the sacrificial animals.' Tang sent him oxen and sheep. The Count of Ge ate them but still did not sacrifice. Tang again sent people to inquire, 'Why do you not perform the ritual sacrifices?' He replied, 'We cannot supply the sacrificial millet.' Tang ordered the people of Bo to go and farm for him, while the young and weak offered the sacrificial food. The Count of Ge led his people to seize those who had food, ale, and millet and take them from them. Those who refused he killed. Among them were children with offerings of millet and meat whom he killed and stole from. The *Documents* is referring to this when it says, 'The Count of Ge took vengeance on those with
5.3   offerings.' When Tang attacked him for killing the children, all within the Four Seas said, 'This was not because he wanted the wealth of the world.
5.4   This was to avenge the common people.' When Tang began his invasions, he started with Ge, and after eleven invasions he had no enemies left in the world. When he invaded in the east, the uncivilized people of the west complained; when he invaded in the south, the uncivilized people of the north complained. They said, 'Why does he leave us for last?' The people looked for him like people looking for rain in a great drought. The traders in the cities did not stop, and the farmers did not cease. He punished their rulers but consoled the people. He came like timely rain. The people were very pleased.
       "Likewise, the *Documents* say of King Wu,

5.5   'We await our lord. When our lord comes, there will be no cruel punishments.' There were some who did not submit. So he invaded toward the east. He brought peace to their men and women. They presented him with silks of black and yellow, saying 'We shall serve our Zhou King and accept his protection, submitting to the great city of Zhou.' 注

       The gentlemen presented black and yellow silks in order to welcome the gentlemen of Zhou. The commoners presented food and broth in order to welcome their commoners. They had rescued their people from the midst of water and fire and executed the one who was cruel to them. 'The Great
5.6   Announcement' says, 'I, Wu, have raised my military might and shall enter his borders, to execute the cruel one, so that my achievement in punishment shall be more glorious than that of King Tang.'

"So the ruler of Song has not been putting into effect benevolent gov-   5.7
ernment. If he would merely put into effect benevolent government, everyone within the Four Seas would lift their heads and watch for him hopefully,
desiring for him to become their ruler. Although Qi and Chu are large, what
would be intimidating about them?" 注

Mengzi was speaking to Dai Busheng, a minister in Song, and said, "Do you   6.1
wish for your king to become good? Let me explain how. Suppose there
were a Chief Counselor of Chu who wished for his son to learn to speak
the dialect of Qi. Would he direct people from Qi to teach him, or would
he direct people from Chu to teach him?"

Dai Busheng said, "He would direct people from Qi to teach him."

Mengzi said, "If one person from Qi teaches him, but a multitude of people
from Chu distract him, even if he strives every day to understand the Qi dialect, he cannot succeed. But if you pick him up and plant him in the midst
of a neighborhood in Qi, after a few years, even if he strives every day to
understand the Chu dialect, he cannot succeed.

"Now, you say that your fellow minister Xue Juzhou is a good noble.   6.2
Suppose you direct him to live in the king's residence. If those in the king's
residence, old and young, common and distinguished, are all like Xue
Juzhou, with whom will the king do what is not good? If those in the king's
residence, old and young, common and distinguished, all oppose Xue Juzhou,
with whom will the king do what is good? What can one Xue Juzhou alone
do with the king of Song?" 注

Dai Yingzhi, a Counselor of Song, said, "To tax at the rate of one-tenth and   8.1
abolish the customs and market taxes is something I currently cannot do.
May I lessen them and wait until next year to stop the current practice? How
would that be?"

Mengzi said, "Suppose there is a person who every day appropriates one   8.2
of his neighbor's chickens. Someone tells him, 'This is not the Way of a gentleman.' He says, 'May I reduce it to appropriating one chicken every month
and wait until next year to stop?' If one knows that it is not righteous, then   8.3
one should quickly stop. Why wait until next year?" 注

Mengzi's disciple Gongduzi said, "Outsiders all describe you as 'fond of dis-   9.1
putation,' Master. May I ask why?"

Mengzi said, "How could I be fond of disputation? I simply cannot do   9.2
otherwise. People have long lived in the world, sometimes with order, sometimes in chaos. During the time of Yao, the waters overflowed and flooded   9.3
the Central States. Snakes and dragons dwelled there. The people had nowhere to settle. On lower ground, they made nests in the trees; on higher

ground, they made dwellings in caves. The *Documents* say, 'The overflowing
9.4   waters warned us.' The 'overflowing waters' were the flooding waters. Yu was
directed to bring order to it. He dredged the earth from the rivers and guided
the water to the sea. He drove the snakes and dragons away and banished
them to the marshes. The water flowed between the channels, making the
Yangtze, Huai, Yellow, and Han rivers. When the flooding had receded, and
attacks by animals had been eliminated, only then did the people live on the
9.5   plains.[5] But after Yao and Shun passed away, the Way of the sages decayed.
Cruel rulers arose one after another, destroying homes to make ponds, so that
the people had nowhere they could rest. They made people abandon the
fields so that they could be made into parks, so that the people could not
get clothes and food. Evil doctrines and cruel practices also arose. As parks,
ponds, marshes, and swamps became more numerous, the animals returned.
By the time of Tyrant Zhou, the world was again in complete chaos.
9.6   "Then the Duke of Zhou assisted King Wu in punishing Tyrant Zhou.
They also attacked the state of Yan, which had supported Tyrant Zhou, and
after three years executed its ruler; they drove Tyrant Zhou's minister Feilian
to a corner by the sea and executed him; they eliminated fifty states that had
supported Tyrant Zhou; they drove tigers, leopards, rhinoceroses, and ele-
phants far off, and the whole world rejoiced. The *Documents* say, 'Greatly enlightened indeed were the plans of King Wen! A great inheritance indeed
was the glory of King Wu! They assist and instruct us descendants. In all things
they are correct, and have no defect.'
9.7   "But eventually decadent successors, the weakening of the Way, evil doctrines, and cruel actions again arose. Ministers murdered their rulers. Sons
9.8   murdered their fathers. Kongzi was afraid and composed the *Spring and Autumn Annals*. Composing a work like the *Spring and Autumn Annals* is the
activity of the Son of Heaven. Hence, Kongzi said, 'Those who appreciate me,
will it not be because of the *Spring and Autumn Annals*? Those who blame
me, will it not be because of the *Spring and Autumn Annals*?'[6]

---

5 Cf. 3A4.7–8.

6 The *Spring and Autumn Annals* is a history that passes ethical judgments on the rulers, ministers, and other figures of the period from 722 to 481 B.C.E. Writing history is the prerogative of
the Son of Heaven, so Kongzi worried that he would be thought presumptuous for doing it. However, Kongzi felt that he had to speak out against wrongdoing. Mengzi is drawing an implicit
comparison between Kongzi's actions in composing the *Spring and Autumn Annals* and his own
practice of "disputation." (The contemporary version of the *Spring and Autumn Annals* is a cryp-
tically terse historical chronicle, seemingly lacking in moral content, so it is possible that it is not
the same as the work Mengzi attributes to Kongzi. However, there is a long tradition that Kongzi
encoded his ethical judgments in this work by subtle choice of wording.)

"Since then, a sage King has not arisen; the various lords are dissipated; 9.9
pundits engage in contrary wrangling; the doctrines of Yang Zhu and Mozi
fill the world. If a doctrine does not lean toward Yang Zhu, then it leans
toward Mozi. Yang Zhu is 'for oneself.' This is to not have a ruler. Mozi is
'impartial caring.' This is to not have a father. To not have a father and to
not have a ruler is to be an animal. Gongming Yi said, 'In your kitchens there
is fat meat, and in your stables there are fat horses. Your people look gaunt,
and in the wilds are the bodies of those dead of starvation. This is to lead
animals to devour people.' 注

"If the Ways of Yang Zhu and Mozi do not cease, and the Way of Kongzi
is not made evident, then evil doctrines will dupe the people and obstruct
benevolence and righteousness. If benevolence and righteousness are ob-
structed, that leads animals to devour people, and then people will begin to
devour one another. Because I fear this, I preserve the Way of the former 9.10
sages, fend off Yang Zhu and Mozi, and get rid of specious words, so that
evil doctrines will be unable to arise. If they arise in one's heart, they are
harmful in one's activities. If they arise in one's activities, they are harmful
in governing. When sages arise again, they will certainly not differ with what
I have said. 注

"Formerly, Yu suppressed the flood, and the world was settled. The Duke 9.11
of Zhou incorporated the uncivilized peoples, drove away ferocious animals, and the common people were at peace. Kongzi completed the *Spring
and Autumn Annals,* and disorderly ministers and brutal sons were afraid. The 9.12
Odes say,

> The uncivilized west and north, he chastised.
> Chu and nearby Shu, he punished.
> Thus no one dared to take us on.

Those who acted as if they have no father and no ruler were those whom
the Duke of Zhou chastised. I, too, desire to rectify people's hearts, to bring 9.13
to an end evil doctrines, to fend off bad conduct, to get rid of specious
words, so as to carry on the work of these three sages. How could I be fond
of disputation? I simply cannot do otherwise. Anyone who can with words 9.14
fend off Yang Zhu and Mozi is a disciple of the sages."[7] 注

Kuang Zhang, a man from Qi, said, "Chen Zhongzi is genuinely a pure 10.1
noble, isn't he? While living in Wuling, in order to avoid eating anything

---

[7] This chapter gives us a synopsis of Mengzi's view of history and his role in it.

obtained illicitly, he did not eat for three days, until his ears did not hear, and his eyes did not see. Above a well there was a plum tree whose fruit had been half-eaten by worms. Crawling, he went over to eat from it, and only after three bites could his ears hear and his eyes see."

10.2   Mengzi said, "Among the nobles of the state of Qi, Zhongzi is outstanding —like a thumb among fingers! Nonetheless, how could Zhongzi be pure? To fill out what Zhongzi is trying to maintain, one would have to be an earth-

10.3   worm. Now, an earthworm eats only dry earth above and drinks only muddy water below. But was the house in which Zhongzi lives built by the sage Bo Yi, or was it in fact built by Robber Zhi? Was the millet that he eats planted by the sage Bo Yi, or was it in fact planted by Robber Zhi? This cannot be known." 注

10.4   Kuang Zhang said, "Why is that a problem? His wife spins hemp that he himself weaves into sandals, which he then exchanges for these other things."

10.5   Mengzi said, "Zhongzi comes from an influential family of Qi. His elder brother Dai received a salary of ten thousand bushels of grain from estates at Ge. He regarded his brother's salary as an unrighteous salary and would not live off of it. He regarded his brother's dwelling as an unrighteous dwelling and would not live in it. He shunned his elder brother, distancing himself from his mother, and lived in Wuling. On a later day, he visited home, and someone had given a live goose to his elder brother as a gift. He furrowed his brow and said, 'What will you use this cackling thing for?!' After that, his mother killed the goose and gave it to him to eat. His elder brother came home and said, 'This is the meat of that *cackling thing*.' Zhongzi went out

10.6   and threw it up. If it comes from his mother, he doesn't eat it, but if it comes from his wife, then he eats it. If it's his elder brother's dwelling, then he won't live in it; if it's in Wuling, then he lives in it. Is this really being able to fill out the category? To fill out what Zhongzi is trying to maintain, one would have to be an earthworm." 注

BOOK 4A

Much of this book consists of short passages discussing the connection between benevolence and government, but there are also several chapters concerning personal ethical cultivation. Among the most interesting and often-discussed passages in this book are 4A10, 4A17, and 4A27.

1.1   Mengzi said, "Even the clear vision of Li Lou and the skillfulness of artisan Gongshuzi will not be able to draw a perfect square or circle if they are not used along with a compass and carpenter's square. Even the hearing of Music Teacher Kuang will not be able to set the five notes if it is not used along with the six pitch pipes. Even the Way of Yao and Shun will not be able to pacify and rule the world if it is not used along with benevolent government. 注

"Suppose there are some who have benevolent hearts and benevolent   1.2
reputations, but the people do not receive their kindness, and they cannot be a model for later generations. This is because they do not put into effect the Way of the Former Kings. Hence it is said, 'Mere goodness is insufficient   1.3
to govern; mere laws do not put themselves into effect.' 注 As the *Odes* say,   1.4

> No excess, no forgetfulness;
> Following the old regulations.

No one has ever gone wrong by honoring the laws of the Former Kings.

"The sages had already done their utmost with their eyes, so they went   1.5
on to use the compass, carpenter's square, balance, and ink-line, so that squares, circles, level surfaces, and straight edges could be used endlessly. They had already done their utmost with their ears, so they went on to use the six pitch pipes, so that the five notes could be set endlessly. They had already done their utmost with the reflection of their hearts, so they went on to use governments that were not unfeeling toward others, and benevolence covered the world.[1] Hence it is said, 'To go high, one must climb the hills   1.6
and mountains; to go low, one must follow the rivers and marshes.' If one governs but does not follow the Way of the Former Kings, can one be called wise? Consequently, it is fitting only for the benevolent to occupy high po-   1.7
sitions. If those who are not benevolent occupy high positions, they will disseminate their evil upon the multitude. If those above lack a Way to assess by,   1.8
those below will lack laws to abide by. If those at court do not have faith in the Way, those in office will not have faith in their rules. When 'gentlemen' violate righteousness, petty people will flaunt punishments. If a state like this survives, it is just luck. Hence, it is said, 'It is not a disaster for a state if   1.9
its city walls are not complete, or if its soldiers are not numerous. It doesn't hurt a country if fields have not been cleared for cultivation, or if there is not much wealth. But if those above lack propriety, and those below have not learned, then thieves will arise, on the eve of the state's demise.' The   1.10
Odes say,

> When Heaven is about to overturn something,
> One should not be behindhand.[2]

---

[1] On "reflection," see also 6A6.

[2] Mengzi cites the ode to illustrate the fact that the situation in his era is dire and requires resolute action.

1.11–1.12   'To be behindhand' is to be lax. Serving one's ruler without righteousness,
             taking and leaving office without propriety, and slandering the Way of the
   1.13   Former Kings in discussion—this is being lax. Hence, it is said, 'To be de-
             manding of one's ruler is what is called being respectful. To display what is
             good and inhibit what is bad is what is called being reverent. To say *My ruler
             is incapable* is what is called being a *thief*.'" 注

   4.1   Mengzi said, "If one loves others and they are not affectionate to oneself,
             one should examine one's own benevolence. If one rules over others and
             they are unruly, one should examine one's own wisdom. If one treats others
             with propriety and they do not respond, one should examine one's own
   4.2   reverence. If in one's actions one does not succeed, one should always seek
   4.3   for it in oneself. If one is proper oneself, the world will turn to one. The
             Odes say,

                    As long as one's doctrines accord with the Mandate
                    One is seeking much good fortune for oneself."[3]

   5.1   Mengzi said, "People have a common saying: 'The world, the state, the fam-
             ily.' The root of the world lies in the state; the root of the state lies in the
             family; the root of the family lies in oneself." 注

   7.1   Mengzi said, "When the world has the Way, those with lesser Virtue are
             servants to those with greater Virtue, and the lesser worthies are servants to
             the greater worthies. When the world lacks the Way, the smaller are servants
             to the larger, and the weaker are servants to the stronger. Both courses of
             action are due to Heaven. Those who follow Heaven survive. Those who
   7.2   oppose Heaven perish. 注 Duke Jing of Qi said, 'Someone who can neither
             command nor take orders is cut off.' He then tearfully gave his daughter in
   7.3   marriage to a leader of the Wu people. 注 Presently, small states take great
             states as their teachers and are ashamed to take orders from them. This is
   7.4   like disciples being ashamed to take orders from their teachers. If they are
             ashamed of it, there is nothing better than taking King Wen as their teacher.
             If they took King Wen as their teacher, a great state in five years, or a small
   7.5   state in seven years, would govern the world. 注 The *Odes* say,

                    The descendants of the Shang
                    Were myriad in number.
                    But the Lord on High had already mandated

---

[3] On the "Mandate," see 5A5.4.

That they submit to the Zhou alone,
So they submitted to the Zhou alone.
The Mandate of Heaven is not constant.
So the discerning ministers of the Shang
Assisted the Zhou with the libations in the capital.[4]

Kongzi commented on this ode, 'Even multitudes of people are no match for benevolence. If the ruler of a state is fond of benevolence, he has no match in the world.'

Presently, those who desire to have no match in the world do so without using benevolence. This is like holding something hot without dowsing one's hands. But as the *Odes* say,   7.6

Who is able to hold something hot,
Oh, without dowsing his hands?"

Mengzi said, "Tyrant Jie and Tyrant Zhou lost the world because they lost   9.1
the people. Losing the people is due to losing their hearts. There is a Way for getting the world: if you get the people, you will then get the world. There is a Way for getting the people: if you get their hearts, you will then get the people. There is a Way for getting their hearts: that which you desire, share with them in accumulating, and that which you dislike, do not inflict on them. 注 People turn toward benevolence like water flowing downward   9.2
or animals running toward the wilds. On the other hand, otters drive fish into   9.3
the depths. Hawks drive sparrows into the thick bushes. So Tyrant Jie and Tyrant Zhou drove the people toward Tang and Wu. At the present time,   9.4
if there were a ruler in the world who was fond of benevolence, then the various lords would all be driven toward him. Even if he did not wish to become King, he would be unable to stop it. Those today who desire to   9.5
become King are like people who have been ill for seven years and seek three-year moxa. If they don't start preparing it, they won't get it before the end of their lives. If one does not set one's will upon benevolence, to the end of one's life one will have worries and shame, until one sinks into death and destruction.[5] The *Odes* say,   9.6

---

[4] On the "Mandate," see 5A5.4.

[5] Moxibustion is a traditional Chinese medical practice, still used today, in which herbal remedies are burned slowly while on the surface of the skin. Some kinds of moxa must be dried and aged to reach full potency. Just as this remedy takes a long time to prepare, so does achieving benevolent government.

How can people who act like that be good?
They just lead each other to drown.

This expresses it."

10.1   Mengzi said, "One cannot have a discussion with those who are destroying themselves. One cannot work with those who throw themselves away. Those whose words slander propriety and righteousness are whom I mean by 'those who are destroying themselves.' Those who say, 'I myself am unable to dwell in benevolence and follow righteousness' are whom I mean
10.2   by 'those who throw themselves away.' Benevolence is people's peaceful abode.
10.3   Righteousness is people's proper path. How sad it is when people vacate their peaceful abode and do not dwell in it, or set aside their proper path and do not follow it!" 注

11.1   Mengzi said, "The Way lies in what is near, but people seek it in what is distant; one's task lies in what is easy, but people seek it in what is difficult. If everyone would treat their parents as parents and their elders as elders, the world would be at peace." 注

12.1   Mengzi said, "If one occupies a subordinate position but does not have the confidence of one's superiors, one cannot bring order to the people. There is a Way for gaining the confidence of one's superiors. If one does not have the faith of one's friends, one will not have the confidence of one's superiors. There is a Way for getting the faith of one's friends. If one serves one's parents but they are not happy, one will not have the faith of one's friends. There is a Way for making one's parents happy. If one examines oneself and one is not Genuine, one's parents will not be happy. There is a Way for making oneself Genuine. If one is not enlightened about goodness, one will not
12.2   make oneself Genuine. For this reason, Genuineness is Heaven's Way. Re
12.3   flecting upon Genuineness is the human Way. There has never been a case of one reaching the ultimate of Genuineness yet not inspiring others. There has never been a case of one not being Genuine yet being able to inspire others." 注

14.1   Mengzi said, "Kongzi's disciple Ran Qiu was Chief Steward of the Ji clan.[6] He was unable to change their character and appropriated double what taxes had been previously. Kongzi said, 'Ran Qiu is no disciple of mine. If you disciples were to sound the drums and attack him, I would not disapprove.'

---

[6]   The Ji were one of the families that had usurped power in Kongzi's state of Lu.

From this we can see that Kongzi rejected those who enrich the rulers who   *14.2*
do not put into effect benevolent government. How much more would he
reject those who encourage war? To wage war to fight for land is to kill
people till they fill the fields. To wage war to fight for cities is to kill people
till they fill the cities. This is what is meant by 'leading the land to eat the
flesh of people.' This is a crime even death cannot atone for. Hence, those who   *14.3*
are good at war deserve the greatest punishment. Those who make strategic alliances among the assorted lords come next. Those who clear the fields
and order forced labor on the lands come after them." 注

Mengzi said, "Of what is present within a person, nothing is more genuine   *15.1*
than the pupils of the eyes. The pupils cannot hide one's evil. If, in one's
bosom, one is upright, the pupils will be bright. If, in one's bosom, one is
not upright, the pupils will be shady. If one listens to people's discussions and   *15.2*
looks at their pupils, how can they hide?" 注

Mengzi said, "Those who are respectful do not humiliate others. Those who   *16.1*
are frugal do not steal from others. A ruler who humiliates and steals is worried only that his subjects may not be agreeable with him. How could they
become respectful or frugal? How can respectfulness and frugality come to
be from fawning voices and servile expressions?"

Mengzi debated Chunyu Kun, who asked, "Does ritual require that men   *17.1*
and women not touch when handing something to one another?"
  Mengzi replied, "That is the ritual."
  Chunyu Kun then asked, "If your sister-in-law were drowning, would you
pull her out with your hand?"
  Mengzi replied, "Only a beast would not pull out his sister-in-law if she
were drowning. It is the ritual that men and women should not touch when
handing something to one another, but if your sister-in-law is drowning, to
pull her out with your hand is a matter of discretion." 注
  Chunyu Kun continued, "Currently, the world is drowning! Why is it that   *17.2*
you do not pull it out?"[7]
  Mengzi replied, "When the world is drowning, one pulls it out with the   *17.3*
Way; when one's sister-in-law is drowning, one pulls her out with one's hand.
How could I save the world with my hand?" 注

Mengzi's disciple Gongsun Chou asked, "Why do gentlemen not instruct   *18.1*
their sons themselves?"

---

[7] Chunyu Kun is suggesting that, in the current era, one must abandon the prohibitions demanded by Confucian ritual and righteousness.

18.2   Mengzi replied, "It would not work because of the circumstances. In order to instruct, you must correct what someone does. If the correction does not work, one must follow it up with reprimands. If one follows it up with reprimands, then it will hurt the feelings of the son, who will say, 'My father instructs me by correcting me. But my father is not always correct himself.' Then father and son will hurt the feelings of each other. For fathers and sons to hurt each other is quite bad.

18.3–18.4   "So the ancients instructed each other's sons. Fathers and sons did not demand goodness of one another. If the one demands goodness of the other, then they will become estranged. There is nothing more inauspicious than for them to become estranged." 注

19.1   Mengzi said, "What is the greatest service? Serving one's parents is the greatest. What is the greatest thing one preserves? Preserving one's self is the greatest. I have heard of being able to serve one's parents without losing one's self. But I have never heard of losing one's self yet still being able to

19.2   serve one's parents. Who does not serve someone? Serving one's parents is the root of all service. Who does not preserve something? Preserving one's self is the root of all preservation. 注

19.3   "Kongzi's disciple Zengzi took care of his father, Zeng Xi. He would always give him meat and ale, and when he was about to clear the table, Zengzi would ask to whom the leftovers should be given. When Zeng Xi asked him whether there were any leftovers, he would always say, 'There are.' After Zeng Xi died, Zengzi was cared for by his son, Zeng Yuan. He would always give him meat and ale, but when he was about to clear the table, he did not ask to whom the leftovers should be given. If Zengzi asked him whether there were any leftovers, he would say, 'They are completely gone,' planning on serving the leftovers to his father later. This is what is meant by 'caring merely for their mouth and limbs.' Someone like Zengzi can be said

19.4   to have satisfied his father's wishes. To serve one's parents as Zengzi did—only that is really acceptable."

21.1   Mengzi said, "There is unwarranted praise, and there is slander that comes from seeking to maintain integrity." 注

22.1   Mengzi said, "People easily switch their side in discussions only because they have never been held responsible."

23.1   Mengzi said, "It is a calamity for someone to be fond of being a teacher to others." 注

27.1   Mengzi said, "The core of benevolence is serving one's parents. The core of
27.2   righteousness is obeying one's elder brother. The core of wisdom is know-

ing these two and not abandoning them. The core of ritual propriety is the adornment of these two. The core of music is to delight in these two.

"If one delights in them, then they grow. If they grow, then how can they be stopped? If they cannot be stopped, then one does not notice one's feet dancing to them, one's hands swaying to them." 注

BOOK 4B

This book ranges over a wide variety of topics. Among the most interesting and often-discussed passages in this book are 4B6, 4B11, 4B12, 4B19, 4B26, and 4B33.

Mengzi said, "Shun was born in Zhu Feng, moved to Fu Xia, and died in Ming Tiao. He was thus of the eastern tribes. King Wen was born in Qi Zhou and died in Bi Ying. He was thus of the western tribes. Their lands were over a thousand leagues apart, and their eras were separated by more than a thousand years. But when they achieved their intentions in the Central States, it was like joining the two halves of a tally. The judgments of the former sage and the later sage are one." 注 *1.1 1.2 1.3*

When Zichan was in charge of the government of the state of Zheng, he used his own carriage to carry people across the Zhen and the Wei rivers.[1] Mengzi commented, "He was kind but did not understand how to govern. By September the foot bridges are to be repaired, and by October the carriage bridges are to be repaired, so the people no longer face the difficulty of wading across the rivers. If gentlemen are equitable in governing, it is acceptable even to order people out of their way while they travel. How can they carry every single person across? Hence, in governing, if one tries to make everyone happy, there will simply not be enough days." 注 *2.1 2.2 2.3 2.4 2.5*

Mengzi said, "If a ruler is benevolent, no one will fail to be benevolent. If a ruler is righteous, no one will fail to be righteous." *5.1*

Mengzi said, "A great person will not engage in 'propriety' that is not propriety, or 'righteousness' that is not righteousness." 注 *6.1*

Mengzi said, "Those who achieve the mean care for those who do not achieve the mean.[2] Those who have talent nurture those who do not have talent. *7.1*

---

[1] On Zichan, see 5A2.4 and the commentary to that passage.

[2] "The mean" is what is neither excessive nor deficient for a particular context (cf. 4B10).

Hence, people will delight in having worthy fathers and elder brothers. If those who achieve the mean abandon those who do not achieve the mean, and those who have talent abandon those who do not have talent, then the worthy and those who do not measure up will be separated from each other by less than an inch."

8.1   Mengzi said, "People must have some things that they do not do, and only then can they really do anything." 注

10.1   Mengzi said, "Kongzi would do nothing that was excessive."

11.1   Mengzi said, "The words of great people are not necessarily faithful, and their actions are not necessarily resolute. They rest only in righteousness." 注

12.1   Mengzi said, "Great people do not lose the hearts of their 'children.'" 注

13.1   Mengzi said, "Caring for the living is not sufficient to be considered a great task. Only sending off the dead may be considered a great task." 注

14.1   Mengzi said, "The gentleman travels deeply, following the Way, desiring to understand it for himself. Understanding it for himself, he dwells in it peacefully. Dwelling in it peacefully, he deeply relies upon it. Deeply relying upon it, he draws upon it left and right, encountering its source. Hence, the gentleman desires to understand it for himself." 注

16.1   Mengzi said, "No one has ever been able to use goodness to force others to submit. Only if one cares for others with goodness will one be able to make the world submit. It has never happened that someone becomes King without the hearts of the world first submitting to him."

19.1   Mengzi said, "That by which humans differ from animals is slight. The masses
19.2   abandon it. The gentleman preserves it. Shun was enlightened about things. He had scrutinized human roles. He acted out of benevolence and righteousness; he did not act out benevolence and righteousness." 注

20.1   Mengzi said, "Yu disliked strong alcohol but was fond of good teachings.
20.2   Tang held to the mean. He put worthies in office regardless of their social
20.3   background. King Wen looked after the people as if they had been injured.
20.4   He looked for the Way as if he had never seen it. King Wu did not neglect those who were nearby, nor did he forget those who were far away.
20.5   "The Duke of Zhou longed to unite the excellences of these Kings in order to bestow upon the people these four actions. If he encountered any-

thing that was inconsistent, he would raise his head and reflect upon it, from the day into the night. When he was fortunate enough to understand it, he would sit and await the dawn." 注

Mengzi said, "In the Eastern Zhou, the influence of the Kings expired, and people lost touch with the *Odes*. When people lost touch with the *Odes*, only then was the *Spring and Autumn Annals* made. The *Carriage* of Jin, the *Ogre* of Chu, and the *Spring and Autumn Annals* of Lu are works of the same kind.[3] Their affairs were those of Hegemons like Huan of Qi and Wen of Jin. Their style was that of a historian. Kongzi said, 'Their significance I have dared to assume.'" 注   *21.1*   *21.2*   *21.3*

.

Mengzi said, "A gentleman's influence lasts five generations and is cut off. Likewise, a petty person's influence lasts five generations and is cut off. I did not succeed in being Kongzi's disciple. I was improved by others." 注   *22.1*   *22.2*

Peng Meng learned archery from Yi, completely fathoming his Way. Thinking that the only person in the world who could defeat him was Yi, he killed him. Mengzi said, "Yi was also at fault in this. Even though Gongming Yi said that he seemed to be without fault, I think the most one can say is that his fault was slight. How could he be without fault? 注   *24.1*

"The state of Zheng sent Zizhuo Ruzi to invade the state of Wei. Wei sent Yugong Si to pursue him. Zizhuo Ruzi said, 'Today my arthritis is acting up, so I am unable to hold my bow. I suppose I shall die.' He asked his chariot driver, 'Who is it that chases me?' When his driver said, 'It is Yugong Si,' he exclaimed, 'I shall live!' His driver said, 'Yugong Si is the best archer of the state of Wei. What do you mean, Master, when you say that you will live?' He replied, 'Yugong Si studied archery under Yin'gong Tuo. Yin'gong Tuo studied archery under me. Now, Yin'gong Tuo is an upright person. Those whom he chooses for friends must be upright.'   *24.2*

"When Yugong Si arrived, he said, 'Why do you not hold your bow, Master?' Zizhuo Ruzi replied, 'Today my arthritis is acting up. I am unable to hold my bow.' Yugong Si replied, 'I am merely a petty person, but I studied archery under Yin'gong Tuo. Yin'gong Tuo studied archery under you, Master. I cannot bear to take your Way and turn it against you. Nonetheless, what I do today is service to my ruler. I dare not cast it aside.' So he pulled out some arrows and hit them against the wheel of his chariot, breaking off the arrowheads. He then shot off a set of four arrows and then returned." 注

---

[3]   The *Carriage* and *Ogre* no longer exist, but the point is that they are historical works that pass judgment on the people and events they describe.

26.1   Mengzi said, "When people in the world discuss 'nature,' they are referring
        simply to what is primordial. What is primordial is based on what happens
26.2   smoothly. 注 In contrast, what I dislike about 'wise' people is that they force
        things. If 'wise' people were like Yu in guiding the waters, then there would
        be nothing to dislike about their wisdom. Yu, in guiding the waters, guided
        them where no effort was required. If 'wise' people also guided things where
        no effort was required, their wisdom would also be great. 注
26.3   "Consider the height of the heavens and the distance of the stars and
        planets. Yet if one merely seeks out their primordial state, one can sit and
        determine the solstice in a thousand years." 注

28.1   Mengzi said, "What distinguishes gentlemen from others is that they pre-
        serve their hearts. Gentlemen preserve their hearts with benevolence and
28.2   preserve their hearts with propriety. 注 The benevolent love others, and
28.3   those who have propriety revere others. Those who love others are gener-
        ally loved by others. Those who revere others are generally revered by others.
28.4   "Here is a person who is harsh to me. A gentleman in this situation will
        invariably examine himself, saying, 'I must not be benevolent. I must be lack-
28.5   ing in propriety. How else could this situation have come upon me?' If he
        examines himself and *is* benevolent, and if he examines himself and *has* pro-
        priety, yet the other person is still harsh, a gentleman will invariably exam-
28.6   ine himself, saying, 'I must not be devoted.' If he examines himself and *is*
        devoted, yet the other person is still harsh, a gentleman says, 'This person is
        simply lost. What difference is there between a person like this and an animal?
        What point is there in rebuking an animal?' 注
28.7   "For this reason, the gentleman has a concern to the end of his life, but
        he does not have a morning's anxiety. He certainly has what concerns him:
        'Shun was a person; I, too, am a person. Shun was a model for the world
        that could be passed down to future generations. Yet I am still nothing more
        than an ordinary person.' This is something to concerned about. How does
        he deal with this concern? By trying to be like Shun.
            "Gentlemen have no anxieties. They do nothing that is not benevolent,
        nor do they put into effect what lacks propriety. If there is a morning's
        calamity, it is not the gentleman's anxiety." 注

29.1   When they were ministers, Yu and Hou Ji lived in a peaceful era, yet they
        passed the doors of their homes three times without entering. Kongzi deemed
29.2   them worthy. Kongzi's disciple Yan Hui lived in a chaotic era, in a narrow
        alleyway, subsisting upon a bowl of food and a gourd of water. Other people
        could not have borne such hardship, and yet it never spoiled Yan Hui's joy.
        Kongzi deemed him worthy.

Mengzi said, "Yu, Hou Ji, and Yan Hui had the same Way. Yu thought that   29.3–29.4
if there were anyone in the world who drowned, it was as if he had drowned
them himself. Hou Ji thought that if there were anyone in the world who
was starving, it was as if he had starved them himself. Hence, they were ur-
gent like this. If Yu, Hou Ji, and Yan Hui had exchanged places, they all would   29.5
have done as the others did. 注

"Now, suppose there is someone from your household involved in an   29.6
altercation outside. It is acceptable to go and help even though you are disheveled and not fully dressed. But if there is someone from your village in-   29.7
volved in an altercation outside, it is foolish to go and help when you are
disheveled and not fully dressed. Even bolting your door is acceptable in this
case." 注

When Kongzi's disciple Zengzi was living in Wucheng, there were bandits   31.1
from the state of Yue, and he was told, "Bandits are coming. Perhaps you
should leave?" Before leaving he said, "Do not house people in my home,
or they may damage the plants and trees in my garden." When the bandits
withdrew, he sent word, "Repair my house, and I shall then return." After
Zengzi had returned, his attendants said, "The Master was treated with so
much devotion and reverence in Wucheng. Yet when bandits came, he was
the first to leave, for all the people to see, and when the bandits withdrew
he returned. This seems inappropriate."

But his disciple Shenyou Xing replied, "How could someone like you
understand this? Previously, when the Master was staying with the Shenyou
family and there was the incident involving Fu Chu, the Master led away
seventy disciples, who thereby escaped."[4]

When Zengzi's disciple Zisi was living in the state of Wei, there were   31.2
bandits from the state of Qi, and he was told, "Bandits are coming. Perhaps
you should leave?" Zisi said, "If I leave, who will defend the state with the
ruler?" Mengzi commented, "Zengzi and Zisi had the same Way. Zengzi was   31.3
a teacher—a father or elder brother. Zisi was a minister—someone less significant. If Zengzi and Zisi had exchanged places, each would have done as
the other." 注

There once were a wife and a concubine who lived in the state of Qi. When   33.1
their husband went out, he would always come back stuffed with meat and

---

[4] It is important that the people stay and defend the city, so the accusation is that Zengzi sets a
bad example by leaving. Shenyou Xing's rebuttal is that one's obligations differ depending upon
whether one is an official guest of a city, a Master caring for his disciples, or a government minister. Zengzi does what is appropriate for his role in a particular situation.

ale. When the wife asked whom he had been eating and drinking with, it was always the richest and most esteemed people. So the wife said to the concubine, "When our husband goes out, he always comes back stuffed with meat and ale. When I ask whom he has been eating and drinking with, it is always the richest and most esteemed people. However, nobody well known has ever come to visit us. I'm going to spy on where our husband goes."

Getting up early, she stealthily followed her husband. No one in all the city stopped to chat with him. He ended up among those performing sacrifices at the tombs beyond the eastern wall. He begged for their leftovers. If that was not enough, he would look around and go to another group. This was his Way of stuffing himself!

His wife returned and told his concubine: "A husband is somebody you look up to for the rest of your life. And now he turns out to be like this!" So she and the concubine cursed their husband and broke down crying in the courtyard. But the husband returned, unaware of what had happened, casually strolling in from outside, strutting proudly before his wife and concubine.

33.2   As a gentleman sees it, it is seldom the case that the manner in which people seek wealth, rank, profit, and success would not shame their wife and concubines and make them break down in tears if they knew about it. 注

BOOK 5A

In this book, Mengzi is asked to explain stories about sages that either present ethical dilemmas or seem to cast the sages in an unfavorable light. Among the most interesting and often-discussed passages in this book are 5A2, 5A5, and 5A9.

1.1   Mengzi's disciple Wan Zhang asked, "Shun 'went into the fields, and cried out and wept to the autumn sky.' Why did he cry out and weep?"

Mengzi replied, "He was bitter over the fact that he did not receive the affection of his parents."[1]

1.2   Wan Zhang then asked, "The saying goes, 'When their parents love them, they rejoice and do not forget them. When their parents dislike them, they work hard to please them and are not bitter.' Was Shun bitter?"

Mengzi replied, "Gongming Gao's disciple Zhang Xi asked him, 'I have heard your explanation of how Shun *went into the fields*. But I still do not understand the fact that he *cried out and wept to the autumn sky, and to his par-*

---

[1] See 5A2.3 on Shun's dysfunctional family.

ents.' Gongming Gao simply replied, 'This is not something that someone like you could understand.'

"Gongming Gao thought that the heart of a filial child could not be so indifferent that he would not cry. Shun thought, 'In exerting my strength to the utmost in plowing the fields, I have merely done my duty as a son. What have I done that my parents do not love me?!' The Emperor Yao directed   1.3
his children, nine sons and two daughters, the various officials, the sacrificial oxen and sheep, the full storehouses and granaries, to serve Shun even while he toiled amid the plowed fields. Many of the nobles of the world went to him. The Emperor planned to oversee the world with him and eventually transfer it to him. But because he was not reconciled with his parents, Shun felt like a poor, homeless person. 注

"To have the nobles of the world delight in oneself is something people   1.4
desire, but it was not sufficient to relieve his concern. To take pleasure in beauty is something people desire, and he married the Emperor's two daughters, but it was not sufficient to relieve his concern. Wealth is something that people desire, and for wealth he had the whole world, but it was not sufficient to relieve his concern. To be esteemed is something that people desire, and he was esteemed by the Son of Heaven, but it was not sufficient to relieve his concern. Others delighting in him, taking pleasure in beauty, wealth, esteem—none of these was sufficient to relieve his concern, because only being reconciled with his parents could relieve his concern.

"When people are young, they have affection for their parents. When   1.5
they come to understand taking pleasure in beauty, then they have affection for those who are young and beautiful. When they have a wife and children, then they have affection for their wife and children. When they take office, then they have affection for their rulers, and if they do not get the approval of their rulers, then they burn within. But people of great filiality, to the end of their lives, have affection for their parents. In the great Shun I have seen a person who had affection for his parents even after fifty years!"

Wan Zhang asked, "The *Odes* say   2.1

> How should one handle taking a bride?
> One must inform one's father and mother.

It seems that no one should be more faithful to such a teaching than Shun. So why did Shun take a bride without informing his father and mother?"

Mengzi responded, "He could not have taken a bride if he had informed them. For a man and a woman to live together is the greatest of human roles. If he had informed his parents, then he would have had to abandon the greatest of human roles, which would have led to enmity with his father and mother. For this reason he did not inform them."[2]

2.2   Wan Zhang said, "I now understand your explanation of Shun taking a wife without informing his parents. But why did Emperor Yao betroth his daughters without informing Shun's parents?"

Mengzi said, "The Emperor also knew that if he informed them Shun could not wed them."

2.3   Wang Zhang said, "Shun's parents ordered him to go up into the granary to finish building it. Then they took away the ladder, and his father set fire to the granary. They ordered him to dig a well. He had left the well, but (not knowing this) they covered the well over. Shun's brother, Xiang, said, 'The plan to bury this *ruler of the capital* was all my achievement! His oxen and sheep—those can go to our parents. His grain storehouses—those can go to our parents. But his shields and spears—mine. His zither—mine. His bow—mine. And his two wives shall service me in my bed!' Xiang then went into Shun's home. Shun was on his couch, playing his zither. His face flushed with embarrassment, Xiang said, 'I was wracked with concern, worrying about you, my lord!'

"Shun said, 'My numerous ministers, rule them with me.'

"I wonder whether Shun did not realize that Xiang planned on killing him?"

Mengzi replied, "How could he have not realized it? But when Xiang was concerned, he was concerned too. When Xiang was delighted, he was delighted too." 注

2.4   Wan Zhang said, "In that case, did Shun feign his happiness?"

Mengzi said, "He did not. Formerly, someone gave a gift of a live fish to Zichan of Zheng. Zichan ordered a groundskeeper to take care of it in the pond. The groundskeeper cooked it instead. But he reported back, 'When I first released it, it seemed uncertain. But in a short time it was at ease. It was satisfied and swam off.' Zichan exclaimed, 'He has found his place! He has found his place!' The groundskeeper left and said to himself, 'Who said that Zichan was wise? When I had already cooked and eaten it, he says, *He has found his place! He has found his place!*' Hence, a gentleman *can* be deceived by what is in line with his path, but it is difficult to trap him with what is not the Way. Xiang came in accordance with the Way of a loving younger brother. Hence, Shun genuinely had faith in and was happy about him. How could he be feigning it?" 注

---

2   Shun's cruel parents would have opposed his marriage so that he would have no wife or children to inherit his property if he died. On the "human roles," see 3A4.8.

Wan Zhang asked, "Shun's brother Xiang took it as his daily task to try to   *3.1*
kill Shun, yet when Shun took office as Son of Heaven, he merely imprisoned him (rather than executing him). Why?"

Mengzi replied, "He actually gave him a territory to administer, although
some mistakenly referred to it as 'imprisonment.'"

Wan Zhang continued, "Shun 'dismissed the Supervisor of Works to You   *3.2*
Zhou and imprisoned Huan Dou on Mount Chong. He killed the rulers
of the Three Miao in San Wei and executed Kun on Mount Yu. He punished these four and so all the world submitted.' This was because he was
executing those who were not benevolent. Xiang was consummately lacking in benevolence, yet he gave him the territory of Youbi to administer.
What crime did the people of Youbi commit?! Is a benevolent person inherently like this? In the case of other people, he punishes them. In the case
of his younger brother, he gives him a territory to administer."

Mengzi replied, "Benevolent people do not store up anger nor do they
dwell in bitterness against their younger brothers. They simply love and treat
them as kin. Treating them as kin, they desire them to have rank. Loving
them, they desire them to have wealth. He gave him Youbi to administer to
give him wealth and rank. If he himself was the Son of Heaven, and his
younger brother was a common fellow, could this be called loving and treating him as kin?"

Wan Zhang said, "May I ask why some referred to it as 'banishment'?"   *3.3*

Mengzi replied, "Xiang did not have effective power in his state. The Son
of Heaven instructed officials to administer the state and collect tribute and
taxes. Hence, it was referred to as 'banishment.' So could Xiang have succeeded in being cruel to his subjects? Nonetheless, Shun desired to see him
often. Hence, Xiang came to court as constantly as a flowing spring. This is
expressed in the phrase, 'He did not await the time of tribute but met the
ruler of Youbi on government business.'" 注

Mengzi's disciple Xianqiu Meng asked, "Among the ancient sayings it states,   *4.1*

> A noble of consummate Virtue does not treat his ruler as a minister
> and does not treat his father as his son. But when Shun stood facing
> south, Yao, leading the various lords, faced north and did obeisance
> to him.[3] And Shun's father, the Blind Man, also faced north and did

---

[3] The ruler faces south, because he is the earthly analogue of the Pole Star (cf. *Analects* 2.1).
At Yao's invitation, Shun took over the reigns of government when Yao became too old to rule.
However, Shun did not assume the title of Emperor until after Yao's death.

obeisance to him. Shun saw his father, and his countenance was disturbed. Kongzi commented, "At this time, the world was in danger! How precarious!"

Could this actually be so?"

Mengzi said, "No. These are not the teachings of a gentleman. They are the sayings of the eastern wilds of Qi. When Yao grew too old, Shun took charge. Then, as 'The Canon of Shun' states, 'In the twenty and eighth year of Shun's rule, Yao passed away. The hundred clans mourned as if for a father or mother. For three years, the eight musical instruments were all silent within the Four Seas.' Kongzi commented, 'There are not two Suns in the Heavens. The people do not have two Kings.' Shun was already the Son of Heaven when he led the various lords of the world in the three years of mourning for Yao. Such was the situation with these two Sons of Heaven."

4.2   Xianqiu Meng continued, "I now understand your explanation of how Shun did not make a vassal of Yao. But the *Odes* say,

> All throughout the world
> Nothing is not the King's land.
> Those within the King's borders
> None are not his vassals.

So how, may I ask, when Shun had become Son of Heaven, was the Blind Man not his vassal?"

Mengzi replied, "That is not what this ode is talking about. It's about working on the King's business but being unable to support one's mother and father. The narrator is saying, 'Nothing I am doing is not the King's business. I alone do work that is worthy.' Hence, in explaining an ode, do not interpret a character to the detriment of the phrase, and do not interpret a phrase to the detriment of the poem's intent. Let your own thought meet the poem's intent. In this manner you will understand it. If you simply read each phrase literally, then consider how 'The Clouds of the Han' says, 'Among the remnants of Zhou / But one was left behind.' If one believed this saying, there would have been no survivors of the Zhou at all. 注

4.3   "In being a filial son, nothing is greater than honoring one's relatives. In honoring one's relatives, nothing is greater than caring for them with the world. So being the father of the world is the ultimate in honor. To use the world to care for someone is the ultimate in care. The *Odes* say, 'Constantly intone *filial and thoughtful* / And one will be a model of filiality and thought-

4.4   fulness.' This expresses it. The *Documents* say, 'Respectfully served was the Blind

Man. Respectful and solicitous was Shun. The Blind Man too was faithful and obedient.' This is a father who was not treated like a son."[4]

Wan Zhang said, "Is it the case that Yao gave the world to Shun?"   5.1

Mengzi said, "It is not. The Son of Heaven cannot give the world to another person." 注

Wan Zhang asked, "In that case, when Shun had the world, who gave it   5.2
to him?"

Mengzi said, "Heaven gave it to him."

Wan Zhang said, "When Heaven gave it to him, did it openly decree it?"   5.3

Mengzi said, "It did not. Heaven does not speak, but simply reveals the   5.4
Mandate through actions and affairs."[5] 注

Wan Zhang asked, "How does it reveal it through actions and affairs?"   5.5

Mengzi replied, "The Son of Heaven can present a person to Heaven, but he cannot make Heaven give him the world. The various lords can present a person to the Son of Heaven, but they cannot make him give that person a state. A Chief Counselor can present a person to one of the various lords, but he cannot make the lord appoint that person Chief Counselor. Formerly, Emperor Yao presented Shun to Heaven, and Heaven accepted him. He made him known to the people, and the people accepted him. Hence, I say that Heaven does not speak but simply reveals the Mandate through actions and affairs."

Wan Zhang continued, "May I ask how he recommended him to Heaven   5.6
and Heaven accepted him, how he presented him to the people and the people accepted him?"

Mengzi replied, "Yao put Shun in charge of the ritual sacrifices, and the various spirits were pleased with him. This was Heaven accepting him. He put Shun in charge of affairs, and the affairs were well ordered, and the people were at ease with him. This was the people accepting him. Heaven gave it to him, and people gave it to him. Hence, as I said, 'The Son of Heaven cannot give the world to another person.' 注 Shun was Prime Minister to   5.7
Yao for twenty and eight years. This is not the doing of a human. It is due to Heaven. After Yao passed away, when the three-year mourning period had been completed, Shun deferred to the son of Yao, going far off to the south of Nanhe. But the various lords and those with official business went to

---

[4] Supposedly, Shun's unremitting love eventually won over his parents and brother, so that they too became virtuous.

[5] Heaven grants a Mandate to those with Virtue, giving them the authority to found a dynasty and rule.

Shun instead of to the son of Yao. Those with cases to try went to Shun instead of to the son of Yao. Singers sang the praises of Shun instead of the son of Yao. Hence, I say it is due to Heaven. It was only after these things that Shun returned to the Central States and assumed the position of the Son of Heaven. Had he simply occupied the palace of Yao and exiled the son of Yao,

5.8 this would have been usurpation, not Heaven giving it to him. 'The Great Announcement' says, 'Heaven sees as my people see; Heaven hears as my people hear.' This expresses what I mean." 注

6.1 Wang Zhang asked, "People have a saying: 'When we come to Emperor Yu, Virtue declined. He did not pass it on to someone worthy but passed it on to his son.' Did this happen?"

Mengzi replied, "No. That is not the case. If Heaven gives it to someone worthy, then it is given to someone worthy; if Heaven gives it to the son, then it is given to the son. Formerly, Shun presented Yu to Heaven. After ten and seven years, Shun passed away. When the three-year mourning period had been completed, Yu deferred to the son of Shun, going far off to the city of Yang. But the people of the world followed him. It was like when Yao passed away, and people followed Shun instead of the son of Yao.

"Yu presented his Prime Minister Yi to Heaven. After seven years, Yu passed away. When the three-year mourning period was completed, Yi withdrew from the son of Yu, going far off to the other side of Mount Ji. Those with business at court and cases to decide went to Qi, the son of Yu, instead of to Yi, explaining 'He is our ruler's son.' Singers sang the praises of Qi instead of Yi, explaining 'He is our ruler's son.'

6.2 "Dan Zhu, the son of Yao, was not worthy. The son of Shun also was not worthy. Shun was Prime Minister to Yao and Yu was Prime Minister to Shun for many years, and their kindness was bestowed upon the people for a long time. In contrast, Qi was worthy and capable of reverently continuing the Way of Yu. And when Yi was Prime Minister to Yu, it was only for a few years, so his kindness was not bestowed upon the people for a long time. The differences in the periods during which Shun, Yu, and Yi were Prime Ministers, and that the sons of the former two were not worthy—these are all due to Heaven. These are not the doings of a human. When no one does it, yet it is done—this is due to Heaven. When no one extends to it, yet it is reached

6.3 —this is fate. 注 For a commoner to have the world, his Virtue must be like that of Shun or Yu, and moreover the Son of Heaven must present him.

6.4 Hence, Kongzi did not get the world. If a dynasty has the world, Heaven will dismiss it only if the rulers are like Tyrant Jie and Tyrant Zhou. Hence, Yi, Yi Yin, and the Duke of Zhou did not get the world. 注

6.5 "Yi Yin was Prime Minister to Tang when he was King of the world. Tang's eldest son, Tai Ding, died before assuming the throne. His next son,

Wai Bing, died after only two years on the throne. His next son, Zhong Ren, died after only four years on the throne. Then Tai Jia, the son of Tai Ding, came to the throne and overturned the statutes and punishments of King Tang. So Yi Yin exiled him to Tong, where the grave of King Tang was. After three years, Tai Jia, regretting his excesses, reproached and corrected himself. After another three years in Tong, he came to dwell in benevolence and move to righteousness. This was through listening to the admonitions of Yi Yin. He was then returned to the capital of Bo.[6]

"The Duke of Zhou's not getting the world is just like Yi in relation to   6.6
the Xia dynasty and Yi Yin in relation to the Shang dynasty. Kongzi said,   6.7
'With Yao and Shun it came about by transmission. With the Xia, Shang, and Zhou it came about by succession. But they were one in their right-eousness.'"

Wan Zhang asked, "People have a story that Yi Yin attracted the attention   7.1
of King Tang with his cooking skills, in order to become his Prime Minister. Did this happen?" 注

Mengzi replied, "No. That is not the case. Yi Yin farmed the fields of the   7.2
ruler of Xin and delighted in the Way of Yao and Shun. If it was not righteous, if it was not the Way, even if you gave him the whole world as his salary,
he could not consider it. Even if you gave him a thousand teams of horses,
he would not glance at it. If it was not righteous, if it was not the Way, he
would not give or accept from others so much as a twig. King Tang sent   7.3
people with gifts to invite him. Calmly, he replied, 'What are the invitation
gifts of Tang to me?' But after Tang had sent people to invite him three times,   7.4
his expression changed and he said, 'Rather than dwell amidst these plowed
fields and from here delight in the Way of Yao and Shun, would I not rather
make this ruler into a ruler like Yao and Shun? Would I not rather make
these people into people like those of Yao and Shun? Would I not rather see
it myself than just read and talk about it? Heaven, in giving birth to the   7.5
people, directs those who first become wise to awaken those who will later
become wise. It directs those who have insight first to awaken those who
will have insight later. Among the people given birth to by Heaven, I am one
of those who has insight first. I shall awaken this people with the Way. If I
do not awaken them, then who will?' 注

"He cared for the people of the world so much that if any ordinary man   7.6
or woman did not receive the kindness of Yao and Shun, he felt as if he
himself had pushed them into a ditch. He undertook the responsibility for
the world this seriously. Hence, he went to King Tang and persuaded him

---

6   On Yi Yin, see also 5A7, 5B1, and 7A31.

7.7   to attack the Xia to save its people. I have never heard of someone who compromises himself rectifying another person. How much less so humiliating himself to rectify the world! The actions of sages are different. Some run off and some come forward. Some flee and some do not. But they all

7.8   maintain their integrity. 注 I have heard of how he sought out King Tang with the Way of Yao and Shun, but I have never heard of him doing it with

7.9   cooking. In 'The Admonitions of Yin' he said, 'Heaven's punitive attack had its origin in the activities within Jie's palace at Mu. I merely started out from the Shang capital of Bo.'"

9.1   Wan Zhang asked, "Some people say that the sage Boli Xi sold himself into servitude to a herder in the state of Qin for five ram skins, and fed the cattle of Duke Mu of Qin because he sought to meet him. Is this story trustworthy?"

     Mengzi said, "No. That is not the case. This was fabricated by those fond

9.2   of gossip. Boli Xi was a person of the state of Yu. The people of the state of Jin, in exchange for fine jade from Chui Ji and a team of fine horses from Qu, gained right of passage through Yu to attack the state of Guo. Qi of Gong

9.3   remonstrated against this, but Boli Xi did not remonstrate against it.[7] 注 He knew that the Duke of Yu could not be remonstrated with, so he left and went to Qin. He was already seventy years old. If he did not yet know that it would be base to feed oxen in order to seek to meet Duke Mu of Qin, could he have been called wise? He knew that the Duke of Yu could not be remonstrated with, so he did not remonstrate with him. Can this be called unwise? He knew that the Duke of Yu was about to perish, so he abandoned him first. This cannot be called unwise. When he was, in good time, raised to prominence in Qin, he knew that Duke Mu was someone with whom he could work, so he became his Prime Minister. Can this be called unwise? He was Prime Minister of Qin and made his ruler distinguished throughout the world, so that he is an example for later ages. Is this something he would be capable of if he were not a worthy person? To sell oneself so as to accomplish things for one's ruler—even a villager who cared for himself would not do this. Can one say that a worthy person would do it?"注

---

[7] Yu was a small state sandwiched between the equally small state of Guo and the powerful state of Jin. Once the Jin army conquered Guo, Yu would be surrounded by Jin, which would easily conquer it.

BOOK 5B

Most of this book deals with the ethical dilemmas faced by nobles in dealing with rulers who may be corrupt. Among the most interesting and often-discussed passages in this book are 5B1, 5B7, 5B8, and 5B9.

Mengzi said, "Bo Yi's eyes would not look upon evil sights, and his ears would not listen to evil sounds. He would not serve someone who was not his ruler; he would not command those who were not his people. When it was well governed, he would take office. When it was chaotic, he would leave office. He could not bear to dwell in situations produced by unruly governments, or where unruly people lived. He regarded being with some rustic like wearing his court cap and gown and sitting down in filth. At the time of Tyrant Zhou, he dwelled on the shores of the Northern Sea, waiting for the world to become pure again. Hence, when they hear of the style of Bo Yi, the unperceptive develop discretion, and the weak develop resolution.[1]

"Yi Yin said, 'Whom do I serve who is not my ruler? Whom do I command who are not my people?' He would take office when it was well governed, and he would take office when it was chaotic. He said, 'Heaven, in producing the people, directs those who first come to understanding to awaken those who will later come to understanding, and directs those who first become aware to awaken those who will later become aware. I am one of Heaven's people who has awakened first. I shall awaken the people with the Way.' He cared for the people of the world, the common men and women, such that if there were those who did not receive the kindness of Yao and Shun, it was as if he himself had pushed them into a ditch. Such was the weight of the personal responsibility he took for the world.[2]

"Liuxia Hui was not ashamed of a corrupt lord and did not consider unworthy a petty office. In taking office, he did not conceal what was worthy and would necessarily act in accordance with the Way. When he was discharged, he was not bitter. In difficult and impoverished circumstances, he was not anxious. If he was in the company of some rustic, he was content

1.1

1.2

1.3

---

[1] Bo Yi's father was the ruler of a state near the end of the Shang dynasty. When his father died, Bo Yi abdicated in favor of his brother, because he believed this was his father's wish. Bo Yi admired King Wen, but when King Wu attacked Tyrant Zhou, he refused to accept any salary from the Zhou dynasty because Tyrant Zhou, while a vicious king, had been his ruler. Bo Yi thus died in poverty of starvation.

[2] Yi Yin lived at the end of the Xia dynasty. Tang, future founder of the Shang dynasty, gave him a position and sent him to serve Tyrant Jie. But Jie had no use for a virtuous minister, so Yi Yin returned to Tang. This happened five more times, and then Yi Yin became Tang's Prime Minister and helped him to overthrow Jie. For more on Yi Yin, see 5A6.5, 5A7, and 7A31.

and unwilling to leave. He said, 'You are you, and I am I. Even if you are stark naked beside me, how can you defile me?' Hence, when they hear of the style of Liuxia Hui, the narrow become tolerant, and the stingy become generous.[3]

1.4   "When Kongzi left the state of Qi, he just scooped up the rice he was about to cook and went. When he left the state of Lu, he said, 'I'm in no hurry.' This is the Way to leave the state of one's parents. When one should go quickly, he went quickly; when one should delay, he delayed; when one should stay, he stayed; when one should remain, he remained; when one should take office, he took office—such was Kongzi.

1.5   "Bo Yi was a sage of purity; Yi Yin was a sage of responsibility; Liuxia Hui
1.6   was a sage of harmony; Kongzi was a sage of timeliness. Kongzi is what is called a complete symphony. In a complete symphony, the bells announce the beginning, and then the jade chimes bring it to a close. The bells' sounding is to begin the harmonious patterns. The jade chimes' being struck is to close the harmonious patterns. To begin the harmonious patterns is the task of wisdom. To end the harmonious patterns is the task of sagacity. 注

1.7   "Wisdom may be compared to skillfulness. Sagacity may be compared to strength. It is like shooting an arrow from beyond a hundred paces: its making it there is due to your strength, but its hitting the bull's-eye is not due to your strength." 注

3.1   Mengzi's disciple Wan Zhang said, "May I ask about friendship?"

        Mengzi replied, "One does not become someone's friend by presuming upon one's age or social status or family relationship. One befriends the Virtue of another person. There may not be anything else one presumes upon.
3.2   Meng Xizi, a worthy official of Lu, had a household that could field a hundred chariots. He had five friends: Yuecheng Qiu, Mu Zhong, and three others whose names I have forgotten. That Xizi was friends with these five men had nothing to do with his household. If these five people had any concern for (the wealth and status of) Xizi's household, he would not have
3.3   been friends with them. This is not only the case with a household of a hundred chariots. Even the ruler of a small state is like this. Duke Hui of Fei said, 'Kongzi's grandson Zisi is my teacher, Yan Ban is my friend, and Wang
3.4   Shun and Zhang Xi are my servants.' This is not only the case with a small state. Even the ruler of a large state is like this. Hai Tang was a worthy of the state of Duke Ping of Jin. When he said 'Enter,' the duke entered. When he

---

[3]   Liuxia Hui was an official in the corrupt government of Kongzi's home state of Lu. Kongzi said of him, "Although he lowered his aspirations and brought disgrace upon his person, at least his speech was in accord with his status and his actions were in accord with his thoughts" (*Analects* 18.8; cf. 15.14 and 18.2).

said 'Sit,' the duke sat. When he said 'Eat,' the duke ate. Even if it were a meal of gruel and vegetable soup, the duke would never fail to eat his fill. How would he dare to not eat his fill? However, this was as far as it went. The duke did not share with him the official position given to him by Heaven. He did not govern with him the responsibility given to him by Heaven. He did not eat with him the salary given to him by Heaven. This is only how a noble honors a worthy, not how a King or duke should honor a worthy. 注

Shun was raised up to see the sovereign Yao. Yao made him his son-in-law   3.5
and installed him in the secondary palace. He first dined as Shun's guest, and then they alternated as guest and host. This was a case of the Son of Heaven befriending a commoner. When those below revere those above, it is called   3.6
'esteeming the prestigious.' When those above revere those below, it is called 'respecting the worthy.' Esteeming the prestigious and respecting the worthy —their righteousness is one." 注

Mengzi's disciple Wan Zhang said, "May I ask what attitude is appropriate   4.1
when exchanging gifts?"

Mengzi replied, "Respectfulness."

Wan Zhang then asked, "When is it disrespectful to repeatedly refuse a   4.2
gift?"

Mengzi replied, "When those who are showing respect give one a gift and one asks oneself whether they obtained this gift righteously or unrighteously, and only then accepts it—this is disrespectful. Hence, one does not refuse it in that manner."

Wan Zhang asked, "What about not refusing it directly, but refusing it in   4.3
one's heart? Suppose one says to oneself that the gift was obtained unrighteously from the people, so one does not accept it oneself by consigning it to someone else. Is this not acceptable?"

Mengzi said, "If the giving is in accordance with the Way, and the acceptance is in accordance with ritual, even Kongzi would accept it."

Wan Zhang asked, "Suppose there were a highway robber, a man answer-   4.4
able to no state, yet his giving was in accordance with the Way, and his presentation was in accordance with ritual. Could one then accept it from the robber?"

Mengzi replied, "That would not be acceptable. 'The Announcement of Kang' says, 'They kill people, making them flee and stealing their goods. They are wild and fear not death. Among all the people, none do not despise them.' People like these should be executed without any effort to instruct them. This teaching, which the Shang accepted from the Xia and the Zhou accepted from the Shang, is something that may not be rejected. It is a standard down to the present. So how could a gift from a robber be accepted?"

4.5   Wan Zhang said, "What the various lords of today obtained from the people is like what a robber obtains. Yet a gentleman will accept it if he approves of the ritual of giving. May I ask what the explanation for this is?"

Mengzi said, "If a King were to arise, do you think that he would line up the various lords of today and execute them? Or would he instruct them, and only execute them if they did not reform? To say that anyone who takes what is not theirs is a simple thief is to go too far in filling out the category of righteousness. When Kongzi took office in Lu, the people of Lu had a custom of contending over the spoils of the hunt. So Kongzi too contended over the spoils of the hunt. If contending over the spoils of the hunt is acceptable, how much more so is accepting gifts!" 注

4.6   Wan Zhang said, "In that case, when Kongzi took office was it not in the service of the Way?"

Mengzi replied, "Of course it was in the service of the Way."

Wan Zhang asked, "How was contending over the spoils of the hunt in the service of the Way?"

Mengzi replied, "(Before trying to reform other practices) Kongzi first made the ritual vessels correct, in accordance with the written standards, and saw to it that the vessels were not filled with rare foods but only with standard ones."

Wan Zhang asked, "Why did he not leave?"

Mengzi replied, "He was testing his Way. If the test showed that it was effective, but people did not put it into effect, only then would he leave. This is why he never stayed more than three years in any one place during his travels. Sometimes Kongzi took office to see whether his Way could be put into effect. Sometimes he took office because he was invited in accordance with ritual. Sometimes he took office for a stipend to live. With Ji Huanzi, Prime Minister of Lu, he took office to see whether his Way could be put into effect. With Duke Ling of Wei, he took office because he was invited in accordance with ritual. With Duke Xiao of Wei, he took office for a stipend to live."

4.7

7.1   Mengzi's disciple Wan Zhang said, "May I ask why it is righteous for you to not meet the various lords?"

Mengzi replied, "Unemployed nobles living in the city are called 'ministers of the markets and wells,' while those living in the countryside are called 'ministers of the plants and grasses.' But they are both just commoners. According to ritual, commoners dare not meet with any of the various lords before they have exchanged the tokens appropriate to becoming genuine ministers."[4]

---

[4]   This chapter should be read in conjunction with 3B1. Regarding the tokens exchanged when someone becomes a minister, see 3B3.1.

Wan Zhang asked, "When a commoner is summoned to perform a ser-   7.2
vice, he goes and does it. If a ruler wants to meet with him and summons
him, how could he not go to meet with him?"

Mengzi replied, "It is right to go and perform a service, but it is not right
to go and meet with him.

"Moreover, *why* does the ruler want to meet with him?"   7.3

Wang Zhang answered, "Because of his great knowledge or his worthiness."

Mengzi said, "If it is because of his great knowledge, even the Son of
Heaven may not summon a teacher. How much less so the various lords! If
it is because of his worthiness, I have never heard of someone *summoning*
a worthy to meet with him. During one of his frequent meetings with   7.4
Kongzi's grandson, Zisi, Duke Mu asked, 'Among the ancients, how would
the rulers of states that could field a thousand chariots befriend the nobles?'
Zisi was not pleased and said, 'When the ancients discussed it, they called it
serving the nobles. How could they have called it *befriending the nobles?*' Since
he was thus displeased, he would have gone on to say, 'In terms of official
position, you are my ruler and I am your minister. How dare I be friends
with my ruler? In terms of Virtue, then it is you who should serve me. How
could you befriend me?'

"So the ruler of a state that could field a thousand chariots could not even
befriend him. How much less could he summon him!

"Once, Duke Jing of Qi was hunting, and he summoned a gamekeeper   7.5
with a plumed staff. The gamekeeper did not come, so the duke was going to
have him killed. Kongzi commented, 'An intent noble does not forget that he
may end up in a ditch. A courageous noble does not forget that he may lose
his head.' What did Kongzi find commendable in the gamekeeper's action?
It was that he would not come when it was not the right kind of summons."

Wang Zhang said, "May I ask how a gamekeeper should be summoned?"   7.6

Mengzi replied, "With a leather cap. Commoners are summoned with a
plain flag, nobles with a dragon flag, and only Chief Counselors with a plumed
staff. When he was summoned with the means appropriate to a Chief Coun-   7.7
selor, the gamekeeper dared not go, even if it meant death. Likewise, if a
commoner were summoned with the means appropriate to a noble, how
could the commoner dare to go? How much less so if a worthy were summoned with the means appropriate to the unworthy! 注

"To want to meet the worthy without according with the Way is like   7.8
wanting someone to enter while shutting the door. Righteousness is the
path and propriety is the door. Only a gentleman can follow this path and
go in and out through this door. The *Odes* say,

> The Way of Zhou is smooth like a whetstone,
> Straight like an arrow.

The gentlemen tread upon it;
The petty people keep their eyes upon it."

7.9   Wan Zhang continued, "When Kongzi's ruler summoned him, he set off without even waiting to hitch horses to his carriage. Was Kongzi wrong then?"
    Mengzi replied, "This refers to when Kongzi held office and had official responsibilities, so he was being summoned in connection with his office."

8.1   Mengzi said to his disciple Wan Zhang, "If you are one of the finest nobles in a village, then befriend the other fine nobles of that village. If you are one of the finest nobles in a state, then befriend the other fine nobles of that state. If you are one of the finest nobles in the world, then befriend the other
8.2   fine nobles of the world. If befriending the other fine nobles of the world is still not enough, then ascend to examine the ancients. Recite their *Odes* and read their *Documents*. But can you do this without understanding what sort of people they were? Because of this, you must examine their era. This is how friendship ascends." 注

9.1   King Xuan of Qi asked about High Ministers. Mengzi replied, "What sort of High Ministers is Your Majesty asking about?"
    The king said, "Are High Ministers not the same?"
    Mengzi said, "They are not. There are High Ministers who are the ruler's distinguished relatives, and then there are High Ministers of other families."
    The king continued, "May I ask about High Ministers who are the ruler's distinguished relatives?"
    Mengzi replied, "If the ruler makes some great mistake, then they remonstrate with him. If he does it repeatedly and does not listen to them, they remove him from office."
9.2   The king blanched, looking shocked.
    Mengzi continued, "Let Your Majesty not be surprised. If Your Majesty asks me, your servant, a question, I dare not answer other than directly."
    When the color returned to the king's face, he asked about High Ministers of other families.
    Mengzi replied, "If the ruler makes some mistake, great or small, then they remonstrate with him. If he does it repeatedly and does not listen to them, they resign." 注

BOOK 6A

This is one of the most philosophically important books in the Mengzi. *In 6A1–5, Mengzi criticizes the rival philosopher Gaozi's claims that human na-*

ture is ethically neutral and that righteousness is "external." In 6A6–15, Mengzi explains his own doctrine that human nature is good. For Mengzi, the "nature" of X is the manner in which X will develop, without coercion or artifice, if given a healthy environment for the kind of thing X is. He argues that human nature is good because we have innate but incipient tendencies toward virtue (2A6, 6A10) that, like the sprouts of a plant, can reach their full potential if given the right environment (1A7.20–24) and some "cultivation" (2A2.12–16). This cultivation is not passive, but requires the effort of the individual (6A15). Human wrongdoing is the result of deformations of one's nature due to a bad environment (6A7–8) or the lack of individual effort (6A9).

Gaozi said, "Human nature is like a willow tree; righteousness is like cups and bowls. To make human nature benevolent and righteous is like making a willow tree into cups and bowls." 注   1.1

Mengzi replied, "Can you make it into cups and bowls by following the nature of the willow tree? You can only make it into cups and bowls by violating and robbing the willow tree. If you must violate and rob the willow tree in order to make it into cups and bowls, must you also violate and rob people in order to make them benevolent and righteous? Your doctrine will surely lead people to regard benevolence and righteousness as misfortunes for them, won't it?" 注   1.2

Gaozi said, "Human nature is like swirling water. Make an opening for it on the eastern side, then it flows east. Make an opening for it on the western side, then it flows west. Human nature not distinguishing between good and not good is like water not distinguishing between east and west." 注   2.1

Mengzi replied, "Water surely does not distinguish between east and west. But doesn't it distinguish between upward and downward? Human nature being good is like water tending downward. There is no human who does not tend toward goodness. There is no water that does not tend downward.[1] 注   2.2

"Now, by striking water and making it leap up, you can cause it to go past your forehead. If you guide it by damming it, you can cause it to remain on a mountaintop. But is this the nature of water? It is only that way because of the circumstances. When humans are caused to not be good, it is only because their nature is the same way." 注   2.3

---

[1] Although water is indifferent to flowing east or west, to make it flow either way, we must follow its natural disposition to flow downward. Likewise, to make humans good, we must work with our natural dispositions.

3.1   Gaozi said, "Life is what is meant by 'nature.'" 注
3.2   Mengzi asked, "Is 'life is what is meant by *nature*' the same as 'white is what is meant by *white*'?"
Gaozi said, "It is."
Mengzi then asked, "Is the white of a white feather the same as the white of white snow, and is the white of white snow the same as the white of white jade?"
Gaozi said, "It is." 注
3.3   Mengzi said, "Then is the nature of a dog the same as the nature of an ox, and is the nature of an ox the same as the nature of a human?" 注

4.1   Gaozi said, "The desires for food and sex are our nature. Benevolence is internal; it is not external. Righteousness is external; it is not internal."[2] 注
4.2   Mengzi asked, "Why do you say that benevolence is internal and righteousness is external?"
Gaozi said, "They are elderly, and we treat them as elderly. It is not that they are elderly because of us. Similarly, that is white, and we treat it as white, according to its being white externally to us. Hence, I say it is external." 注
4.3a   Mengzi replied, "Elderliness is different from whiteness. The whiteness of a white horse is no different from the whiteness of a gray-haired person. But surely we do not regard the elderliness of an old horse as being no differ-
4.3b   ent from the elderliness of an old person? 注 Furthermore, do you say that the one who is elderly is righteous, or that the one who treats another as elderly is righteous?" 注
4.4   Gaozi said, "My younger brother I love; the younger brother of a person from Qin I do not love. I take the explanation for this to lie in me. Hence, I say that it is internal. I treat as elderly an elderly person from Chu, but I also treat as elderly my own elderly. I take the explanation for this to lie in the elderly person. Hence, I say that it is external."[3] 注
4.5   Mengzi replied, "Savoring the roast of a person from Qin is no different from savoring my roast. So what you describe is also the case with objects. Is savoring a roast, then, also external?" 注

---

[2]   Zhu Xi says that "righteousness is external" means that one need not act out of any particular emotion in order to act righteously. In contrast, to say that righteousness is internal means that "in treating people as elderly, the feeling of genuine respect manifests itself from within, and one makes it fully genuine by respecting them." Zhu Xi, *Zhuzi yulei*, vol. 4, 1379. (Cf. 6A5.2.)

[3]   Possible alternative translation of 6A4.4: "My younger brother I love; the younger brother of a person from Qin I do not love. In this case, it is I who feel happy (because of my love for my brother). Hence, I say that it is internal. I treat as elderly an elderly person from Chu, and I also treat as elderly my own elderly. In this case, it is the elderly person who feels happy (because of the respect shown him). Hence, I say that it is external."

Gaozi's disciple Meng Jizi asked Mengzi's disciple Gongduzi, "Why do you   5.1
say that righteousness is internal?"

Gongduzi replied, "I act out of my respect, hence I say that it is inter-   5.2
nal." 注

Meng Jizi asked, "If a fellow villager is older than your eldest brother by   5.3
a year, then whom do you respect?"

Gongduzi replied, "I respect my brother."

Meng Jizi asked, "When you are pouring wine, then whom do you serve
first?"

Gongduzi replied, "I first pour wine for the fellow villager."

Meng Jizi concluded, "The one whom you respect is the former, but the
one whom you treat as elder is the latter. Hence, it really is external. It does
not come from how you feel internally." 注

Gongduzi was not able to answer. He told Mengzi about it. Mengzi said,   5.4a
"Next time, ask him,

"'Do you respect your uncle, or do you respect your younger brother?'

"He will say, 'I respect my uncle.'

"Then you say, 'When your younger brother is playing the part of the
deceased in the sacrifice, then whom do you respect?'

"He will say, 'I respect my younger brother.'[4]

"Then you say, 'What happened to the respect for your uncle?'   5.4b

"He will say, 'My respect changes because of the role my younger brother
occupies.'

"Then you also say, '(In the case you asked about in our previous discussion,) the reason why my respect changes has to do with the role the fellow villager occupies. Ordinary respect is directed toward my brother, but
temporary respect is directed toward the fellow villager.'" 注

Meng Jizi, upon hearing all this, said, "Regardless of whether it is *your*   5.5
uncle or *your* younger brother, it is the same respect. So it really is external.
It does not come from how you feel internally."

Gongduzi replied, "On a winter day, one drinks hot broth. On a summer
day, one drinks cool water. So are drinking and eating external too?" 注

Mengzi's disciple Gongduzi said, "Gaozi says, 'Human nature is neither good   6.1
nor not good.' Some say, 'Human nature can become good, and it can be-   6.2
come not good.' Therefore, when Wen and Wu arose, the people were fond
of goodness. When Tyrant You and Tyrant Li arose, the people were fond
of destructiveness. Some say, 'There are natures that are good, and there   6.3

---

[4]   In a particular ritual, a descendant of a deceased ancestor stands in for him, to symbolically
accept the offerings of food and expressions of respect for the ancestor.

are natures that are not good.' Therefore, with Yao as ruler, there was Shun's evil brother Xiang. With the Blind Man as a father, there was Shun. And with Tyrant Zhou as their nephew, and as their ruler besides, there were

6.4 Viscount Qi of Wei and Prince Bigan.[5] Now, you say that human nature is good. Are all those others, then, wrong?"

6.5 Mengzi said, "As for what they are inherently, they can become good.
6.6 This is what I mean by calling their natures good. 注 As for their becom-
6.7 ing not good, this is not the fault of their potential. 注 Humans all have the feeling of compassion. Humans all have the feeling of disdain. Humans all have the feeling of respect. Humans all have the feeling of approval and disapproval. The feeling of compassion is benevolence. The feeling of disdain is righteousness. The feeling of respect is propriety. The feeling of approval and disapproval is wisdom. Benevolence, righteousness, propriety, and wisdom are not welded to us externally. We inherently have them. It is simply that we do not reflect upon them. Hence, it is said, 'Seek it and you will get it. Abandon it and you will lose it.' Some differ from others by two, five, or countless times—this is because they cannot fathom their potentials. 注

6.8 "The *Odes* say,

> Heaven gives birth to the teeming people.
> If there is a thing, there is a norm.
> This is the constant people cleave to.
> They are fond of this beautiful Virtue.

Kongzi said, 'The one who composed this ode understood the Way!' Hence, if there is a thing, there must be a norm. It is this that is the constant people cleave to. Hence, they are fond of this beautiful Virtue." 注

7.1 Mengzi said, "In years of plenty, most young men are gentle; in years of poverty, most young men are violent. It is not that the potential that Heaven confers on them varies like this. They are like this because of what sinks and
7.2 drowns their hearts. Consider barley. Sow the seeds and cover them. The soil is the same and the time of planting is also the same. They grow rapidly, and by the time of the summer solstice they have all ripened. Although there are some differences, these are due to the richness of the soil and to unevenness
7.3 in the rain and in human effort. 注 Hence, in general, things of the same kind are all similar. Why would one have any doubt about this when it comes
7.4 to humans alone? We and the sage are of the same kind. Hence, Longzi said, 'When one makes a sandal for a foot one has not seen, we know that one

---

[5] On Xiang and the Blind Man, see 5A1 ff. On Bigan, see 2A1.8.

will not make a basket.' The similarity of all the shoes in the world is due to the fact that the feet of the world are the same. 注

"Mouths have the same preferences in flavors. Master Chef Yi Ya was the first to discover what our mouths prefer. If it were the case that the natures of mouths varied among people—just as dogs and horses are different species from us—then how could it be that throughout the world all tastes follow Yi Ya when it comes to flavor? When it comes to flavor, the reason the whole world looks to Yi Ya is that mouths throughout the world are similar.   7.5

"Ears are like this too. When it comes to sounds, the whole world looks to Music Master Shi Kuang. This is because ears throughout the word are similar. Eyes are like this too. No one in the world does not appreciate the handsomeness of a man like Zidu. Anyone who does not appreciate the handsomeness of Zidu has no eyes. Hence, I say that mouths have the same preferences in flavors, ears have the same preferences in sounds, eyes have the same preferences in attractiveness. When it comes to hearts, are they alone without preferences in common?   7.6 7.7 7.8

"What is it that hearts prefer in common? I say that it is order and righteousness. The sages first discovered what our hearts prefer in common. Hence, order and righteousness delight our hearts like meat delights our mouths." 注

Mengzi said, "The trees of Ox Mountain were once beautiful. But because it bordered on a large state, hatchets and axes besieged it. Could it remain verdant? Due to the respite it got during the day or night, and the moisture of rain and dew, there were sprouts and shoots growing there. But oxen and sheep came and grazed on them. Hence, it was as if it were barren. Seeing it barren, people believed that there had never been any timber there. But could this be the nature of the mountain? 注   8.1

"When we consider what is present in people, could they truly lack the hearts of benevolence and righteousness? The way that they discard their genuine hearts is like the hatchets and axes in relation to the trees. With them besieging it day by day, can it remain beautiful? With the respite it gets during the day or night, and the restorative effects of the morning qi, their likes and dislikes are sometimes close to those of others.[6] But then what they do during the day again fetters and destroys it. If the fettering is repeated, then the evening qi is insufficient to preserve it. If the evening qi is insufficient to preserve it, then one is not far from an animal. Others see that he is an animal, and think that there was never any capacity there. But is this what a human is like inherently? 注   8.2

---

[6] Qi is an energetic fluid that flows between us and our environment. (See also the commentary.)

8.3 "Hence, if it merely gets nourishment, there is nothing that will not grow. If it merely loses its nourishment, there is nothing that will not vanish.
8.4 Kongzi said, 'Grasped then preserved; abandoned then lost. Its goings and comings have no fixed time. No one knows its home.' Was it not the heart of which he spoke?" 注

9.1–9.2 Mengzi said, "Do not be surprised at the king's failure to be wise. Even though it may be the easiest growing thing in the world, if it gets one day of warmth and ten days of frost, there has never been anything that is capable of growing. It is seldom that I have an audience with the king, and when I withdraw, those who 'freeze' him come. What can I do with the sprouts that
ʹ are there? 注
9.3 "Now, Go is an insignificant craft.[7] But if one does not focus one's heart and apply one's intention, then one won't get it. 'Go Qiu' was the best at Go throughout the world. Suppose you told Go Qiu to teach two people Go, and one focuses his heart and applies his will to it, listening only to Go Qiu. The other, although he listens to him, with his whole heart thinks about hunting swans, reflecting only upon drawing his bow to shoot them. Although he learns together with the other person, he will not be as good as he. Will this be because his intelligence is not as great? I answer that it is not." 注

10.1 Mengzi said, "Fish is something I desire; bear's paw is also something I de-
sire.[8] If I cannot have both, I will forsake fish and select bear's paw. Life is something I desire; righteousness is also something I desire. If I cannot have
10.2 both, I will forsake life and select righteousness. Life is something I desire, but there is something I desire more than life. Hence, I will not do just any-thing to obtain it. Death is something I hate, but there is something I hate
10.3 more than death. Hence, there are calamities I do not avoid. 注 If it were the case that someone desired nothing more than life, then what means that could obtain life would that person not use? If it were the case that some-one hated nothing more than death, then what would that person not do
10.4 that would avoid calamity? From this we can see that there are means of ob-taining life that one will not employ. From this we can also see that there are
10.5 things that would avoid calamity that one will not do. Therefore, there are things one desires more than life, and there are also things one hates more than death. It is not the case that only the worthy person has this heart. All humans have it. The worthy person simply never loses it. 注

---

7 Go is an ancient board game, played with black and white stones on a grid.
8 Bear's paw was a kind of culinary delicacy.

"A basket of food and a bowl of soup—if one gets them, then one will   *10.6*
live; if one doesn't get them, then one will die. But if they're given with contempt, then even a homeless person will not accept them. If they're tram-
pled upon, then even a beggar won't take them. 注 However, when it comes   *10.7*
to a salary of ten thousand bushels of grain, then one doesn't notice propriety and righteousness and accepts them. What do ten thousand bushels
add to me? Do I accept them for the sake of a beautiful mansion? for the
obedience of a wife and concubines? to have poor acquaintances be indebted to me? 注 In the previous case, for the sake of one's own life one   *10.8*
did not accept what was offered. In the current case, for the sake of a beautiful mansion one does it. In the previous case, for the sake of one's own life
one did not accept what was offered. In the current case, for the obedience
of a wife and concubine one does it. In the previous case, for the sake of
one's own life one did not accept what was offered. In the current case, in
order to have poor acquaintances be indebted to oneself one does it. Is this
indeed something that one can't stop doing? This is what is called losing
one's fundamental heart." 注

Mengzi said, "Benevolence is the human heart and righteousness is the hu-   *11.1*
man path. To leave one's path and not follow it, or to lose one's heart and   *11.2*
not know to seek for it—these are tragedies! If people lose their chickens   *11.3*
or dogs, they know to seek for them. But if they lose their hearts, they do
not know to seek for them. The Way of learning and inquiry is no other   *11.4*
than to seek for one's lost heart."

Mengzi's disciple Gongduzi asked, "We are the same in being humans. Yet   *15.1*
some become great humans and some become petty humans. Why?"
    Mengzi replied, "Those who follow their greater part become great hu-
mans. Those who follow their petty part become petty humans." 注
    Gongduzi continued, "We are the same in being humans. Why is it that   *15.2*
some follow their greater part and some follow their petty part?"
    Mengzi replied, "It is not the function of the ears and eyes to reflect, and
they are misled by things. Things interact with other things and simply lead
them along. But the function of the heart is to reflect. If it reflects, then it
will get it. If it does not reflect, then it will not get it. This is what Heaven has
given us. If one first takes one's stand on what is greater, then what is lesser
will not be able to snatch it away. This is how to become a great person." 注

Mengzi said, "There are Heavenly honors, and there are human honors.   *16.1*
Benevolence, righteousness, devotion, faithfulness, delighting in goodness
without tiring—these are Heavenly honors. Being a duke, High Minister, or
Chief Counselor—these are human honors. The ancients cultivated Heavenly   *16.2*

16.3 honors, and human honors followed upon them. Nowadays, people cultivate Heavenly honors because they want human honors. So when they have
obtained the human honors, they cast away the Heavenly honors. This is the
extreme of confusion! In the end they will lose everything."

17.1 Mengzi said, "The desire to be esteemed is a heart humans have in common.
But every person has what is esteemed within him. It is simply that he has
17.2 not reflected upon it. That which humans esteem is not what is genuinely
esteemed. Those whom a High Minister like Zhao Meng esteems, Zhao
17.3 Meng can also debase. The *Odes* say, 'Both drunk from your ale / And satiated with your Virtue.' This means that they were satiated with his benevolence and righteousness. This is why they did not long for the taste of
marbled meat or fine grain. With a fine reputation and justified praise one
does not long for fine clothes."

19.1 Mengzi said, "The five domesticated grains are the finest of seeds. But if they
are not mature, they are not as good as wild plants. Similarly, benevolence
depends on reaching maturity."

BOOK 6B

*This book discusses a variety of topics, including ritual propriety and issues
in applied ethics and government policy. Among the most interesting and
often-discussed passages in this book are 6B1, 6B4, and 6B15.*

1.1 A person from the state of Ren asked Mengzi's disciple Wuluzi, "Which is
more important, ritual or food?"
Wuluzi said, "Ritual is more important."
1.2 The person then asked, "Which is more important, sex or ritual?"
1.3 Wuluzi said, "Ritual is more important."
Then the person said, "Suppose that if you try to eat in accordance with
ritual, you will die of hunger, but if you do not eat in accordance with ritual, then you will get food. Must you then act in accordance with ritual? Or
suppose that if you try to formally receive your bride at her parents' home,
then you will not get a wife, but if you do not formally receive your bride,
then you will get a wife. Must you then formally receive your bride?"
1.4 Wuluzi was unable to answer. The next day he went to the state of Zou
to tell Mengzi about this. Mengzi said, "What difficulty is there in answering
1.5 this? If one lines up their tops without evening out their bottoms, a square
inch of wood can be made to be taller than the top of a tower!

"Consider the statement, 'Metal is heavier than feathers.' Could that refer to a single metal buckle and a wagonload of feathers? If you compare them, focusing on a case in which food is important and ritual is insignificant, why stop at food being merely important? If you compare them, focusing on a case in which sex is important and ritual is insignificant, why stop at sex being merely important? *1.6* *1.7*

"Go and respond to him, 'Suppose that if you twist your elder brother's arm to snatch his food, then you will get food. But if you do not twist it, you will not get food. Then will you twist it? If you climb over your neighbor's wall and seize his maiden daughter, you will get a wife. If you do not seize her, you will not get a wife. Then will you seize her?'" 注 *1.8*

When Song Keng was about to go to Chu, Mengzi encountered him at Stone Hill.[1] Mengzi said, "Where are you about to go, venerable sir?" *4.1* *4.2*

Song Keng replied, "I have heard that Qin and Chu are at war. I plan to have an audience with the king of Chu, to persuade him to abandon this. If the king of Chu is not agreeable, I plan to have an audience with the king of Qin, to persuade him to abandon this. I shall certainly meet with success between the two kings." *4.3*

Mengzi said, "I am not asking for details, but I wonder if I could hear the main point you will use in persuading them." *4.4*

Song Keng said, "I shall explain the unprofitability of what they plan."

Mengzi said, "Your intention, venerable sir, is indeed great. But your slogan is unacceptable. If you persuade the kings of Qin and Chu by means of profit, the kings of Qin and Chu will set aside the commanders of their armies because they delight in profit. This is for their armies to delight in being set aside because they delight in profit. Those who are ministers will embrace profit in serving their rulers. Those who are children will embrace profit in serving their fathers. Those who are younger brothers will embrace profit in serving their elder brothers. This is for rulers and ministers, fathers and children, elder and younger brothers to end up abandoning benevolence and righteousness. It has never happened that people embrace profit in their contact with one another yet fail to be destroyed. *4.5*

"If you persuade the kings of Qin and Chu by means of benevolence and righteousness, the kings of Qin and Chu will set aside their armies because of their delight in benevolence and righteousness. This is for the officers of their armies to delight in being set aside because they delight in benevolence *4.6*

---

[1] Song Keng (also known as Song Xing or just Songzi) was a pacifist philosopher who taught that conflict occurs only because people fail to recognize that "the genuine desires of humans are few," and hence easy to satisfy.

and righteousness. Those who are ministers will embrace benevolence and righteousness in serving their rulers. Those who are children will embrace benevolence and righteousness in serving their fathers. Those who are younger brothers will embrace benevolence and righteousness in serving their elder brothers. This is for rulers and ministers, fathers and children, elder and younger brothers to abandon profit. It has never happened that people embrace benevolence and righteousness in their contact with one another, yet their ruler fails to become King. Why must one say 'profit'?" 注

14.1   Mengzi's disciple Chen Zhen asked, "When would the gentlemen of ancient times take office?"

    Mengzi replied, "There were three situations in which they took office, and
14.2 three in which they left office. First, they took office if they were invited with the utmost reverence and ritual, and were told that their teachings would be put into effect. But if their teachings were not put into effect, then
14.3 even if there were no decline in propriety, they would leave office. Second, they took office if they were invited with the utmost reverence and ritual, even if their teachings were not put into effect. But if there were a decline
14.4 in propriety, they would leave office. Third, suppose they were starving to the point that they could not even go out their door, not eating either breakfast or supper, and a ruler heard of it and said, 'I cannot do what is most important—putting into effect his Way or following his teachings. But I am ashamed to have him starve in my territory.' If the ruler assists him, he may accept it, but only if it is needed to avoid dying." 注

15.1   Mengzi said, "King Shun arose from the plowed fields. Prime Minister Fu Yue was raised to office from a construction site. Prime Minister Jiao Ge was raised to office from the salted fish market. Prime Minister Guan Zhong was raised to office from the custody of the jailer. Prime Minister Sunshu Ao was raised to office from the coastland. Prime Minister Boli Xi was raised
15.2 to office from the marketplace. 注 Hence, when Heaven is about to bestow a great responsibility on a particular person, it will always first subject one's heart and resolution to bitterness, belabor one's muscles and bones, starve one's body and flesh, deprive one's person, and thwart and bring chaos to what one does. By means of these things it perturbs one's heart, toughens
15.3 one's nature, and provides those things of which one is incapable. One must often make mistakes, and only then can one improve. One must be troubled in one's heart and vexed in one's deliberations, and only then rise up. These things must show in one's face and be expressed in one's voice, and then others will see them in you.
15.4   "If, internally, a state has no model families or able nobles, and, externally, it has no enemies or foreign problems, the state will usually perish.

"Only in these ways do we know that we live through adversity but die   15.5
through ease."

Mengzi said, "There are many techniques of instruction. My scorning to in-   16.1
struct someone is also instructing him."

BOOK 7A

*This book consists primarily of brief aphorisms, reminiscent in style of the
Analects. Among the most interesting and often-discussed passages in this
book are 7A1, 7A4, 7A15, 7A17, 7A26, 7A35, and 7A45.*

Mengzi said, "To fully fathom one's heart is to understand one's nature. To   1.1
understand one's nature is to understand Heaven. To preserve one's heart and   1.2
nourish one's nature is the way to serve Heaven. To not become conflicted   1.3
over the length of one's life but to cultivate oneself and await one's fate is
the way to take one's stand on fate." 注

Mengzi said, "Everything is fate. But one only accepts one's proper fate. For   2.1–2.2
this reason, someone who understands fate does not stand beneath a crum-
bling wall. To die through fathoming the Way is one's proper fate. To die as   2.3–2.4
a criminal is not one's proper fate." 注

Mengzi said, "'Seek it and you will get it. Abandon it and you will lose it.'   3.1
In this case, seeking helps in getting, because the seeking is in oneself. 'There   3.2
is a Way to seek it, but getting it depends on fate.' In this case, seeking does
not help in getting, because the seeking is external." 注

Mengzi said, "The ten thousand things are all brought to completion by   4.1
us. 注 There is no greater delight than to turn toward oneself and discover   4.2
Genuineness. Nothing will get one closer to benevolence than to force one-   4.3
self to act out of sympathetic understanding." 注

Mengzi said, "People may not be shameless. The shame of being shameless   6.1
is shameless indeed!"

Mengzi said, "Shame is indeed important for people! Those who are crafty   7.1–7.2
in their contrivances and schemes have no use for shame. If one is not   7.3
ashamed of not being as good as others, how will one ever be as good as
others?" 注

10.1   Mengzi said, "The people must await someone like King Wen to be inspired. However, an outstanding person is inspired even if there is no King Wen."

11.1   Mengzi said, "If someone had been given the wealth of the Han and Wei families but could still see his own inadequacies, he would be far beyond most people." 注

12.1   Mengzi said, "Follow the Way leading to ease when you put the people to work, and they will not be bitter even though they labor. Follow the Way leading to life when you kill people, and they will not be bitter even if they die."[1]

14.1   Mengzi said, "Benevolent teachings do not enter people as deeply as the
14.2   report of benevolent actions. Good regulations do not win over the people
14.3   as well as good instruction. People are in awe of good regulations, but they love good instruction. Good regulations will get material resources from the people, but good instruction will win over the hearts of the people."

15.1   Mengzi said, "That which people are capable of without learning is their genuine capability. That which they know without pondering is their gen-
15.2   uine knowledge. 注 Among babes in arms there are none that do not know to love their parents. When they grow older, there are none that do not
15.3   know to revere their elder brothers. Treating one's parents as parents is benevolence. Revering one's elders is righteousness. There is nothing else to do but extend these to the world." 注

16.1   Mengzi said, "When he was young and lived deep in the mountain wilds, Shun lived among trees and rocks and traveled with deer and pigs. He differed only slightly from the wild people of the deep mountains. But as soon as he heard one good saying or saw one good deed, it was like a river overflowing its banks, torrential, so that nothing could stop it." 注

17.1   Mengzi said, "Do not do that which you would not do; do not desire that which you would not desire. Simply be like this." 注

18.1   Mengzi said, "Those who have often dealt with difficulties and problems have the intelligence that comes with Virtue and the shrewdness that comes with
18.2   wisdom. Only the minister who must stand alone and the son who has been

---

[1] In other words, only make the people do public works projects that will ultimately benefit them, and only kill people (via execution or war) when it is necessary to save other lives.

disinherited can hold on to their hearts in precarious situations and be steady when thinking through calamities. Hence, they succeed."

Mengzi said, "A gentleman takes joy in three things, and being King of the world is not one of them. His first joy is that his parents are both alive and his siblings have no difficulties. His second joy is that looking up he is not disgraced before Heaven, and looking down he is not ashamed before humans. His third joy is getting the assistance of and cultivating the brave and talented people of the world. The gentleman takes joy in three things, and being King of the world is not one of them." 20.1 20.2 20.3 20.4 20.5

Mengzi said, "If you make the management of their fields easy and their taxes light, the people can be made wealthy. If you keep them fed and only employ them in accordance with propriety, there will be more than enough material resources. The people will not live without water and fire. But if you can knock on people's doors in the evening, asking for some water or hot embers, and not be refused, then there is enough. Similarly, when sages rule the world, they make grain be as plentiful as water and fire. When the people have as much grain as they have water and fire, how can they fail to be benevolent?" 23.1 23.2

Mengzi said, "When Kongzi ascended its eastern hills, the state of Lu seemed small. When he ascended Mount Tai, the world seemed small. Hence, once one has observed the ocean, it is hard to regard anything else as a body of water. Once one has traveled through the gates of the sages, it is hard to take anything else as a teaching. There is a technique to observing water: one observes where the waves come from. Likewise, when the sun or moon is bright, at least a beam of light must shine through. Flowing water does not advance without filling up everything before it. Likewise, when a gentleman has his will set on the Way, he does not advance until he has achieved success." 24.1 24.2 24.3

Mengzi said, "If you are earnestly devoted to goodness from the moment you wake up in the morning, you are a disciple of Shun. If you are earnestly devoted to profit from the moment you wake up in the morning, you are a disciple of Robber Zhi. If you wish to know what separates Shun from Robber Zhi, it is nothing other than the distance between profit and goodness." 注 25.1 25.2 25.3

Mengzi said, "Yang Zhu favored being 'for oneself.' If plucking out one hair from his body would have benefited the whole world, he would not do it. Mozi favored 'impartial caring.' If scraping himself bare from head to heels 26.1 26.2

26.3 would benefit the whole world, he would do it. Zimo held to the middle. Holding to the middle is close to it. But if one holds to the middle with-
26.4 out discretion, that is the same as holding to one extreme. 注 What I dislike about those who hold to one extreme is that they detract from the Way. They elevate one thing and leave aside a hundred others." 注

27.1 Mengzi said, "Those who are starving find their food delicious; those who are parched find their drink delicious. They have no standard for food and drink, because their hunger and thirst injure it. Is it only the mouth and belly that hunger and thirst injure? Human hearts, too, are subject to injury.
27.2 If one can prevent the injury of hunger and thirst from being an injury to one's heart, then there will be no concern about not being as good as other people."

29.1 Mengzi said, "Being effective is like digging a well. Even if you dig down ninety feet, if you stop without reaching the spring, you have given up on the well."

30.1 Mengzi said, "Yao and Shun always treated it as their nature. Tang and Wu
30.2 made themselves into it. The Five Hegemons feigned it. But if one feigns it for a long time without turning back, how can anyone know that they do not have it?" 注

31.1 Mengzi's disciple Gongsun Chou asked, "Prime Minister Yi Yin banished his king, Tai Jia, saying, 'I cannot stand by while he is so intractable.' The people were greatly pleased by this. When Tai Jia became worthy, he returned him
31.2 to the throne, and the people were again greatly pleased. When a worthy is a minister to a ruler who is not worthy, can he definitely banish him?"
31.3   Mengzi replied, "If one has the intention of Yi Yin, then one can; but if one lacks the intention of Yi Yin, then it is usurpation."

33.1 Dian, son of the king of Qi, asked, "What is the task of a noble?"
33.2   Mengzi replied, "He aims his will high."
33.3   Dian asked, "What does it mean to 'aim one's will high'?"
    Mengzi replied, "Let him simply be benevolent and righteous. To kill one innocent person is to fail to be benevolent. To take something that one is not entitled to is to fail to be righteous. Where does he dwell? Benevolence. Where is his path? Righteousness. If he dwells in benevolence and follows righteousness, the task of a great person is complete."

34.1 Mengzi said, "If you offered Zhongzi the state of Qi but it was not right-eous to accept it, he would not do so. Everyone has faith in him about this.

But this is no more than the righteousness of refusing a basket of grain or a bowl of soup. Nothing is greater for a human than these relations: between relatives, between ruler and ministers, and between superiors and inferiors. How can one have faith in someone's great achievements on the basis of his petty achievements?"[2]

Mengzi's disciple Tao Ying asked, "When Shun was Son of Heaven and Gao Yao was his Minister of Crime, if the Blind Man had murdered someone, what would they have done?"[3]

    Mengzi said, "Gao Yao would simply have arrested him."

    Tao Ying asked, "So Shun would not have forbidden it?"

    Mengzi said, "How could Shun have forbidden it? Gao Yao had a sanction for his actions."

    Tao Ying asked, "So what would Shun have done?"

    Mengzi said, "Shun looked at casting aside the whole world like casting aside a worn sandal. He would have secretly carried him on his back and fled, to live in the coastland, happy to the end of his days, joyfully forgetting the world." 注

When traveling from the city of Fan to the capital of Qi, Mengzi happened to see the king's son at a distance. Sighing, he said, "One's position alters one's *qi* as food alters one's body.[4] How important is one's position! After all, are we not all just someone's children? The mansion, carriage, and clothes of the king's son are like those of many other people. What makes the king's son like that is his position being what it is. How much more so if one dwells in the most grand position in the world! When the ruler of Lu went to Song, he called at the gate, and the guard commented, 'This is not our ruler. So how is it that his voice sounds like that of our ruler?' This was due simply to the similarity in the position of the rulers."

King Xuan of Qi wanted to shorten the period of mourning. Mengzi's disciple Gongsun Chou asked, "Isn't mourning for a year better than stopping completely?"

Marginal references: 35.1, 35.2, 35.3, 35.4, 35.5, 35.6, 36.1, 36.2, 36.3, 39.1

---

[2] See 3B10 on Zhongzi and why Mengzi regards him as petty. See 6A10 and 7B11 on refusing some grain or soup.

[3] The "Blind Man" was Shun's father. According to some commentators, he was called this because of his lack of ethical understanding (as illustrated by 5A1–4).

[4] On *qi*, see 2A2.8–16 and the Introduction, "Mengzi's Philosophy."

39.2   Mengzi replied, "This is as if someone were twisting his elder brother's arm, and you said to him, 'How about doing it more gently?' Simply instruct him in filiality and brotherliness."

39.3   One of the imperial sons had a mother who died. His tutor asked on his behalf to let him mourn for a few months. Gongsun Chou asked, "How about this case?"[5]

39.4   Mengzi replied, "In this case, he desires to mourn the full period, but he cannot. Even doing it one extra day would be better than stopping completely. What I had been talking about before was a case in which he did not do it, even though nothing prevented it."

40.1   Mengzi said, "There are five means by which a gentleman instructs others.
40.2–40.3 There is transforming them like timely rain. There is bringing their Virtue
40.4   to completion. There is developing their talent. There is question and an-
40.5–40.6 swer. There is private cultivation. These five are the means by which a gentleman instructs." 注

41.1   Mengzi's disciple Gongsun Chou said, "The Way is certainly lofty and fine! But it seems as if it mounts Heaven itself, so that it cannot be reached. Why not make it so that it can be reached and pursued earnestly every day?"

41.2   Mengzi replied, "A great carpenter does not warp the plumb-line for the sake of an inept worker. The great Yi did not change how he taught to draw
41.3   the bow for the sake of an inept archer. A gentleman draws back the bow, but before he lets the arrow fly, he stands in the middle of the way: let those who are able follow him."

42.1   Mengzi said, "When the world has the Way, the Way stays with you to the grave. When the world lacks the Way, you stay with the Way to the grave.[6]
42.2   But I have never heard of the Way staying with you while you follow others."

43.1.   Mengzi's disciple Gongduzi said, "When Prince Geng of Teng attended your school, he seemed to deserve propriety, but you would not even answer his questions. Why is this?"

43.2   Mengzi replied, "I will not answer those who presume upon their status, those who presume upon their 'worthiness,' those who presume upon their age, those who presume upon their achievements, or those who presume

---

[5]   The son's mother was a "secondary wife" of the king, and the king's primary wife opposed letting him mourn for the full three-year period.

[6]   "An intent noble does not forget he may end up in a ditch; a courageous noble does not forget he may lose his head" (3B1.2)

upon former acquaintance. I will not answer any such people. Prince Geng was guilty of two of these."

Mengzi said, "One who gives up in one case where one may not give up will give up anything. One who is stingy to those who are deserving will be stingy in everything. He will move forward too fast and he will move backward too quickly." 44.1

44.2

Mengzi said, "Gentlemen, in relation to animals, are sparing of them but are not benevolent toward them. In relation to the people, they are benevolent toward them but do not treat them as kin. They treat their kin as kin, and then are benevolent toward the people. They are benevolent toward the people, and then are sparing of animals." 注 45.1

BOOK 7B

This book consists mainly of brief aphorisms on a variety of topics, in the style of the Analects. *Among the most interesting and often-discussed passages in this book are 7B16, 7B24, 7B26, 7B31, and 7B37.*

Mengzi said, "How unbenevolent is King Hui of Liang! Those who are benevolent extend from what they love to what they do not yet love. Those who are unbenevolent extend from what they do not love to what they do love." 1.1

Mengzi's disciple Gongsun Chou asked, "What do you mean?" 1.2

Mengzi replied, "King Hui of Liang led his people to war and slaughtered them for the sake of land. When he was defeated, he did it again. Fearing that he would be unable to win, he urged his beloved son to his death in battle. This is what I mean by extending from what he does not love to what he does love." 注

Mengzi said, "There are no righteous wars in the *Spring and Autumn Annals*.[1] There are only cases of those that are better than others. A punitive war is when a superior attacks a subordinate. When hostile states attack one another, it is not a punitive war." 2.1

2.2

Mengzi said, "It would be better not to have the *Documents* than to believe everything in it. I accept only two or three passages in 'The Completion of 3.1

3.2

---

[1] For the *Spring and Autumn Annals*, see 3B9.8.

3.3 the War' chapter. A benevolent person has no enemies in the world. When the one who was supremely benevolent attacked the one who was supremely unbenevolent, how could it be that 'the blood flowed till it floated the threshing sticks?'"²

4.1 Mengzi said, "There are people who say, 'I am good at arranging military
4.2 formations,' or 'I am good at waging war.' These are great crimes. If the ruler of a state is fond of benevolence, he will have no enemies in the world.
4.3 'When King Tang attacked in the east, the tribes of the west were bitter. When he attacked in the south, the tribes of the north were bitter. They
4.4 said, *Why does he make us last?*' And when King Wu attacked the Shang, he
4.5 had three hundred war chariots and three thousand infantry. But the King said, 'Fear not! I bring you peace! I am no enemy of the people.' Then the
4.6 people bowed their heads, like animals shedding their horns. To launch a 'punitive attack' means to correct. If each wishes to correct itself, of what use is war?"³

5.1 Mengzi said, "A carpenter or a wheelwright can give another his compass or T-square, but he cannot make another skillful." 注

7.1 Mengzi said, "It is only now that I understand the severity of killing someone's parent. If you kill someone's father, he will also kill your father. If you kill someone's brother, he will also kill your brother. Although you did not kill your father or brother yourself, there is just a moment's time between the two."

10.1 Mengzi said, "Just as one who is well supplied with wealth cannot be killed by a bad year, so one who is well supplied with Virtue cannot be disordered by an evil era."

11.1 Mengzi said, "If one is fond of making a name for oneself, one may be able to relinquish a state that can field a thousand chariots. But if one is just not that kind of person, relinquishing a basket of grain or a bowl of soup would show in one's face."

14.1 Mengzi said, "The people are the most important, the altars to the land and
14.2 grain are next, and the ruler is the least important. For this reason, one who wins over the common people becomes the Son of Heaven. One who wins

---

² This section of the *Documents* refers to how King Wu overthrew Tyrant Zhou.
³ The words "punitive attack" (*zhēng* 征) and "correct" (*zhèng* 正) are etymologically related.

over the Son of Heaven becomes one of the various lords. One who wins over one of the various lords becomes a Chief Counselor.

"So when one of the various lords endangers the altars to the land and *14.3* grain through his misrule, he is replaced. But when there are plenty of sac- *14.4* rificial animals, the vessels of millet are pure, and the sacrificial rituals are performed on time, yet there is still drought or flooding, then one replaces the altars to the land and grain." 注

Mengzi said, "A sage is a teacher for a hundred generations. Such were Bo *15.1* Yi and Liuxia Hui. Hence, when they hear of the style of Bo Yi, the unperceptive develop discretion, and the weak develop resolution. And when they hear of the style of Liuxia Hui, the stingy become generous, and the narrow become tolerant. These two were distinguished a hundred generations ago, and a hundred generations from now all those who hear of them will be inspired. Could they have done this if they were not sages? How much more so did they affect those who knew them personally!"[4]

Mengzi said, "Benevolence is simply being human. The Way is simply to *16.1* harmonize with benevolence and put it into words." 注

A certain Mo Qi said, "I am not articulate in speech at all." *19.1*
    Mengzi replied, "There is no harm in that. Nobles dislike those who talk *19.2* too much. The *Odes* say, 'I am sad, / Hated by the rabble.' This could be said *19.3* of Kongzi. It also says, 'He did not quell their hatred, / But neither did he lose his honor.' This could be said of King Wen."

Mengzi said, "Worthies use their own insight to make others insightful. *20.1* But nowadays people try to make others insightful with only their own ignorance."

There was a famine in Qi, and Chen Zhen said to Mengzi, "The people of *23.1* the state all think that you will again ask for the granaries to be opened. I wonder whether you will be able to do so?"
    Mengzi replied, "That would be to act like Feng Fu. In the state of Jin *23.2* there was a certain Feng Fu who was skilled at capturing tigers. Later, after he had become a distinguished official, he was traveling in the countryside and there was a mob chasing a tiger. The tiger was cornered, and no one dared to approach it. But when the people saw Feng Fu, they rushed over and greeted him. So Feng Fu rolled up his sleeves and got out of his carriage to

---

[4] Cf. this passage to 5B1.

assist with the tiger. The mob was pleased, but those who were officials laughed at him." 注

24.1   Mengzi said, "The mouth in relation to flavors, the eyes in relation to sights, the ears in relation to notes, the nose in relation to odors, the four limbs in relation to comfort—these are matters of human nature, but they are also fated. Nonetheless, a gentleman does not refer to them as 'human nature.'

24.2   "Benevolence between father and son, righteousness between ruler and minister, propriety between guest and host, wisdom in relation to the worthy, the sage in relation to the Way of Heaven—these are fated, but they also involve human nature. Nonetheless, a gentleman does not refer to them as 'fated.'" 注

26.1   Mengzi said, "Those who defect from the Mohists always turn toward Yang Zhu. Those who defect from Yang Zhu always turn toward Confucianism.

26.2   When they turn toward us, we should simply accept them. 注 But nowadays those who dispute with followers of Yang Zhu and the Mohists act like they are chasing escaped pigs: even after they have gotten them back in the fold, they go ahead and hog-tie them! 注

29.1   A certain Pencheng Kuo took office in Qi. Mengzi commented, "Pencheng Kuo is a dead man."

When Pencheng Kuo was killed, the disciples asked, "Master, how did you know that he would be killed?"

Mengzi replied, "He was a person of little talent who had never heard the great Way of a gentleman. He had just enough ability to hasten his own death."

30.1   Mengzi went to the state of Teng and was lodged in the upper palace. Someone had left a pair of unfinished sandals by the window, and when he came back for them he could not find them.

30.2   Someone asked Mengzi, "Is this what your followers are like—thieves?"

Mengzi said, "Sir, do you actually think they came here to steal sandals?"

He replied, "Perhaps not. But when you give lessons, Master, you do not chase after those who leave, nor refuse any who come. You simply accept anyone who comes with the right heart." 注

31.1   Mengzi said, "People all have things that they will not bear. To extend this reaction to that which they will bear is benevolence. People all have things that they will not do. To extend this reaction to that which they will do

31.2   is righteousness. 注 If people can fill out the heart that does not desire to harm others, their benevolence will be inexhaustible. If people can fill out the heart that will not trespass, their righteousness will be inexhaustible. 注

If people can fill out the core reaction of refusing to be addressed disrespect- 31.3
fully, there will be nowhere they go where they do not do what is righteous. 注 If a noble speaks when he may not speak, this is tricking someone 31.4
with speech. If one does not speak when he should, this is tricking someone with silence. These are both in the category of trespassing." 注

Mengzi said, "The best teachings are those that discuss what is near but with 32.1
significance that is far-reaching. The best Way is the one that preserves what
is crucial but has broad application. Although the teachings of a gentleman
come from nowhere but his bosom, the Way exists in them. The gentleman 32.2
maintains his own self-cultivation and so the world is at peace. The prob- 32.3
lem with other people is that they abandon their own fields and weed the
fields of others. They demand much of others, while putting little responsibility on themselves."

Mengzi said, "Yao and Shun always treated it as their nature. Tang and Wu 33.1
turned toward it.[5] The height of Virtue is for every turn of one's movements 33.2
and expressions to precisely accord with ritual. When one cries and mourns
for the dead, it is not to impress the living. When one follows the path of
Virtue without turning back, it is not for the sake of a salary. When one's
words are necessarily faithful, it is not in order to justify one's actions. A gen- 33.3
tleman simply acts in accordance with the proper norm and awaits his fate."

Mengzi said, "For cultivating the heart, nothing is better than having few 35.1
desires. If someone has few desires, although there will be times when he
does not persevere, they will be few. If someone has many desires, although
there will be times when he perseveres, they will be few."[6]

Wan Zhang asked, "When in the state of Chen, Kongzi said, 'Perhaps I should 37.1
return home. The scholars of my school are wild and hasty, advancing and
grasping but failing to forget their former behavior.' When in Chen, why
did Kongzi think of the wild scholars of his home state of Lu?"
  Mengzi replied, "Kongzi said, 'If I do not get to associate with those who 37.2
attain the Way exactly, then must it not be those who are wild or squeamish?[7] Those who are wild advance and grasp. Those who are squeamish have
some things that they will not do.' Did Kongzi not want those who attained

---

[5] Contrast 7A30.
[6] "To persevere" means to "preserve one's heart" (4B28).
[7] To "attain the Way exactly" is more literally to "hit the mean of the Way" (*zhòng dào* 中道).

the Way exactly? But he could not be sure of getting them. Hence, he thought of the next best."

37.3   Wan Zhang said, "May I ask what those called 'wild' were like?"

37.4   Mengzi replied, "Those like Qin Zhang, Zeng Xi, and Mu Pi are the ones Kongzi called 'wild.'" 注

37.5   Wan Zhang said, "Why did he call them 'wild'?"

37.6   Mengzi replied, "Their resolutions were grand. They chanted, 'The ancients! The ancients!' But if one calmly examines their conduct, it does not

37.7   match their resolutions and words. If he also failed to get those who are wild, he wanted to associate with those who disdain to do what is not pure. These are the squeamish. They are the next best. 注

37.8   But Kongzi said, "'The only ones who pass by my door without entering my home whom I do not regret having as associates are the village worthies. The village worthies are the thieves of virtue.'"

Wan Zhang said, "What must one be like to be called a 'village worthy'?"

37.9   Mengzi replied, "The village worthies are those who say,

> Why are (the resolutions of the wild scholars) so grand? Their words take no notice of their actions, and their actions take no notice of their words. Then they chant, "The ancients! The ancients!" And why are the actions (of the squeamish) so solitary and aloof? Born in this era, we should be for this era. To be good is enough.

Eunuch-like, pandering to their era—these are the village worthies." 注

37.10   Wan Zhang said, "If the whole village declares them worthy people, there is nowhere they will go where they will not be worthy people. So why did Kongzi regard them as thieves of virtue?"

37.11   Mengzi replied, "If you try to condemn them, there is nothing you can point to; if you try to censure them, there is nothing to censure. They are in agreement with the current customs; they are in harmony with the sordid era in which they live. They seem to dwell in devotion and faithfulness; their actions seem to be blameless and pure. The multitude delight in them; they regard themselves as right. But you cannot enter into the Way of Yao and Shun with them. Hence, Kongzi said they are 'thieves of virtue.'

37.12   "Kongzi said, 'I hate that which seems but is not. I hate weeds out of fear that they will be confused with grain sprouts. I hate cleverness out of fear that it will be confused with righteousness. I hate glibness out of fear that it will be confused with faithfulness. I hate the tunes of the state of Zheng out of fear that they will be confused with proper music. I hate purple out of fear that it will be confused with vermillion. I hate the village worthies out of fear that they will be confused with those who have Virtue.' 注

"The gentleman simply returns to the standard. If the standard is correct,   37.13
then the multitudinous people will be inspired. When the people are inspired,
then there will be no evil or wickedness."[8] 注

Mengzi said, "From Yao and Shun to Tang was more than five hundred years.   38.1
So while Yu and Shun's minister Gao Yao understood the former sages by
seeing them, Tang understood the former sages only by hearing about them.
    "From Tang to King Wen was more than five hundred years. So while   38.2
Tang's ministers Yi Yin and Lai Zhu understood the former sage by seeing
him, King Wen understood the former sages only by hearing about them.
    "From King Wen to Kongzi was more than five hundred years. So while   38.3
King Wen's ministers Taigong Wang and San Yisheng understood the former
sage by seeing him, Kongzi understood the former sages only by hearing
about them.
    "From Kongzi to the present time is a little more than one hundred years.   38.4
It is not long from the era of a sage, and we are close to the home of a sage.
Yet where is he? Where is he?" 注

[Translator's comment: Mengzi taught that those who are talented have an
obligation to use their skills for the betterment of society and not merely
their own self-aggrandizement. He said that we must look within ourselves
to find our best inclinations and develop them. He argued that loving families with good values produce caring adults who have integrity. He asserted
that government must aim at the well-being of all the people not just the
well-off. He declared that rulers who punish those who steal because they
live in poverty and lack education are merely setting traps for the people.
He claimed that war is a final resort that usually causes more troubles than
it solves. We have advanced beyond Mengzi's Iron Age, agrarian, aristocratic
society in many ways. But his basic ethical teachings are as relevant today as
they were two millennia ago. So why not take up Mengzi's challenge and
carry forward the Way of the ancients?]

---

[8] Kongzi and Mengzi divide the world into the noble, the wild, the squeamish, and the village
worthies. Which are you?

COMMENTARY

Book 1A

Zhu Xi comments, "If one accords with the Heavenly Pattern, one will not seek profit, but one will naturally never fail to profit. If one submits to human desires, then one will never obtain profit though one seeks it, and harm will follow upon it. This is what is meant by the expression, 'A hair's breadth mistake leads to a thousand league error.' This is the profound meaning with which the *Mengzi* begins. This is something learners should carefully examine and clearly understand."   1.6

Cheng Yi said, "A gentleman never fails to desire profit, but if one is single-mindedly focused on profit, then it leads to harm. If there is only benevolence and righteousness, then one will not seek profit, but one will never fail to profit."

1A1 can be read as a criticism of Mohism, a consequentialist philosophy that encouraged people to judge actions in terms of the benefits (or "profit") they bring to people in general and not just to oneself or one's group. The Mohists aimed at impartial consequences rather than individual self-interest. But Mengzi argues that this practice is self-undermining: aiming directly at profit is, paradoxically, unprofitable.[1]

King Wen was the virtuous ruler of the Zhou people. Zhu Xi comments, "Mengzi explains that although King Wen used the people's labor, the people actually delighted in it. They gave what they built for him fine names and also delighted in his having them. This was because King Wen was able to love his people. Hence, the people delighted in his delight and King Wen was able to enjoy his delights."   2.3

Jie was the evil last ruler of the Xia dynasty. Zhu Xi explains, "Jie once said of himself, 'I have the world, like the Heavens have the Sun. When the Sun perishes, only then shall I perish!' The people resented his ferociousness. Hence, they judged him in accordance with his description of himself, saying, 'When will this Sun perish? If it will perish then I am willing to perish with it.'"   2.4

Zhu Xi explains, "He moves the people in order to get them to the food. He moves the grain to give it to those too old or young to move."   3.1

Notice the subtle irony in Mengzi's comment, "Your Majesty is fond of war, so allow me to use war as an illustration." Mengzi's general point is that King Hui only understands a small part of good government. He goes on to explain other policies   3.2

---

[1] Cf. 6B4 and Van Norden, *Virtue Ethics and Consequentialism in Early Chinese Philosophy*, 301–5.

that the king needs to enact. Notice his interest in environmental conservation and concrete farming policies in the following passages.

"Fifty paces laughing at a hundred paces" (*wǔshí bù xiào bǎi bù* 五十步笑百步) has become a proverbial expression in contemporary Chinese, roughly equivalent to "the pot calling the kettle black."

3.4　　Zhu Xi comments, "When the people's clothes and food are insufficient, they have no leisure to learn propriety and righteousness. But when they are warm and well fed yet lack instruction, they become like animals. Hence, when they have been made wealthy and are instructed about filiality and brotherliness, then people will know to love their parents and revere their elders. Then they will work for them and will not let them carry loads on the roadways."

6.2　　Zhu Xi comments, "'He did not seem like a ruler' and 'I did not see anything awe-inspiring' mean that he lacked majesty. In general, one's appearance and manner of speech correspond to one's Virtue. If he is like this on the outside, then what exists inside him can be known."

6.6　　This is the first reference to Mengzi's sprout metaphor (cf. 2A6). Zhu Xi comments, "Being fond of life and hating death is something human hearts have in common (6A10). Hence, if a ruler of people does not have a taste for killing people, the world will be pleased with and turn to him."

7.2　　Mengzi is telling a strategic lie here, since he himself mentions Confucian records of Huan and Wen in 4B21. Regarding "being King," Zhu Xi explains that it "means the Way of being the true King of the world." (Both Hui of Liang and Xuan of Qi illegitimately usurped the title of "King," which properly belongs to the reigning ruler of the Zhou dynasty.)

7.5　　Zhu Xi links this passage to 2A6: "The king saw the ox's frightened appearance and could not bear to kill it. This is just what is meant by 'the heart of compassion is the sprout of benevolence.' If he can 'expand and fill it up,' then he can 'care for all within the Four Seas.' Hence, Mengzi refers to this, desiring the king to examine this and fill it out."

7.7　　Zhu Xi says, "This means that the ox and the sheep are both going to die although innocent. In what way does one distinguish between them and exchange the sheep for the ox? Mengzi intentionally sets up this difficulty, desiring the king to examine himself and seek his fundamental heart. The king seems unable to do so. Hence, in the end, he is unable to resolve for himself what the commoners have said."

7.8　　Zhu Xi comments, "On the one hand, killing the ox was something that the king could not bear to do. On the other hand, anointing the bell was something that could not be dispensed with. . . . When he saw the ox, this heart had already been expressed and could not be repressed. But he had not yet seen the sheep, so the Pattern had not yet taken form and there were no feelings to hinder. Hence, exchanging the sheep for the ox allowed for the two (i.e., the heart and the ritual) to be complete without harm. This is how it is a technique of benevolence. . . . Now, humans are the same as animals in being alive but are different categories of things. Hence, we use animals for rituals, and our heart that does not bear their suffering applies only as far as they are seen and heard. Keeping one's distance from the kitchen is a technique used to cultivate this heart and broaden one's benevolence."

Mengzi and Zhu Xi say nothing about how slaughtering animals will affect the hearts of the commoners who work in the kitchen. Is there some hypocrisy in their willingness to allow others to do work that would damage the benevolent heart of a noble? Notice that the "Daoist" Zhuangzi uses a cook who slaughters an ox as a paradigm for human excellence. This may be an intentional jab at Mengzi.[2]

Zhu Xi comments, "Because of Mengzi's words, the king's heart from the previous day sprouts again. Consequently, he understands that this heart does not come from outside, but he still does not understand how to examine its root and extend it."   7.9

Hair is supposedly especially fine during the autumn, so it is used as an example of something hard to see. Zhu Xi comments, "People have the most valuable natures of anything in Heaven and Earth. Hence, people are in the same category as other people and are affectionate to each other. Consequently, the expression of compassion to the people is very immediate, but to animals it is slow. As one extends and broadens it through benevolent techniques, being benevolent to the people is easy, but being sparing of animals is difficult. In the present case, the king is already able to extend this heart to animals. So his failure to care for the people and become King is not because he is unable to act. It only comes from his not being willing to act." (Cf. 7A45; I am less confident than Mengzi and Zhu Xi that it is easier for humans to have compassion for other humans than for nonhuman animals.)   7.10

Zhu Xi comments, "We have this heart inherently; it does not need to be sought externally. Whether we 'fill it out' (2A6) lies only in ourselves. What difficulty could there be?"   7.11

Zhu Xi explains, "'To treat as elders' is to serve the elderly. 'Your elders' means your father and elder brothers. 'The elders of others' means the fathers and elder brothers of others. 'To treat as young ones' is to nurture young ones. 'Your young ones' means your children and younger brothers. 'The young ones of others' means the sons and younger brothers of others. . . . If one is unable to extend one's kindness, then the multitude will rebel, and one's relatives will be separated. Hence, one 'will lack the wherewithal to care for one's wife and children.' Now, flesh and blood relatives are originally of one qi.[3] They are not like other people who are merely of the same species. Hence, the ancients extended it from treating their parents as parents, and only then reached being benevolent to the people. Next they extended it till there was enough left over, and only then reached to being sparing of animals (7A45). This was all a matter of going from what is near and reaching to what is far, from what is easy and reaching to what is difficult. In the present case, if the king examines it, he will discover this phenomenon. Thus, Mengzi again extends the root (by explaining this to the king) and once more asks him."   7.12

David S. Nivison has noted that the word "extend" in "extend one's kindness" is a technical term in the Mohist theory of argumentation, where it means "infer" and is defined as "getting someone to grant what that person has not accepted when it is the

---

[2] *Zhuangzi* 3, "The Key to Nourishing Life," in *Readings in Classical Chinese Philosophy*, eds. Ivanhoe and Van Norden, 224–25; hereafter referred to as *Readings*.

[3] Here, *qi* is the underlying stuff out of which people are composed as physical entities. See 2A2.8–9 and the Introduction ("From Mengzi to Zhu Xi") for more on *qi*.

same as something that that person does accept."[4] This insight has led to considerable discussion over what extension is for Mengzi. Is it a form of argumentation? ("You have compassion in case A, therefore you ought to have compassion in case B.") Is it a way of addressing weakness of will? ("You say that you cannot do B, but you can do A, which is actually harder than B. Therefore you can do B after all.") Is it a technique for ethical cultivation? ("You feel compassion in case A but not in case B. Focus on the similarities between these two cases as a way of helping your emotions flow from one case to the other.") How is extension consistent with Mengzi's demand that we not force ourselves to do what we do not feel ready to do (2A2.16)?[5] (See also 7A15, 7A17, and 7B31.)

7.14   Zhu Xi comments, "Mengzi thinks that the reason that the king's heart of love for the people is light and short must be that he thinks these three things will make him happy. But these three things are actually not what make people's hearts happy—even less so than killing a frightened ox. Hence, he refers to them, desiring that the king will measure them."

7.15   Zhu Xi comments, "It is correct for the heart to not delight in these. It must be that he does these because desires tempt him."

7.16   "To climb a tree in search of a fish" (*yuán mù qiú yú* 緣木求魚) has become a proverbial expression in modern Chinese for using impractical means to reach a goal.

7.18   Zhu Xi comments, "If those near are happy, those far away will come. So one need not discuss large or small, strong or weak. If the king forcefully seeks what he desires, then he will not get it. If he can turn toward the root, then he will reach what he desires, though he does not seek it. This is the same as the meaning of the opening chapter" (1A1).

7.20   Zhu Xi comments, "Nobles have engaged in learning and inquiry, and they understand the Pattern of righteousness. Hence, even if they lack a constant livelihood, they have a constant heart. The people are unable to be like this."

7.21   Zhu Xi comments, "This explains the people's having constant hearts because they have constant livelihoods."

7.22   Zhu Xi comments, "This is what is meant by, if they lack a constant livelihood, they will lack a constant heart."

7.24   Zhu Xi comments, "This chapter explains that a ruler of people should reject the achievements of a Hegemon and put into effect the Kingly Way. The most important part of the Kingly Way is nothing other than extending 'a heart that is not unfeeling toward others' in order to put into effect 'a government that is not unfeeling toward others' (2A6.2). The king of Qi was not without this heart, but it was stolen by his selfish desire for profit and achievements. He was unable to fill it out to put into effect benevolent government. Even though Mengzi repeatedly and carefully explained it to him in this way, his understanding was still deeply obscured. In the end, he was unable to become enlightened. How sad!"

---

[4]   *Mozi* 44–45, "Names and Objects." Cf. Angus C. Graham, *Later Mohist Logic, Ethics, and Science* (Hong Kong: Chinese University Press, 1978), 487–89.

[5]   See Nivison, "Motivation and Moral Action in Mencius," in *The Ways of Confucianism*, 91–119, and the discussion in the Introduction, "Mengzi's Philosophy."

Book 1B

King Tang founded the Shang dynasty. "King Tai" is the posthumous title of Duke   3.1
Danfu, whose descendants Wen and Wu founded the Zhou dynasty. On the service
of Tang, see 3B5. On King Tai, see 1B5.5.

"Heaven" here has both normative and descriptive aspects. It should be the case   3.2
(normatively) that the powerful are generous enough to serve the weak. But it should
be the case (prudentially) that the weak are wise enough to serve the strong. As Zhu
Xi puts it, "When people naturally accord with the Pattern, he says they 'delight in
Heaven.' When people do not dare to violate the Pattern, he says they 'are in awe of
Heaven.'"

Zhu Xi comments, "'Small courage' is a product of only blood and *qi*. Great   3.5
courage is an expression of the Pattern of righteousness." (See also 2A2.3–8 for more
on courage in relation to *qi*.)

Zhao Qi said, "The Bright Tower on Mount Tai is the place where the Son of Heaven   5.1
during the Zhou would summon to court the various lords when making his eastern
inspection tour. In the time of the Han dynasty the old site still existed. Those who
want to destroy it probably think that, since the Son of Heaven no longer makes inspection tours of the various lords, one should not occupy it. The king asks whether
he should destroy it or leave it."

Zhu Xi explains, "'Nine-one' is the well field system. One square league was a field   5.3
of nine hundred acres. One would lay out a pattern in the shape of the character *jǐng*
井 ('well'), to divide it into nine sections. In each section was a field of one hundred
acres. The center one hundred acres was the public field, and the outer eight hundred acres were private fields. Eight clans would each receive a private field of one
hundred acres and cultivate in common the public field. This was dividing it into
'nine' and taxing 'one.'"

Zhu Xi comments, "Mengzi means that Duke Liu's people were satisfied with their   5.4
wealth because, although he was fond of wealth, he was able to extend his own heart
so that it reached to the people. In the present case, if the king is also able to be like
this, then what difficulty is there in his becoming the King of the world?"

Duke Danfu (posthumously known as King Tai) was a descendant of Duke Liu. Zhu   5.5
Xi comments, "There were none who were 'bitter or unmarried' because King Tai was
fond of sex but was able to extend his own heart so that it reached to the people."

Zhu Xi comments, "In my humble opinion, from the opening chapter of the book
down to this one, the general idea is the same. Whether it is the delights of making
music (1B1), parks (1B2), touring (1B4), or the heart that is fond of courage (1B3),
wealth, or sex (1B5), these are all part of the Heavenly Pattern that human feelings
cannot lack. Nonetheless, the Heavenly Pattern and human desires 'proceed from the
same source yet are different feelings.' To accord with the Pattern and be impartial to
the world is the manner in which sages fully use their natures. To give free reign to
one's desires and be selfishly interested in oneself alone is the way in which the masses
extinguish the Heavenly in themselves. One may not make merely a hair's-breadth
error in distinguishing the two: their rightness and wrongness, their gains and losses,
are quite far from each other. Thus, when Mengzi questions the rulers of his time, he

examines things, making very fine distinctions, so as to restrain their human desires and preserve their Heavenly Pattern. His method seems abstract, but it is actually specific; the actions seem easy, but are actually demanding. Learners can, by the standard within themselves, recognize that his doctrines oppose unorthodox teachings and his pandering era, and they can understand the starting point of 'restraining yourself and returning to the rites'" (*Analects* 12.1).

6.3 Zhu Xi comments, "The king is reluctant to hold himself responsible, even though he is made to feel ashamed by his subordinate's line of questioning. From this we can recognize that he is unworthy to work with."

The king's refusal to answer Mengzi's final question shows that he lacks the willingness to reform that is characteristic of the worthy (cf. 2A8). He is thus one of "those who throw themselves away" (4A10).

8.3 Zhu Xi comments, "If all within the Four Seas turn toward someone, then he becomes the Son of Heaven. If the world turns against him, then he becomes 'a mere *fellow*.'" Wang Mian said, "This teaching is acceptable only if those in subordinate positions have the benevolence of Tang and Wu, and those in superior positions have the cruelty of Jie and Tyrant Zhou. Otherwise, you will simply be committing the crime of regicide."

This passage is often seen as an illustration of "correcting names," as mentioned in *Analects* 13.3 and Xunzi's essay by that title.[1]

10.3 King Wen tolerated the actions of vicious Tyrant Zhou, but his successor, King Wu, overthrew Tyrant Zhou. Zhang Zai explained why: "There is less than a hair's-breadth difference between these two situations. If the Mandate of Heaven has not been broken, then one is the minister of one's ruler. But on the day that the Mandate is broken, then he is 'a mere *fellow*' (1B8). How can one know whether the Mandate has been broken or not? Simply by people's feelings. When eight hundred of the various lords unexpectedly assembled to support King Wu, how could King Wu stop it?"

10.4 As is often the case, Mengzi takes the happiness of the people to be the ultimate indicator of Heaven's will (cf. 5A5–6). As Zhao Qi explained, "The Way for invading is that one should follow the people's hearts. If the people's hearts are happy, then one has followed the intention of Heaven."

11.4 Fan Zuyu said, "When Mengzi served the rulers of Qi and Liang, if he discoursed on the Way and Virtue, then he would always invoke Yao and Shun. If he discoursed on attacks and invasions, then he would always invoke Tang and Wu. In general, in ruling the people, if you do not model yourself on Yao and Shun, then you will become cruel. In carrying out punitive actions, if you do not model yourself on Tang and Wu, then you will become chaotic. How can one say, 'My ruler is incapable' (of such Virtue) and set aside what one has learned to follow him?"

The saga of Mengzi's efforts to reform King Xuan of Qi continues in 2B2, and the conclusion of the invasion of Yan is recounted in 2B9.

16.3 Zhu Xi comments, "When a person acts, that person causes it, and when a person stops, that person causes it. Nonetheless, that by means of which a person acts, and

---

[1] See *Xunzi* 22, in *Readings*, 292–98.

that by means of which a person stops, definitely involves the Heavenly Mandate. It is not something that this particular person is capable of causing, nor is it something that this particular person is capable of stopping. So how could Mengzi's not meeting the duke be something Zang Cang is capable of causing? This chapter means that the comings and goings, successes and failures of sages and worthies are made by the Heavenly Mandate, not something that human power can attain."

See also 2B13 on trusting in Heaven, and 7A1–3 on fate. For more on the controversy surrounding Mengzi's funeral for his mother, see 2B7.

Book 2A

Mengzi gives a more positive impression of Yanzi in 1B4 (not included in this translation). Perhaps the primary target of Mengzi's criticisms here in 2A1 is Guan Zhong, whom Gongsun Chou carelessly lumps together with Yanzi.   *1.2–3*

Zilu was not one of Kongzi's most talented disciples, and Guan Zhong succeeded in making his ruler Hegemon (see 2A3). So why would a Confucian rather be compared to the former? Yang Shi explained, "Compare it to being a chariot driver in a ritual hunt. Zilu 'drove . . . in the prescribed manner' but we caught nothing; Guan Zhong's achievement was simply to get birds by having 'violated the rules' (3B1.4)."

Gongsun Chou is praising Mengzi's courage by comparing it to that of Meng Ben.   *2.2*
But, as Mengzi goes on to explain, the courage of Meng Ben or Gaozi is a shallow kind that is easily obtained.

Cheng Yi explained, "If the heart is dominated by something, then it can be unperturbed." In each of the following cases, a person's heart is dominated by something different.   *2.3*

Zhu Xi explains, "Bogong You is an assassin. The necessity of winning is what dominates him, so he has an unperturbed heart."   *2.4*

Zhu Xi explains, "Meng Shishe is an aggressive soldier. Lacking fear is what dominates him, so he has an unperturbed heart."   *2.5*

Notice that the account of Bogong You is largely a third-person description of his actions, while with Meng Shishe we have a first-person account of how he feels and thinks.

Zhu Xi comments, "Bogong You concentrated on his enemy. Meng Shishe focused   *2.6*
on maintaining himself. Zixia had firm faith in Kongzi. Zengzi '(sought) for it in himself' (2A7, 4A4; *Analects* 15.21). Hence, although Bogong You and Meng Shishe are not on a level with Zengzi and Zixia, nonetheless, in terms of the manifestation of their *qi*, each is similar to one of them in a certain respect. Between the former two, Mengzi does not know whose courage is preferable. But in terms of what they preserve, Meng Shishe gets what is more crucial than what Bogong You gets." (On *qi*, see the commentary on 2A2.8.)

Zengzi's comment is consistent with Kongzi's statement that "to see what is right,   *2.7*
but to fail to do it, is to be lacking in courage" (*Analects* 2.24).

As A. C. Graham explains, in Mengzi's era, *qi* "is like such words in other cultures   *2.8*
as Greek *pneuma* 'wind, air, breath.' It is the energetic fluid which vitalises the body,

in particular as the breath, and which circulates outside us as the air." Later, this concept is "adapted to cosmology as the universal fluid . . . out of which all things con-
dense and into which they dissolve."[1] (This late sense is how thinkers such as Zhu Xi
understood it.) *Qi* is thus the physical medium through which one's emotions and personal character are manifested. So to "preserve one's *qi*" is to control one's emotions.
Meng Shishe was similar to Zengzi in that both focused on something inside themselves, as opposed to Bogong You and Zixia, who focused on something external to
themselves. However, as Zhu Xi explains, "what Meng Shishe preserved was just the
qi of one's self. This is not as good as Zengzi's examining himself and following the
Pattern (of the Way). He preserved what is especially important. Mengzi's unperturbed
heart has its source in this."[2]

2.9a   Zhu Xi explains this difficult passage as follows: "Gaozi said that if there is something that one does not understand in doctrines, then one should set the doctrine aside
and need not examine and search for the Pattern in one's heart. If one is not at peace
in one's heart, then one should regulate one's heart with force and need not further
seek for help from the *qi*. This is the way in which he firmly maintained his heart and
quickly became unperturbed. Having recited Gaozi's doctrines, Mengzi passes judgment on them: When Gaozi says that what you do not get from your heart you should
not seek for in the *qi*, this is being concerned about the root and relaxed about the
branches—that is acceptable. When he says that what you do not get from doctrines
you should not seek from the heart, then he is already lost due to external things, and
so has left behind what is internal. This is necessarily unacceptable."

David S. Nivison offered an alternative interpretation, based on a parallel between
this passage and Zhuangzi's fictional dialogue between "Kongzi" and "Yan Hui": Gaozi
recommends that we completely commit ourselves to following correct ethical doctrines, forcing our heart and our *qi* to follow what they dictate. In contrast, Mengzi
recommends that we not only follow ethical doctrines but seek further to find the basis for these doctrines in the reactions of our heart (2A6, 6A10), which will then guide
our *qi*. Finally, Zhuangzi recommends that we ultimately eschew doctrines, empty
our hearts, and follow the promptings of the *qi*, which unites us with other things.[3]

2.10   Zhu Xi comments, "Mengzi explains that if the direction of the will is unified, the
qi will definitely follow it. Nonetheless, if that which the *qi* rests in is unified, then it
will move the will. For example, if someone is running and stumbling, the *qi* is focused on this and it will move the will. This is why one must both maintain one's will
but also not injure the *qi*."

2.11   Zhu Xi suggests that Gongsun Chou is asking specifically about how Mengzi's
unperturbed heart is better than Gaozi's unperturbed heart. He then comments, "By
'understanding doctrines' one has the wherewithal to understand the Way and right-

---

[1]   Graham, *Disputers of the Tao*, 101.

[2]   For more on *qi*, see the Introduction. For a discussion of 2A2.1–8, see Van Norden, "Mencius on Courage," in *The Philosophy of Religion*, ed. Peter A. French et al., *Midwest Studies in
Philosophy*, vol. 21 (Notre Dame, IN: University of Notre Dame Press, 1997), 237–56. For more
on courage, see 1B3.

[3]   See David S. Nivison, "Philosophical Voluntarism in Fourth Century China," in *The Ways
of Confucianism*, 121–32, and *Zhuangzi* 4, "The Human Realm," in *Readings*, 228.

eousness and to not be in doubt about any situation in the world. By 'cultivating the *qi*' one has the wherewithal to harmonize with the Way and righteousness and to not be in fear about any situation in the world. This is the manner in which he can assume a great responsibility yet have an unperturbed heart. Gaozi's learning is the exact opposite of this. His unperturbed heart is nothing more than being ignorantly unaware and stubbornly unmindful." (See 2A2.17 for more on "understanding doctrines.")

Zhu Xi uses language suggestive of mystical insight to explain the "floodlike *qi*": *2.12–15* "Mengzi's heart has attained it by itself, and it has no form or sound to give evidence for it. It has aspects that are not easy to put into words. Hence, Cheng Yi said, 'If one considers this one statement, we can tell that Mengzi genuinely has this *qi*.'"

Cheng Yi also remarked, "Heaven and humans are one. There is no division. The floodlike *qi* is just my *qi*. If it is nurtured and not harmed, then 'it will fill up the space between Heaven and Earth' (2.13). But as soon as there is the obscuration of the tiniest selfish thought, one is discontented and 'starved.'"

Regarding the relationship between righteousness and the *qi* (2.14–15), Zhu Xi explains, "If people can nurture this *qi* to completion, then their *qi* will harmonize with the Way and righteousness and assist them, so that, in one's actions, one will have a courage and resoluteness that lacks any doubts or fears. Without this *qi*, then even if one's actions do not necessarily diverge from the Way and righteousness, nonetheless one's body will not be filled with *qi*, so that one cannot avoid doubts and fears, and one will be unable to be effective. . . . The beginning of nurturing it is to have every action accord with righteousness. If one examines oneself and is constantly upright, one will be ashamed of nothing, and this *qi* will naturally be produced from within. One cannot do only a single action that accidentally accords with righteousness and then get it by a 'seizure' of what is external. 'If some of one's actions leave one's heart unsatisfied, it will starve' means that as soon as what one does is not in accord with righteousness and one examines oneself and is not upright, then there will be an inadequacy in one's heart, and one's body will not be filled. This being the case, how could righteousness be external? Gaozi did not understand the Pattern of this, so he said, 'Benevolence is internal,' 'righteousness is external' (6A4–5), and because he did not regard becoming righteous as a task, he was necessarily unable to accumulate righteousness in order to produce the floodlike *qi*. The earlier verse, 'What you do not get from doctrines, do not seek for in your heart' (2A2.9a), is precisely the meaning of treating righteousness as external."

We might say that the farmer from Song is someone who "acts out benevolence and *2.16a–b* righteousness," rather than "acted out of benevolence and righteousness" (4B19.2). Zhu Xi comments, "Those who nurture their *qi* must take accumulating righteousness as their task but not anticipate its effectiveness. If they happen to fail to be filled (with floodlike *qi*), they should simply not forget what they are in service to, and may not do anything to 'help' it grow. This is the process for accumulating righteousness and nurturing the *qi*."

Zhu Xi summarizes the two kinds of errors in ethical cultivation: "Those who abandon the sprouts and do not weed forget what they are working for. Those who pull on them and 'help' them to grow assume they have it, and when they do not get it, they act recklessly. If one does not weed, then one will only fail to nurture it, but if one pulls on it, then one will, on the contrary, harm it. If one avoids these two things, then one's *qi* will be nurtured and will not be injured. If like Gaozi one is unable to accumulate righteousness but desires to force one's heart to be regulated, then one will be unable to avoid the twin faults of assuming and assisting. Not only will he not be good at cultivating the 'floodlike,' but he will even harm it."

2.17   Zhu Xi comments, "Gaozi did not understand doctrines, yet he was unwilling to seek for it in his heart. He reached the point of the theory that 'righteousness is external,' and then he naturally could not evade those four disabilities. How could he understand the doctrines of the world and have no doubts about them?!"

2.18   Cheng Hao takes Kongzi's comment to be a strategic lie: "Kongzi said of himself that he was incapable in regard to rhetoric simply because he desired to make learners focus on the root."

2.24   Mengzi (and Zhu Xi) place great emphasis on using "discretion" (4A17) to flexibly respond to complex circumstances. However, this verse makes clear that there are some absolute prohibitions that one may not violate.

2.26   Cheng Yi said, "Yao and Shun ruled the world, but the Master extended their Way, holding it up to instruct ten thousand generations. How could later generations have based themselves on the Way of Yao and Shun without Kongzi?"

2.28   Cheng Yi and Cheng Hao said, "In this chapter, Mengzi develops what has not been expressed before by previous sages. Learners should immerse their hearts and delve into it."

5.6   This passage illustrates that Mengzi was not a purely theoretical philosopher. He was a "public intellectual," concerned with the concrete details of government reform and public policy. Zhu Xi comments, "This chapter means that if one is capable of putting into effect Kingly government, then bandits and barbarians will become like one's father and sons. If one does not put into effect Kingly government, then even children will be one's enemies."

6.1   There are various causal accounts of why humans have this "heart." For Mengzi, this heart is implanted in us by Heaven, a sort of semipersonal higher power (7A1). For Zhu Xi, benevolence is not only a personal virtue but a basic cosmological principle underlying even the natural world: "The heart of Heaven and Earth is giving birth to things. These things each get this as their heart. This is why humans all have hearts that are not unfeeling toward others."

6.2   This verse illustrates how Mengzi's philosophical psychology relates to his political philosophy.

6.3   Note that Mengzi does not say that every human would necessarily *act* to save the child. All he claims is that any human would have at least a momentary feeling (literally, "heart") of genuine compassion, and that the reaction would occur "suddenly" (which shows that it is not the result of calculations of self-interest). This passage is, in part, a response to the "ethical egoist" Yang Zhu, who seems to have claimed that only self-interested motivations are part of human nature. (See 3B9.9 and the Introduction, "Mengzi's Philosophy," for more on this philosopher.)[4]

---

[4]   For a dialogue that may represent something like Yang Zhu's position, see "Robber Zhi," in *Readings*, 369–75. See also Van Norden, *Virtue Ethics and Consequentialism in Early Chinese Philosophy*, 200–11.

On these feelings (literally, "hearts") see also 6A6. With the story of Ox Mountain   6.4–5
(6A8), Mengzi explains how someone could lose these hearts and become "not human."
Zhu Xi believes that righteousness, propriety, and wisdom are manifestations of
benevolence, and that this is why Mengzi goes on to discuss each of them here, after
giving an illustration of only benevolence. Zhu Xi thus interprets Mengzi as holding
the doctrine of "the unity of the virtues" (see commentary on 2A7.2). He also suggests,
"Compassion, disdain, deference, and approval and disapproval are emotions. Benevolence, righteousness, propriety, and wisdom are human nature. The heart is what
links the nature and emotions." (See "Zhu Xi's Reinterpretation," in the Introduction,
for more on how he understands this verse.)

A "normal," healthy human has four limbs. Similarly, a normal human has the four   6.6–7
"sprouts." But, as the comparison to limbs suggests, it is possible to lose the sprouts
(6A8).

Mengzi thinks the capacity for virtue is innate in humans, but it must be cultivated
("filled out") in order for us to become fully virtuous. He discusses this process of filling out (which he also calls "extending") in many passages, including 1A7.12, 7A15,
7A17, and 7B31.

The arrow-maker and the coffin-maker are born with the same heart of benevolence   7.1
as the armor-maker and the shaman-healer. But their choices of career and way of life
determine whether they want humans to live or die.

Zhu Xi explains this paragraph in terms of the unity of the virtues: "Benevolence   7.2–3
is the heart of Heaven and Earth in giving birth to things. One gets it first of all, and
it links all four virtues together. . . . Because one is not benevolent, one is not wise.
Because one is not wise, one does not understand wherein propriety and righteousness lie."

Zhu Xi comments, "He does not discuss wisdom, propriety, and righteousness, be-   7.4–5
cause benevolence encompasses the entire substance. If one can become benevolent,
then the other three are in its midst." And as Kongzi asked, "Does becoming benevolent come from oneself, or does it come from others?!" (*Analects* 12.1)

Zhu Xi explains how the people mentioned form a hierarchy. "Zilu was pleased   8.1–5
that he heard about his faults so he could reform them. Such was his courage in self-
cultivation." Zhou Dunyi commented, "Nowadays, when people have a fault, they are
not pleased to be corrected by others. This is like concealing an illness and shunning
medicine." Zhu Xi continues, "In contrast, King Yu did not wait to have a fault, but
was capable of humbling himself to accept what was good in the world." Finally, Shun
was greater than Zilu or King Yu, because he did not await being *told* criticisms or
hearing good advice. Zhu Xi comments, "If I copy what is good in someone else and
do it myself, then it encourages him to do good too. This is my helping him to do
good. What greater good is there for the gentleman than to be capable of encourag-
ing all the people of the world to do good?"

Bo Yi's disdain to do what is wrong is a manifestation of the heart of righteousness   9.1
(2A6, 6A6). Consequently, he is highly commendable. However, he has extended his
heart too far. (On "extension," see 1A7.12. For more on Bo Yi, see 5B1.)

Zhu Xi explains that "'without losing himself' is without losing his uprightness."   9.2
Liuxia Hui's willingness to adapt to circumstances shows the "discretion" that is so

central to Confucianism (4A17). However, he ends up compromising too much. (For more on Liuxia Hui, see 5B1.)

9.3   Zhu Xi comments, "The actions of Bo Yi and Liuxia Hui definitely both reached the highest level. Nonetheless, since they have some biases, they definitely have an obscured view (of the Way). Hence, they cannot be followed as models."

Book 2B

2.2   Zhu Xi compares this to *Analects* 17.20, where Kongzi excused himself from meeting someone on the grounds of illness but then made sure the messenger heard him playing his zither and singing along. Cheng Hao said of the latter passage, "This is what Mengzi means by 'scorning to instruct someone' (6B16). By means of this he instructs him deeply."

2.3   Zhu Xi comments, "Zhongzi replied with discreet expressions, and then sent people to seek for Mengzi and instruct him to not return but to get to the court, in order to make what he had already said true."

2.4   Zhu Xi comments, "What Jingzi is discussing is petty reverence. What Mengzi is discussing is great reverence."

2.6   Zhu Xi comments, "In the present case, the king of Qi only has rank. How could one be disrespectful of (Mengzi's) age and Virtue on account of this?"

2.7   This is perhaps Mengzi's most direct statement of why he is so insistent that rulers treat him with ritual courtesy if they wish to consult with him. As Cheng Yi and Cheng Hao explained, "The ancients would come to rulers only after the rulers had expressed reverence through the utmost ritual. This was not because they desired to be highly respected themselves, but only for the reason Mengzi states."

2.8   Zhu Xi comments, "First, they studied under them and treated them as teachers. Afterward, they regarded them as ministers and gave them responsibilities."

2.9   Zhu Xi comments, "'Those whom they instruct' means those who listen to them, whom they can make servants. 'Those from whom they receive instruction' means those whom they follow and learn from."

2.10   On Mengzi's unwillingness to be like Guan Zhong, see 2A1.1–6. On Yi Yin, see 5A7. Zhu Xi comments, "This chapter illustrates that a guest-teacher does not regard scurrying along to comply as respectful, but instead regards offering challenging responsibilities and displaying what is good as reverent." ("Respect" and "reverence" are the two aspects of the "heart of propriety" that Mengzi discusses in 6A6.)

3.4–5   Zhu Xi explains, "At that time, there were those who desired to harm Mengzi, so he set up guards (in Xue) as a precaution." Yin Tun said the lesson of this chapter is that "a gentleman's declining, accepting, taking, and giving simply correspond to the Pattern." The considerations that Mengzi describes have analogues in contemporary considerations about whether to accept gifts, donations, and grants from individuals or foundations with questionable motives. (See also 6B14 on Mengzi's interlocutor here, Chen Zhen.)

4.2   As Zhu Xi explains, Kong Juxin is blaming the king for this, rather than accepting personal responsibility.

Chen Yang said, "With one saying from Mengzi, the ruler and minister of Qi both   *4.4*
understood their faults. This is inherently sufficient to inspire a state. Nonetheless, Qi
in the end did not succeed in becoming a good state. Was the reason for this not that
they 'were pleased (with his teachings) but did not persist, they followed them but did
not reform'?" (*Analects* 9.24)

King Zikuai of Yan resigned his throne to his minister Zizhi (in 315 B.C.E.). The king   *8.1*
probably intended this as a purely symbolic demonstration of his humility and had
arranged to resume the throne immediately, but his devious Prime Minister used it as
an opportunity to seize power, leading to a chaotic political situation. Shen Tong was
a minister in Qi who asked about this situation "on his own behalf," meaning that this
was not an official inquiry from the king about what *he* should do. Zhu Xi comments,
"The various lords, the land, and the people were all received from the Son of Heaven
and passed down from former rulers. If someone gives it on his own behalf, then the
giver and the receiver are both guilty" (cf. 5A5).

On "the agent of Heaven," see 2A5.6. Zhu Xi comments, "This last part means that   *8.2*
Qi does not have the Way; it is no different from Yan. So it is like Yan invading Yan."

Yang Shi said, "It certainly was permissible to invade Yan. Hence, Mengzi said, 'It
is.' If the king of Qi were able to punish its ruler and console its people, why should
he not do it? But he killed their fathers and elder brothers, seized their sons and
younger brothers, and then the Yan people rebelled against him. To then turn and
blame Mengzi for what he said is quite mistaken."

Benevolence and wisdom are paired, and their importance in governing is similarly   *9.2*
explained in *Analects* 12.22.

Mengzi here acknowledges that even sages can make mistakes but suggests that their   *9.3*
mistakes arise out of their virtues. (Compare 5A2–3 on King Shun's treatment of his evil
brother Xiang.) Zhu Xi comments, "The Duke of Zhou and Guan Shu were younger
and elder brother. That being so, there was an element of inevitability in the Duke of
Zhou's mistake in assigning Guan Shu and not knowing that he was going to revolt."

On the eclipse metaphor, compare *Analects* 19.21. Zhu Xi comments, "Mengzi is   *9.4*
blaming Chen Jia for being unable to encourage his ruler to move toward the good
and correct his faults. Instead, Chen Jia instructs him to stick to his wrongs and gloss
over his faults."

Lin Zhiji said, "That the king of Qi was ashamed before Mengzi is 'the feeling of
disdain' (2A6.4, 6A6). To a certain extent, one cannot stop it. If it were the case that
among his ministers there were some who were able to follow this heart and make him
accord with it, then his righteousness would be inexhaustible. But this fellow Chen
Jia stooped to rationalizing for him and injured his heart that would move toward the
good and correct his faults. Instead, he increased his tendency to gloss over his mistakes
and reject criticism. Hence, Mengzi held him deeply responsible."

Zhu Xi comments, "Mengzi had been in Qi a long time, and the Way had not been   *10.1*
put into effect. Hence, he was leaving."

As Zhu Xi explains, "Mengzi is saying, 'Suppose I did desire wealth. I was previ-   *10.5*
ously a High Minister, and I declined a salary of one hundred thousand bushels by re-
signing. If I were to take this stipend of ten thousand now, even if I desired wealth, I
obviously would not be doing it for *that* reason.'"

10.6   Zhu Xi comments, "Mengzi cites this in order to make clear that, when the Way has not been put into practice, for him to turn and accept the stipend would be no different from this." (We do not know anything else about Ji Sun and Zishu Yi.)

10.7   Cheng Yi said, "The manner in which the king of Qi *treated* Mengzi was appropriate. And Mengzi was willing to be a respected model for the people of the state. However, the king of Qi did not genuinely desire to respect Mengzi. He just desired to tempt him with profit. Hence, Mengzi refused him and would not accept it."

13.3–4 Zhu Xi explains, "From Yao and Shun to Tang, and from Tang to Wen and Wu, were both five hundred odd years, after which a sage appeared. . . . 'Our era' means a day when chaos is at its most extreme and one who longs to bring order can be effective. Yet we get no one with the capacity."

13.5   Zhu Xi comments, "He means, 'I did not meet with success at this time in Qi because Heaven does not yet desire to pacify the world. Although the intention of Heaven cannot be known, I am its instrument. Why should I be unhappy?' Thus, although Mengzi seemed to be unhappy, he was actually never unhappy. We see here that sages and worthies have a will that is concerned about their time, but also a genuine delight in Heaven, and that these are not contradictory."[1]

Book 3A

1.2–3   See 6A1 ff. and the Introduction ("Mengzi's Philosophy") on the concept of the "nature" of a thing. Zhu Xi interprets Mengzi's doctrine in the light of his distinctive metaphysical view: "'Nature' is the Pattern with which humans are endowed by Heaven at birth. It is purely good without any evil. In the beginning, people have not the slightest difference from Yao or Shun. However, the mass of people sink into selfish desires and lose it. Yao and Shun did not have any obscuration by selfish desires, so they were able to fill out their natures."

Zhu Xi also comments, "People of that time did not understand the original goodness of the nature, and regarded being a sage or worthy as something one could not aspire to. Hence, the Heir Apparent was incapable of being without doubt about Mengzi's teachings, so he came again and sought to meet him. Perhaps he thought there might be some other account, one that was less exalted and less demanding."

Notice that Mengzi says human nature is "good," *simpliciter*, whereas Zhu Xi substitutes "original goodness." See the Introduction, "Zhu Xi's Reinterpretation," for the metaphysical and textual assumptions underlying Zhu Xi's comments on this and the previous verse.

1.4–5   Zhu Xi comments, "Mengzi had already informed the Heir Apparent that the Way does not have two destinations. He then cites these three sayings to illuminate this,

---

[1]   On the five-hundred-year cycle of sage Kings, see David W. Pankenier, "The Cosmo-Political Background of Heaven's Mandate," *Early China* 20 (1995): 121–76, and Douglas J. Keenan, "Astro-Historiographic Chronologies of Early China Are Unfounded," *East Asian History* 23 (2002): 61–68. For a general discussion of this passage, see Philip J. Ivanhoe, "A Question of Faith: A New Interpretation of *Mencius* 2B.13," *Early China* 13 (1988): 153–65.

desiring the Heir Apparent to have firm faith and apply effort, so as to take sages and worthies as his teachers and not to turn and seek other accounts." (Gongming Yi was a disciple of Kongzi's disciple who is also cited in 3B3, 3B9.9, and 4B24.)

Zhu Xi endorses the view of the Cheng brothers that one of Mengzi's greatest contributions was to state explicitly that human nature is good. He also suggests that, although this passage and 6A6 are the only ones stating outright that human nature is good, it is implicit throughout the text. Although many later interpreters have followed Zhu Xi in thinking that the goodness of human nature was central to the thought of Kongzi as well, a good case can be made that Kongzi had no explicit view on human nature, and that his implicit view was actually closer to that of Xunzi, who stated that "human nature is bad." (See 3A2–3 for more on Duke Wen of Teng.)

Zhu Xi suggests that the Heir's advisers are only familiar with later, decadent practices of mourning, rather than the authentic practices that Mengzi describes.   2.3

Zhang Zai made the refreshingly radical comment, "If poverty and wealth are un-   3.20
equal, and there is no method to instruction or cultivation, though one desires to discuss ruling, it will be nothing more than acting recklessly. Those who regard strong measures as problematic always take seizing the fields of the wealthy as an excuse for not acting. However, putting this method into effect pleases many. If one merely has a technique for doing so, within a few years, without punishing a single person, one can recover from it. What is problematic is only that superiors do not put it into effect."

See Angus C. Graham, "The Nung-chia 'School of the Tillers' and the Origins of   4.1
Peasant Utopianism in China," *Studies in Chinese Philosophy and Philosophical Literature* (Albany: State University of New York Press, 1990), 67–110.

Zhu Xi comments, "This means that the ruler should cook his meals for himself,   4.3
along with ruling the people. With this teaching, Xu Xing probably desires to obscure and destroy Mengzi's rules about distinguishing between gentlemen and the uncultivated."

Zhu Xi explains, "To 'feed others' is to pay out taxes to superiors. If the gentlemen   4.6
did not have the petty people, they would starve. If the petty people did not have the gentlemen, then there would be chaos. For them to exchange these two things is just like farmers exchanging grain for tools with the potters and blacksmiths. This is just the means by which they help each other, and not the means by which they harm each other. Why should those who rule the world have to plow as well?"

Zhu Xi comments, "To distinguish people according to their talents is only minor   4.10
kindness. To instruct people about goodness, although it is a part of loving the people, nonetheless attains what is limited and difficult to sustain for a long time. But things like Yao employing Shun and Shun employing Yu and Gao Yao—these are what is called employing people for the sake of the world. In this case, the kindness is broad and the instruction is limitless. This is the manner in which they were benevolent."

Chen Liang came from Chu, which was considered to be only partially "civilized,"   4.12
and became a Confucian (which Mengzi identifies with genuine Chinese culture). Chen Xiang had the advantage of studying under Chen Liang but then changed to "barbarian" practices. Zhu Xi concludes, "Chen Liang used Chinese culture to transform the uncivilized, while Chen Xiang was transformed by the uncivilized."

4.17   As Zhu Xi explains, "Xu Xing wants to make it so that the goods in the marketplace
—regardless of whether they are fine or crude, beautiful or ugly—will be priced only
on the basis of their length, weight, or quantity."

4.18   Mengzi is making an insightful point about economics. (How sad the Chinese
Marxists did not listen to him!) But notice that it is part of a general observation about
differences in quality among things of the same kind. Just as a big shoe is worth more
than a small shoe, so is a high-quality shoe worth more than a shoddy shoe, and so is
a sage more worthy than an uncultivated person. (The essay "On Equalizing Things"
by the Daoist Zhuangzi may be a response to Mengzi's claims about the inherent in-
equality of things.)[1]

5.2   According to the received Chinese text, the quotation from Mengzi in 3A5.2 begins,
"I *can* see him today." However, this does not make sense because Mengzi never sees
Yi Zhi. The simplest explanation is that a "not" has dropped out of the text. But for an
alternative explanation see my "Textual Notes to the *Mengzi*." (Go to www.hackett
publishing.com and look under "Title Information" for "Title Support Pages.")

5.3a–c   Yi Zhi cites a passage from the *Documents* that he claims demonstrates that the ancient sage Kings practiced impartial caring. Mengzi responds that the point of the passage is that sages treat the people like infants only in the respect that the people need
care and guidance in order to avoid hurting themselves or engaging in wrongdoing.
(The paternalism of Confucian political theory is very clear here.)

        David S. Nivison offers a clear explanation of Mengzi's comment about "one
source" versus "two sources." People naturally love their own family members. This
is the "one source" of love that gradually extends outward to encompass friends,
strangers, and even nonhuman animals. Mengzi holds that, because our compassion
for others grows out of this source, it will naturally have gradations, being stronger for
relatives than for strangers. Yi Zhi acknowledges that this is the psychological source
of human compassion, and that he acted out of it in giving his parents a lavish funeral.
However, Yi Zhi insists that there is also a second source of benevolence, which is the
Mohist doctrine of "impartial caring." We should take our innate feelings of love for
our family members (the first source) and extend that love to everyone equally, thereby
achieving the impartial caring dictated by Mohist teachings (the second source). Yi
Zhi is effectively saying, Yes, you can only learn to love within a family, but you are
obligated to extend that love to everyone equally.[2]

5.4   It is not immediately obvious how this is a rejoinder to the Mohists, since they agree
that the deceased should be buried. And even Yi Zhi himself seems to say that lavish
burials are acceptable as expressions of the "one source," as long as this love is extended to everyone impartially. However, Mengzi's point may be that if we acknowledge that it is right to follow one's natural instinct to bury one's deceased parents, we
cannot consistently deny that it is also right to follow one's instinct to love one's family members more than strangers.

---

[1] See Zhuangzi 2, in *Readings*, 213–24.

[2] For this interpretation, see David S. Nivison, "Two Roots or One?" in *The Ways of Confucianism*, 133–48.

Book 3B

Zhu Xi comments, "As soon as one has a heart that calculates profit, then even if it is *1.3* a matter of profiting by bending a lot to reach a little, will one not do it?"

In this passage, Mengzi offers three justifications for his insistence on being treated *1.5* with respect by rulers. First, it is intrinsically wrong to allow oneself to be treated in a demeaning manner. (This is what Western philosophers would call a "deontological" constraint.) Second, compromising righteousness in the name of profit is intrinsically corrupting of one's character (cf. *Analects* 4.16). (Western philosophers would classify this as a "virtue ethics" consideration.) Third, a minister who is not treated with respect will not have the standing to influence his ruler for good anyway. (This is, paradoxically, a "consequentialist" argument against thinking in consequentialist terms, similar to those Mengzi gives in 1A1 and 6B4.)[1] This chapter should be read in conjunction with 5B7.

Zhu Xi comments, "This means that the two men mentioned earlier were flatterers *2.2–3* who covertly assumed power. This is the submissive Way of concubines and wives. It is not the action of a man."

The sexist assumptions of this passage are evident and should not be ignored: submissiveness is assumed to be fitting for a woman but inappropriate for a man. But while acknowledging the sexism of Mengzi's rhetoric, we should not lose sight of the ethical point that he aims to make: genuinely great people do not stoop to gaining power by submissive flattery. Rather, they maintain their integrity even if it costs them office and political influence.

Gongming Yi was a disciple of Kongzi's disciple who is also cited in 3A1, 3B9, and *3.1* 4B24.

Zhu Xi comments, "It is not that parents do not wish for their children to get mar- *3.5* ried, but they disdain their not doing it in accordance with the Way. Likewise, a gentleman will not sully himself with improper relationships, but he also will not forget about righteousness through chasing after profit." (Cf. 7B31.)

Zhu Xi comments, "Desiring to become Hegemon of the world, the king of Song tried *5.1* to destroy Teng, invade Xue, and defeat the soldiers of Qi, Chu, and Wei. I suspect that this passage is from this period."

Zhu Xi suggests that the phrase "'There were some who did not submit' refers to *5.5* those who assisted Tyrant Zhou in wrongdoing and therefore did not submit to the Zhou" (cf. 3B9.6).

Song was later destroyed by Qi and its king was killed. Recent history has demon- *5.7* strated the wisdom of Mengzi's general doctrine: the use of military force in other states will be effective only if the people of those states uniformly regard the army as liberators rather than invaders.

---

[1] On the distinctions between deontology, virtue ethics, and consequentialism, see Van Norden, *Virtue Ethics and Consequentialism in Early Chinese Philosophy*, 29–37.

6.2   Zhu Xi comments, "This means that when petty people are numerous, a gentleman lacks the wherewithal, by himself, to succeed in the task of correcting a ruler." (Cf. 6A9.)

8.3   Here, Mengzi tells us that we must simply start doing (or not doing) certain things right away. But in 2A2.16 he warns us not to force ourselves to do what we are not yet ready to do.
        On taxing at one-tenth, see 3A3.15.

9.9   Yang Zhu and Mozi represent two extreme positions that Mengzi rejects. Yang Zhu held that benevolence and righteousness are unnatural, the products of artificial social conditioning. A human who follows his nature will act only in his own self-interest. Thus, in modern terms, Yang Zhu may be classified as an "ethical egoist." Mozi was at the opposite extreme, advocating impartial concern for everyone. He thus rejected "differentiated love," as well as the ritual practices that Confucians saw as cultivating virtue. (For more on Yang Zhu, see 2A6; on Mozi, see 3A5; on both, see 7A26, 7B26, and the Introduction, "Mengzi's Philosophy." Gongming Yi was a disciple of Kongzi's disciple, who is also cited in 3A1, 3B3, and 4B24. His saying is explained in 1A4.4.)

9.10   Cheng Yi suggests that Yang Zhu's doctrine primarily calls into question righteousness, while Mozi's Way raises doubts about benevolence. (I would have said that it was the other way around.) Cheng Yi adds that the Buddhist teachings of his own era are not as mistaken as those of Yang Zhu and Mozi, but paradoxically this makes them even more dangerous, since they may mislead those close to understanding "the Pattern."

9.14   Zhu Xi comments, "If one merely has the ability to oppose the teachings of Yang Zhu and Mozi, then one is headed in the correct direction. Although one may not necessarily understand the Way yet, one is still a disciple of the sages."

10.3   Zhu Xi explains, "An earthworm is self-sufficient and does not seek anything from people. But Zhongzi cannot evade living in a house and eating grain. But as for where those came from, perhaps it was something that was not righteous. In this case, he is incapable of being as pure as an earthworm." (On Bo Yi, see 5B1. On the notorious Robber Zhi, see 7A25.)

10.6   Zhongzi prides himself on his "purity," because he supposedly avoids benefiting from any ill-gotten gains. However, it is impossible to consistently follow this standard while living in human society, because one cannot verify the righteousness of everything one accepts. Fan Zuyu suggested that Zhongzi is also unfilial, because he shunned his elder brother and mother. (On Zhongzi, see also 7A34.)

Book 4A

1.1   Personal virtue is necessary for good government but not sufficient. One must combine it with the right institutions and policies. Mengzi discusses these in a number of passages, including 3A3.

1.2–3   Fan Zuyu noted that King Xuan of Qi showed a benevolent heart in sparing an ox being led to slaughter (1A7.4–5), yet his state was not well-ruled, because he did not put into effect the specific policy recommendations that Mengzi gave him (1A7.20–24).

Zhu Xi observes, "To have the heart but to lack the government, this is called 'mere goodness.' To have the government but to lack the heart, this is called 'mere laws.'"

Fan Zuyu said, "The highest honor ministers can give a ruler is to demand chal-   1.13
lenging things of him, to make their ruler become like Yao or Shun. The height of reverence for one's ruler is to display the Way of goodness in order to inhibit the ruler's bad heart, only fearing lest one's ruler sink into excess. The ultimate of stealing from and harming one's ruler is to fail to inform him about the Way of goodness because one says that he is unable to put it into effect."

This is similar to the view expressed in the *Greater Learning*, which says, "Those of   5.1
antiquity who wished that all people throughout the empire would let their inborn luminous Virtue shine forth put governing their states well first; wishing to govern their states well, they first established harmony in their households; wishing to establish harmony in their households, they first cultivated themselves."[1]

It is a better situation when those with lesser Virtue serve those with greater Virtue,   7.1
but in a disordered and chaotic world (one that "lacks the Way"), it is prudent for the less powerful to serve the more powerful. Hence, as Zhu Xi explains, "Heaven" here refers to "what should happen because of the Pattern of the situation."

Zhu Xi explains, "Wu was a barbarian state. Duke Jing was ashamed to marry his   7.2
family into them, but he was intimidated by their strength. Hence, he cried and gave his daughter to them."

King Wen was initially less powerful than Tyrant Zhou, but because of his Virtue,   7.4
King Wen amassed a large group of followers. Throughout his reign, whether power-ful or not, he served Tyrant Zhou. Zhu Xi notes that Mengzi is here appealing to the "heart of shame" (2A6, 6A6) of rulers in order to encourage them to cultivate their Virtue.

On sharing what one desires, see 1B5. On not inflicting on others what one dislikes,   9.1
see *Analects* 15.24.

This is an important passage, because it sketches Mengzi's account of moral failure.   10.1–3
(See also 6A15 and 7B37.) Zhu Xi comments, "Those who are destroying themselves do not know that propriety and righteousness are fine things, so they slander them. Even if one has a discussion with them, they will never have faith. Those who throw themselves away know that benevolence and righteousness are fine things, but they sink into sloth. They say of themselves that they are definitely unable to act. If one takes action with them, one will definitely be unable to encourage them to persevere."

A simple yet profound saying!   11.1

Mean 25 states that "To be Genuine is to make oneself complete" (*chéng zhě zì chéng*   12.3
yě 誠者自成也).[2] In other words, to be Genuine is to realize fully one's own good

---

[1] Translation by Gardner, *The Four Books*, 4–5, citing *Daxue*, Classic 4.

[2] Cf. Gardner, *The Four Books*, 126.

potential. Once one has done this, one will hate what is bad and love what is good "like hating a hateful smell or loving a lovely sight" (*Greater Learning*, Commentary 6).

14.3 Zhu Xi suggests that Sunzi (author of *The Art of War*) is an example of "those good at war." "Those who make strategic alliances" include advocates of realpolitik such as Su Qin and Zhang Yi, ministers on opposing sides of the pro-Qin and anti-Qin military alliances. (These were the primary strategic alliances of the Warring States period.) "Those who clear the fields" include Legalist thinkers like Shang Yang, who destroy the traditional farming communities.[3]

15.2 This reflects the belief, common to Confucianism and other traditions that emphasize the virtues, that a wise person can "read" a person's true character from his demeanor. (See also 1A6 and 7B11.)

17.1 "Discretion" is literally "weighing," as on a scale. This passage makes clear that there are certain standard ethical requirements that can be suspended in exigent circumstances. But only the wise person knows the difference between exercising discretion and compromising righteousness. A modern analogy to the situation Mengzi describes is this: a prudent professor will avoid even casual physical contact with students, but this would hardly inhibit him or her from performing CPR if it were needed. (See 4B29, 4B31, and 6B1 for additional discussions.)

17.3 Zhu Xi paraphrases Mengzi's point as, "You want me to save the world, but you want to make me bend the Way in order to get along with people. This is to lose at the start the tool that you use to save it" (cf. 3B1).

18.4 To "demand goodness" is to be uncompromising in one's expectations. As Mengzi states in 4B30.3–4 (not in this translation), one demands goodness of friends, not one's father or son. This does not mean that a father ignores his son's faults, though. As Wang Mian said, "How should a father be toward his son? When he is not righteous, let him simply warn him."

19.1–2 Zhu Xi explains that "To preserve one's self is to not allow it to sink into unrighteousness. As soon as one loses one's self, one has corrupted one's substance and disgraced one's parents. Even if one sacrifices three animals a day to care for them, it won't be sufficient to be filial. . . . If one serves one's parents with filiality, then one's devotion can be transferred to one's ruler, and one's agreeableness can be transferred to one's elders. If one's self is correct, then one's family will be ordered, one's state will be well-ruled, and the world will be at peace" (paraphrasing the *Greater Learning*, Classic 4).[4]

21.1 Lu Dalin said, "Praise and slander are not necessarily grounded in what is actual. Because of this, those who cultivate themselves should not easily become offended or pleased."

---

[3] On Legalism, see Graham, *Disputers of the Tao*, 267–92, and Schwartz, *The World of Thought in Ancient China*, 321–49.

[4] Cf. Gardner, *The Four Books*, 4–5.

George Savile made a similar point: "The Vanity of teaching often tempteth a Man to   23.1
forget he is a Blockhead."[5]

Mengzi holds that humans innately have incipient dispositions toward virtue. Benev-   27.2
olence is manifested in such things as spontaneous acts or feelings of compassion
(1A7.4, 2A6), and love of one's parents (here and 7A15). Righteousness is manifested
in disdain to do shameful things (6A10), and respect or deference to elders (here and
7A15). But these incipient feelings have to be cultivated so that they "grow" or "extend"
(1A7.12) to all relevantly similar situations. This passage suggests that part of what
helps this growth is delighting in the manifestations of the sprouts, instead of denying
that one has them or condemning them (4A10).
     Wisdom is here presented as a "meta-virtue," which consists in the proper under-
standing of and commitment to benevolence and righteousness (see also 5A9 and
5B1.7 on wisdom). It is not clear whether "ritual" here refers to ritual *actions* (i.e., the
rites) or propriety as a *disposition* (i.e., the virtue). (The character is the same, and I
hedged by translating it as "ritual propriety.") However, the fact that "ritual" is paired
with music and described as an "adornment" to benevolence and righteousness suggests that Mengzi is here thinking of ritual actions.

Book 4B

Zhu Xi explains that "a 'tally' is made out of jade. One carves characters into it and   1.3
splits it in half. Two people each keep half, and if there is a reason to, they can match
the two pieces to each other to establish trust" (in the messenger who brings the tally).
This is one of several passages that demonstrates that Mengzi thought there is one right
Way to live (4B29). We must flexibly respond to the details of particular circumstances
(4A17), but there is a "best" way to respond to a given situation. As Fan Zuyu said, "Although there are distinctions of earlier and later or near and far in the births of the
sages, nonetheless their Way is one."

Mengzi's admonition (to avoid political "stunts" that do little besides give one an   2.5
empty reputation) is still relevant today. Zhuge Liang, the famed strategist of the
Three Kingdoms era, once said, "One rules the world with great Virtue, not with small
kindnesses."

We must distinguish between genuine propriety and righteousness and their specious   6.1
semblances (cf. 7B37).

If people will do anything to get or maintain power and wealth, it is really circumstances   8.1
and not they who are the agents of change. In this sense, *they* never do anything. In
addition, Virtue gives one an ability to influence others that mere power lacks.

---

[5]   George Savile, *The Complete Works of George Savile, First Marquess of Halifax*, ed. Walter
Raleigh (Oxford: Clarendon Press, 1912), 240.

11.1   I follow the interpretation of Zhao Qi, according to which a great person can lie or fail to follow through on his commitments if the situation dictates it. (This would be a case of "discretion," as discussed in 4A17.) As an illustration, Zhao Qi refers to *Analects* 13.18, in which Kongzi endorses a son covering up his father's crime to protect him.[1] In contrast, Zhu Xi holds that great people are always faithful and resolute, but this is not because they aim to be. He reads the passage in the light of *Analects* 4.10 and approvingly quotes Yin Tun: "If one is focused upon righteousness, then faithfulness and being resolute are in its midst. If one is focused on faithfulness and being resolute, then one will not necessarily accord with righteousness."

12.1   I follow the interpretation of Zhao Qi, according to which "children" refers to the ruler's subjects, whose hearts the ruler must win over.[2] However, many translators follow Zhu Xi, who interprets the passage as meaning, "Great people are those who do not lose their childlike heart." He comments that "The heart of a child is pure unity without artificiality." I think that Zhu Xi is led to this reading because of the Buddhist influence on his thought, which encouraged him to seek for something akin to a pure, underlying Buddha nature as the source of the Way.

13.1   This passage illustrates the Confucian emphasis on the proper performance of funerals and mourning rituals. (Cf. 3A5 and *Analects* 1.9.)

14.1   Cheng Hao explained that Mengzi is referring to a sort of insight that goes beyond doctrines or texts: "To understand it through wordless learning is to understand it for oneself."

19.2   Zhu Xi's explanation is incisive: "Benevolence and righteousness were already based in Shun's heart, and all that he did came from them. It is not that he regarded benevolence and righteousness as fine things and only then forced himself to act." (On the "human roles," see 3A4.8. Cf. this passage to 2A2.16.)
        Zhu Xi plausibly suggests that 4B19 through 4B22 form a continuous historical narrative, from the pre-dynastic sovereign Shun down to the time of Mengzi himself.

20.5   Zhu Xi explains, "Their times are different and circumstances vary, hence there may be something inconsistent in their actions. But when he engaged in reflection and got it, their Pattern was no different from the start. 'He would sit and await the dawn,' because he was anxious to put it into effect." (For examples of the kinds of "inconsistent" actions a person might reflect upon, consider 4B29, 4B31, and 5A2. On "reflection," see 6A6.7 and its commentary.)

21.3   Yin Tun said, "This means that Kongzi created the *Spring and Autumn Annals* in the style of the historians to record the affairs of his time, and the significance was to settle what is perverse and what is correct, to set a great standard for a hundred Kings." (For more on Kongzi's decision to compose the *Spring and Autumn Annals*, see 3B9.8.)

---

[1] Zhao Qi, *Mengzi zhu*, Commentary on 4B11. (Compare also 1A7.2 and *Analects* 13.20.)

[2] Zhao Qi, *Mengzi zhu*, Commentary on 4B12. Compare 3A5, in which Mengzi says that good rulers treat their subjects like "babies," using the same term that I render as "child" in this passage. On winning over the hearts of the people, see 4A9 and 4B16.

Kongzi had Zengzi as a disciple, who had Kongzi's grandson, Zisi, as a disciple.   22.2
Mengzi was a disciple of either Zisi himself or one of Zisi's disciples. So he was either
a fourth- or fifth-generation disciple of Kongzi. Zhu Xi comments that, "Although
Mengzi's expression is very humble, nonetheless the burden he has assumed is heavy,
and he cannot fully express it."

Gongming Yi was a disciple of Kongzi's disciple who is also cited in 3B3 and 3B9.   24.1
    This chapter illustrates the Confucian fondness for seeking creative solutions to eth-   24.2
ical dilemmas. (Cf. 4A17 and 7A35.)

The meaning of the word I have here rendered "primordial" is disputed. I am taking it   26.1
to mean something like the original direction (or even "trajectory") of something active.
    Shun put Gun in charge of flood control, but his use of dams only exacerbated the   26.2
situation. Shun then gave authority to Yu, who dredged rivers and built canals, using
the natural flow of water to his advantage (cf. 3B9.3–4 and 6A2).
    By tracking how the stars naturally move, we can predict celestial events even a   26.3
millennium away. As Zhu Xi explains, the general point of this passage is that we find
out what the nature of a thing is by following how it develops in an unforced way from
its original state. Thus, water reveals its nature when it flows downward unimpeded,
not when we force it uphill (6A2). And if we are genuinely wise, we will take advantage of the nature of things in interacting with them (just as Yu did in his flood control projects).[3]

Zhu Xi suggests that this means that "they preserve benevolence and propriety in their   28.1
hearts and do not forget them."
    Zhu Xi suggests that "devotion" here refers to making one's best effort at loving and   28.5–6
revering others.
    Confucians encourage people to look at their own faults before they blame others.
However, as this passage makes clear, there are limitations to how far this should go.
    A "calamity" (a troubling situation) produces "anxiety" (a mental state) in most   28.7
people. However, the gentleman is "unperturbed" (2A2) by calamities because he is
concerned only with being the best person that he can.

Zhu Xi comments, "The Way of sages and worthies is that when they enter office, they   29.3–5
save others, and when they leave office, they cultivate themselves. But their hearts are
one." (On Yu and Hou Ji, see 3A4.7–8.)
    This passage illustrates very clearly the difference between Confucian "discretion"
(4A17, 4B31) and either relativism or pluralism. The correct action is very context-
sensitive, but there is one right response to a situation, so different sages would all do
the same things in the same situation.
    Zhu Xi suggests that verse 29.6 is an analogue to the actions of Yu and Hou Ji, and   29.6–7
29.7 to Yan Hui.

Kong Wenzhong said, "The words and actions of the sages and worthies of ancient   31.3
times were not the same, and their tasks were also different. But their Ways never failed

---

[3] For a challenging alternative explanation, see Graham, "The Background of the Mencian
Theory of Human Nature."

to be the same. If learners understand this, then they will respond to what they encounter like a scale weighing things, rising and falling through many changes, with no injury to its being the same." (Cf. 4A17, 4B29.)

33.2   Mengzi accepted the patriarchal assumptions of his society (3B2). However, the fact that the wife and concubine in this story have a better sense of ethical shame than their husband shows that women have the "sprout of righteousness" (2A6, 6A6) that is part of the basis for Virtue in human nature. Indeed, this story shows that sometimes women have an even more developed "heart of shame" than men.

Book 5A

1.2–3   Gongming Gao was a disciple of Kongzi's disciple Zengzi. Yang Shi said, "Shun only feared that he was not agreeable to his parents. He never regarded himself as filial. If he had regarded himself as filial, then he would not have been filial." (Shun is a paradigm of filial piety. But, paradoxically, the later tradition praises him for systematically underestimating his own virtue.)

In the *Records of the Historian*, Sima Qian says that the Emperor Yao "betrothed his two daughters to him, in order to observe how he was at home. He had his nine sons serve him, to observe how he was in public." It also says, "After one year, the place Shun lived had become a community. After two years, it had become a city. After three years, it had become the capital."[1] (This was because the people of the world were drawn to his Virtue.)

2.3   Sima Qian's *Records of the Historian* provides more details of what Shun's parents and brother did: "They ordered Shun to climb up and finish sealing the roof of the granary. His father set fire to the granary. Shun then used a pair of conical hats and drifted off, escaping death. Later, they ordered Shun to dig a well. But Shun dug a hidden side tunnel out of the well. Once Shun had gone deep inside the well, his father and Xiang filled up the well with dirt. But Shun escaped from the hidden side tunnel." Zhu Xi explains that "Xiang was Shun's younger brother by a different mother. After Shun had lived in that place for three years, it became the capital (5A1.3, commentary), hence he calls him 'ruler of the capital.' 'Xiang then went into Shun's home' desiring to get his cut of Shun's possessions. Xiang simply hated Shun, so he never came to his home. Hence, Shun was delighted when he saw him come and directed him to rule over his numerous ministers. Mengzi is saying that it is not that Shun does not know that Xiang planned on killing him, but when he sees him concerned, he is concerned; when he sees him delighted, he is delighted. The feelings between brothers naturally cannot be stopped."

2.4   Zichan was a skillful minister who was praised by Kongzi (*Analects* 5.16; cf. 4B2). Zhu Xi explains that "Xiang coming 'in accordance with the Way of a loving younger

---

[1]   On this and the following stories about Shun, see Sima Qian, *Shiji*, "Basic Annals" 1, in Ssu-ma Ch'ien, *The Grand Scribe's Records*, vol. 1, 8–16.

brother' is an example of deceiving him by what is in line with his path." He adds, "Shun fundamentally did not realize that his brother was feigning it. Hence, he was genuinely happy about him. What feigning was there on Shun's part?"

This is a psychologically complex and philosophically intriguing passage. Shun knows that Xiang tried to kill him. So why is Shun so happy to discover Xiang in his home, and why does he share Xiang's "concern"? Perhaps Shun has convinced himself that Xiang looks sad because he felt remorse over trying to kill him and came to Shun's home to mourn. Although this is a cognitive error, Mengzi (and Zhu Xi) take it to be highly admirable. This illustrates the extreme to which Confucianism is an ethics that evaluates actions in terms of the character they express, rather than evaluating character in terms of the actions it leads to. (In Western terms, Mengzian Confucianism is a radical form of virtue ethics, rather than rule-deontology or consequentialism.)[2]

Zhu Xi comments, "By handling him in this way, Shun did not lose the heart of treating as kin and loving, yet Xiang was unable to be cruel to the people of Youbi." Wu Huo said, "Sages do not harm personal generosity for the sake of public righteousness, but they also do not harm public righteousness for personal generosity. Shun's relationship with Xiang was a case of both consummate benevolence and the utmost righteousness."   3.3

This passage illustrates the Confucian commitment to "differentiated love." It figures in contemporary debates over whether Confucianism is committed to an immoral policy of favoritism or nepotism. (On differentiated love, see 3A5, *Analects* 13.18, and the Introduction.)

Mengzi here sketches a fundamental hermeneutic principle: holism of meaning. Zhu Xi notes that, "In the ode that Xianqiu Meng cites, the following lines state, 'The Chief Counselor is unfair. / I alone work hard and well.' So the author of the ode is saying of his situation, 'All in the world are the King's vassals. So why am I alone made to work hard and with skill?' This does not mean that a Son of Heaven can make a vassal of his father."   4.2

As Zhu Xi explains, "The world belongs to the world. It is not the private possession of any one person."   5.1

The term *ming*, which refers in this passage to a Mandate to rule, can also refer to the ethical Way that Heaven *decrees*. (Thus, the *Mean* begins, "What Heaven mandates is called the 'nature.' To follow the nature is called the 'Way.'") Finally, what Heaven decrees can also be conceptualized as *fate*.[3]   5.4

It is not clear how the "various spirits" indicated that they were pleased with Shun. However, "The Canon of Shun" states that he "was appointed to be Grand Recorder,   5.6

---

[2]   On virtue ethics, rule-deontology, and consequentialism, see Van Norden, *Virtue Ethics and Consequentialism in Early Chinese Philosophy*, 29–37.

[3]   For the context of the quotation from the *Mean*, see Gardner, *The Four Books*, 110. For the Mandate as fate, see 5A6.2, 7A1, and 7A2; cf. 1B16.3 and 2B13.

and there were no bewitchments by violent wind, thunder, and rain."[4] (But contrast 7B14.4.)

5.8 Zhu Xi comments, "Heaven has no concrete form. Its seeing and listening follow upon the seeing and listening of the people. Because the people went to Shun like this, we can understand that Heaven gave it to him."

6.2 Zhu Xi gives the distinction between Heaven and fate an interesting metaphysical interpretation: "In general, if one discusses it in terms of the Pattern, one calls it 'Heaven.' If one discusses it from the perspective of humans, one calls it 'fate.' But their underlying reality is one." (The word "fate" can also refer to the "Mandate" to rule.)

6.4 Kongzi had the Virtue to be King, but he did not have the opportunities that would allow him to ascend to that position. Zhu Xi comments, "Those like King Yu's son Qi, King Tang's grandson Tai Jia, and King Wu's son Cheng, although they did not come up to the worthiness and sagacity of Yu's Prime Minister Yi, Tang's Prime Minister Yi Yin, and King Wu's brother the Duke of Zhou, they were nonetheless able to preserve the former accomplishments of their ancestors, so Heaven did not dismiss them. Hence, Yi, Yi Yin, and the Duke of Zhou, although they had the Virtue of Shun and Yu, did not get the world."

7.1 In Chinese cooking, the cook is also the butcher. Recall that Mengzi regards butchering as an unsuitable job for a gentleman (1A7.8). But according to Sima Qian's *Records of the Historian*, Yi Yin wanted to reach the ruler but had no access. So he became a kitchen servant to the ruling family of the state of Xin, from which Tang's wife came. He pleased King Tang with the dishes he made, and then told him about the Way of a King.[5] Zhu Xi suggests that this story dates from the Warring States Period, long after the actual time of Tang and Yi Yin, so it is likely to be fabricated.

7.5 Zhu Xi suggests that "Wisdom refers to understanding how affairs ought to be. Insight refers to becoming enlightened about how the Pattern is."

7.7 Zhu Xi comments, "If Yi Yin had cooked to seek out King Tang, this would be humiliating himself in the extreme. How could he rectify the world?"

9.2 See *Zuozhuan*, Duke He 5 (Legge, *The Ch'un Ts'ew with the Tso Chuen*, vol. 5 of *The Chinese Classics*, 145–46). See also Legge's helpful map, which may be found between pages 112 and 113 of the Prolegomena, showing the locations of Yu, Jin ("Tsin"), Guo ("Kwoh"), and Qin ("Ts'in").

9.3 Fan Zuyu said, "When ancient sages and worthies were down on their luck, they were not ashamed to do menial work. So it would not have been surprising if Boli Xi had tended oxen. It is simply that, if the ruler had not treated him with the highest respect and the utmost propriety, then he could not have obtained an audience with him. How could he have first humiliated himself in order to seek to meet the ruler?" This passage is fascinating for several reasons. First, it gives what is perhaps Mengzi's most detailed account of the virtue of wisdom. From Mengzi's comments about Boli Xi, we learn that a wise person (1) can properly evaluate the character of others; (2) is

---

[4] "The Canon of Shun," from the *Documents of Tang*, in the *Documents*. (For a somewhat different translation, see Legge, *The Shoo King*, vol. 3 of *The Chinese Classics*, 32.)

[5] Sima Qian, *Shiji*, "Basic Annals" 3, in Ssu-ma Ch'ien, *The Grand Scribe's Records*, vol. 1, 43.

skillful at finding the best means to achieve a goal; (3) understands and avoids what is base; and (4) has a prudent concern for his own well-being.[6]

In addition, Zhu Xi comments that, "Already by the time of Mengzi, there was no evidence of what Boli Xi actually did. Mengzi simply thought over the Pattern of the situation and extended it, so he knew that the story Wan Zhang asked about was necessarily not the case." This illustrates the fact that, as David S. Nivison observes, Mengzi is a "speculative" rather than an "empirical" historian.[7] Although he is concerned with what the truth is (several times in this book he makes clear that certain things were "not the case"), Mengzi's method for discovering the truth is not the sifting of empirical evidence but rather the use of ethical insight into the minds of sages.

Book 5B

Mengzi frequently cites Bo Yi, Yi Yin, and Liuxia Hui as examples of three individuals   *1.5–6* who each attained one aspect of sagehood but failed to achieve the complete sageliness of Kongzi. (For more on Bo Yi and Yi Yin, see 2A2.22; on Bo Yi and Liuxia Hui, see 2A9 and 7B15.)

Zhu Xi comments, "Wisdom is the goal of understanding, and sagacity is the goal of Virtue. When one plays a single instrument, it is a small performance with its own beginning and end; so is the understanding of the other three masters partial, and their goal is also partial. Likewise, just as the small performances are harmonized into one great symphony, so does Kongzi's understanding extend everywhere and his Virtue lacks nothing."

Zhu Xi comments, "One sees that Kongzi's skillfulness and strength are both com-   *1.7* plete, and his sagacity and wisdom are complete. The other three masters have more than enough strength, but their skillfulness was insufficient to match Kongzi. Therefore, although they achieved sagehood in one respect, their wisdom was insufficient to perfectly achieve timeliness. . . . The three other masters were like Spring, Summer, Autumn, and Winter, each of which has its own time. Kongzi was the harmonizing, original *qi* that flows throughout all four seasons."

Fan Zuyu commented, "The text calls the duke's position 'the position from Heaven';   *3.4* it calls his responsibility 'the responsibility from Heaven'; it calls his salary 'the salary from Heaven.' This means that Heaven directs the worthy to govern the people of Heaven. This is not something that the rulers of people may arrogate to themselves" (cf. 5A5).

Mengzi has a thoughtful philosophy of friendship. As Aristotle also said, genuine   *3.6* friendship is based on shared Virtue. Friendship can obtain between those of differing social status, but only if neither friend seeks to presume upon these differences.

---

[6] On wisdom, see also 4A27 and Van Norden, *Virtue Ethics and Consequentialism in Early Chinese Philosophy*, 273–77.

[7] David S. Nivison, "Mengzi as Philosopher of History," in Chan, *Mencius: Contexts and Interpretations*, 282–304.

Otherwise, the friendship cannot manifest the virtue of "faithfulness" (3A4.8). As Zhu Xi explains, "Friendship is one of the human relationships by means of which one supports benevolence. Hence, the Son of Heaven need not debase himself in order to befriend a commoner. A commoner need not have an ulterior motive to befriend the Son of Heaven." (For more on friendship, see especially 5B7.4 and 5B8; also see 3A4.8 and 4A12.1.)

4.5 Mengzi thinks that ethical growth involves recognizing paradigmatic instances of righteousness (or benevolence) and then "extending" to "fill out the category" of similar cases (e.g., 2A6, 3B3.5, 6A10). But as this passage makes clear, one can err through both overextension and underextension (cf. 3B10).

7.6–7 When the gamekeeper explained why he did not answer the summons, the duke let him go.[1] Nonetheless, from our contemporary perspective, the gamekeeper's risk of his life over such a small principle seems puzzling, and Kongzi's praise seems exaggerated. There are at least two ways to understand this incident, though. (1) The gamekeeper's refusal to answer an improper summons may be immensely significant in his own cultural context, because it symbolized, for all concerned, the more general obligations and prerogatives of ruler and subjects (cf. *Analects* 3.19). Perhaps the gamekeeper was taking a stand (both literally and figuratively) against the unlimited authority of the duke. (2) Kongzi's praise may be intentional hyperbole. Perhaps Kongzi does not think that the gamekeeper's refusal was ethically obligatory but merely holds up this humble official's quixotic fastidiousness as an inspiration to nobles who are tempted to violate more serious principles. (This incident is also mentioned in 3B1.2.)

8.2 For Mengzi, friendship, Virtue, and textual understanding are intimately related. Genuine friendship is based on shared Virtue (5B3 and 5B7.4), so the friendship of the Virtuous extends outward to more and more people, including the Virtuous of ancient times. We can only befriend them through the texts that they have left behind, but these have to be interpreted in terms of the contexts in which they were composed (cf. 5A4.2).

9.2 Zhu Xi comments, "What is righteous for great ministers is different for relatives and nonrelatives. Following a standard rule and using one's discretion each have their own place." (In this case, the "standard" would be to simply resign if a ruler errs and does not listen to good advice, while replacing a bad ruler to whom one is related is using "discretion" [4A17] in a special case.)

Book 6A

1.1 Zhu Xi comments, "Gaozi means that human nature fundamentally lacks benevolence and righteousness and must await straightening and bending before it can be-

---

[1] See *Zuozhuan*, Duke Zhao 20 (Legge, *The Ch'un Ts'ew with the Tso Chuen*, vol. 5 of *The Chinese Classics*, 684).

come complete. This is like Xunzi's theory that 'human nature is bad.'" (Xunzi was a later Confucian critical of Mengzi. He compared ethical cultivation to "steaming and bending . . . wood straight as a plumb line into a wheel.")[1]

As Zhu Xi explains, the problem with Gaozi's position is that, "if one's doctrine is like this, then the people of the world will regard benevolence and righteousness as things that harm their nature, so they will be unwilling to engage in them."   1.2

Gaozi's response to Mengzi's counterargument in 6A1 is that, just as it does not "harm" water to make it flow east or west, so it does not harm human nature whether we make it good or bad.   2.1

The key to appreciating this chapter (and the adjacent ones) is that the similes are not intended as mere rhetorical window dressing without cognitive content. Mengzi's objection is that Gaozi's simile fails to do justice to the natural characteristics of water, and thereby presents a misleading impression of human nature.   2.2

When humans become bad, it is due to artificial interference with their natural tendencies, similar to the manner in which water can be forced uphill (6A7–8).   2.3

As Zhu Xi explains, "'Life' refers to that by means of which humans and animals have awareness and move."   3.1

Mengzi is trying to establish that Gaozi wishes to state a strict equivalence between the "nature" of a thing and its "life." If he does wish to claim that "nature" is identical with "life," then, as Zhu Xi explains, Gaozi's position "means that everything that has life shares one nature."   3.2

Mengzi has skillfully performed a reductio ad absurdum of Gaozi's position. As Zhu Xi explains, if what Gaozi claims "really is so, then because dogs, oxen, and humans all have awareness and are capable of motion, their natures have no differences." But it sounds as absurd in Chinese as it does in English to say that the nature of an ox is no different from the nature of a human.   3.3

There are three major interpretations of what it would mean to claim that righteousness is internal. (1) Many agree with Jiao Xun, who takes it to be another way of saying that "in human nature there is originally no righteousness."[2] In contrast, righteousness would be *internal* if it were part of human nature. (2) Kwong-loi Shun argues that for righteousness to be external is for one's knowledge of righteousness to derive from certain features of the external world. In contrast, righteousness would be *internal* if one's knowledge of it comes from certain features of one's "heart" or "mind."[3] (3) I agree with Zhu Xi, who says "righteousness is external" means that one need not act out of any particular emotion in order to act righteously. In contrast, to say that righteousness is internal means that "in treating people as elderly, the feeling of genuine respect manifests itself from within, and one makes it fully genuine by respecting   4.1

---

[1] *Xunzi* 1, "An Exhortation to Learning," in *Readings*, 256; see also *Xunzi* 23, "Human Nature Is Bad," in *Readings*, 298–306.

[2] Jiao Xun, *Mengzi zhengyi*, Commentary on 6A4.

[3] Shun, *Mencius and Early Chinese Thought*, 98–99.

them."[4] (Cf. 6A5.2.) On Jiao Xun's reading, the external/internal debate is over *human nature*; on Shun's reading, it is about ethical *epistemology*; and on Zhu Xi's reading, it is about *motivation*.

4.2   If we want to ride a white horse, the fact that we choose "Silver" from our stable rather than "Chestnut" depends only upon the whiteness of the former horse, something external to us. Now, treating the elderly with deference is a paradigmatic example of righteousness. Gaozi argues that, similarly to the case of whiteness, our righteous treatment of an elderly person depends solely upon their elderliness, a property external to us.

4.3a   Mengzi notes that, when we show righteousness toward an elderly person, we are not merely responding to the external property of elderliness, or else we would treat old horses with the same reverence that we treat elderly people.

4.3b   Zhu Xi explains, "Righteousness does not lie in their elderliness, but rather it lies in my heart that treats them as elderly. So it is obvious that righteousness is not external."

4.4   Loving one's younger brother is a paradigmatic example of benevolence. One does not feel fraternal love toward other people's siblings. Hence, benevolence depends upon how you feel toward others. In the case of righteousness, you owe deference to an elderly person, regardless of whether it is your grandmother or a stranger of your grandmother's age. Hence, deferring to the elderly depends upon a quality they have, not upon how we feel toward them. As Zhu Xi puts Gaozi's point, "Love is determined by me, hence benevolence lies in what is internal. Respect is determined by elderliness, hence righteousness lies in what is external."

4.5   Enjoying the taste of a fine, roasted piece of meat is a paradigm of something "internal." Now, Gaozi's argument assumed that it is impossible to feel respect for every elder, because one has no special bond with most of them. However, Mengzi's example illustrates that it is quite possible to have the same internal response to a wide range of things that one has no special connection with. It doesn't have to be *my* roast for me to find it delicious, nor does someone need to be *my* grandmother for me to feel respect for her.

5.2   This is a clear, unambiguous statement: righteousness is internal because it requires acting out of a particular feeling (cf. 4B19). In contrast, if it were *external*, then righteousness would be purely a matter of external behavior and would not require any particular emotion or attitude.

5.3   We naturally respect our elder siblings, but righteousness requires that we defer to different people in different circumstances. For example, I defer to my elder siblings most of the time, but one serves guests at a feast in order of strict seniority. Consequently, Meng Jizi argues, our feeling of respect will have to diverge from our righteous behavior.

5.4b   Meng Jizi's argument was that feelings of respect cannot track the objects of righteous behavior, because the latter vary so much. So Mengzi comes up with an example to illustrate how the object of feelings of respect can vary, depending on the "role" those objects occupy.

---

[4]   Zhu Xi, *Zhuzi yulei*, vol. 4, 1379.

Meng Jizi suggests that respect must be external because it tracks something ex-   5.5
ternal. However, Gongduzi gives an example of something else that varies depending
upon external factors yet is paradigmatically internal: thirst.[5]

Many interpreters follow Zhu Xi in translating the first part of this verse, "Their innate   6.5
emotions can only be good." By these emotions, Zhu Xi means the "hearts" referred
to later in the chapter.
    See 6A8, 6A9, and 6A15 for Mengzi's account of how the human potential for virtue   6.6
can fail to develop.
    We find a similar account of the four feelings (literally, "hearts") and their correla-   6.7
tion with Mengzi's four cardinal virtues in 2A6, except that the feelings are there said
to be merely the "sprouts" of the virtues. Zhu Xi suggests that the difference in phras-
ing is because in the earlier passage Mengzi is stressing the need to cultivate these
reactions, whereas here he is emphasizing the fact that they are innate. "Reflection"
is focusing one's attention upon and thinking about one's feelings and the situations
that elicit them. It is an activity that involves feelings, thoughts, and perception. Thus,
Mengzi helped King Xuan to reflect upon his decision to spare an ox (1A7.4–9), he
encouraged Yi Zhi to reflect upon the lavish burial he had given his own parents
(3A5), and he assisted Wan Zhang in reflecting upon the stories of sage Shun (5A2).
(Cf. 4A1.5, 4B20.5, 6A15, and *Analects* 2.15, 15.31, 19.6, and see the Introduction,
"Mengzi's Philosophy.")
    Zhu Xi explains, "If there is a thing, there is a standard for it. For example, there   6.8
are ears and eyes, so there are the Virtues of good hearing and keen eyesight. There
are fathers and sons, so there are the feelings of love and filiality. This is the constant
nature that the people cleave to. Hence, people's emotions never fail to be 'fond of
this beautiful Virtue.' Looking at it this way, we can see that human nature is good
and understand the three other theories Gongduzi asked about without needing to
dispute them."

Note that Mengzi stresses two distinct factors in cultivation (whether it is agricultural   7.2
or ethical): environment and individual effort.
    We do not know any definite details about Longzi, except that he is also cited fa-   7.4
vorably by Mengzi in 3A3.7 (a passage not in this volume).
    We know more about cultural diversity in standards of taste than did Mengzi.   7.8
However, the fact that connoisseurs appreciate great pieces of music, delicious dishes,
and attractive people from other cultures supports Mengzi's claim for common human tastes.
    "Order" is the same word the School of the Way used to refer to the Pattern of
the universe (see the Introduction, "From Mengzi to Zhu Xi"). Consistent with this
metaphysical view, Cheng Yi claimed that "order" and "righteousness" are two

---

[5] On *Mengzi* 6A1–5, see also D. C. Lau, "On Mencius' Use of the Method of Analogy in Argument," in *Mencius*, Appendix 5, 1970; David S. Nivison, "Problems in the *Mengzi*: 6A3–5,"
in *The Ways of Confucianism*, 149–66; Kwong-loi Shun, "Mencius and the Mind-Dependence
of Morality," *Journal of Chinese Philosophy* 18 (June 1991): 169–93; Van Norden, *Virtue Ethics
and Consequentialism in Early Chinese Philosophy*, 278–301.

manifestations of the same entity: "In a thing, it is the 'Pattern.' In dealing with things, it is 'righteousness.'"

8.1 Remember that Mengzi uses the metaphor of "sprouts" (2A6, 6A9) to describe our innate but incipient ethical inclinations.

8.2 Chinese thinkers show a keen understanding of the interrelationship between one's environment and one's mental state. The "morning *qi*" is thought to be especially pure and invigorating. And the restorative effects of a good night's sleep are obvious. On *qi*, see the commentary to 2A2.8 and also the Introduction, "Mengzi's Philosophy"; on one's "genuine heart," compare 7A15.

8.3–4 The story of Ox Mountain is Mengzi's reply to the objection that some people seem to lack the virtuous inclinations that he claims are part of human nature (2A6, 6A10). Mengzi argues that such people (whom we would label psychopaths or sociopaths) were born with a good nature, but it was stunted by some combination of a bad environment and their own repeated bad actions.

9.1–2 In these verses, Mengzi emphasizes the role of environment (bad advisers who "freeze" the sprouts of virtue of the king of Qi) in explaining human wrongdoing.

9.3 The object of Go is to capture one's opponent's pieces by encircling them with one's own (cf. *Analects* 17.22). A child can play it, but it is difficult to master. Mengzi uses learning Go as a metaphor for how ethical development can depend upon individual agency (such as the king's choosing to not focus and "reflect" upon the message Mengzi gives him). Verses 9.1–2 and 9.3 thus present two complementary explanations of human moral failure.

10.2 Zhu Xi explains how this relates to Mengzi's doctrine of the goodness of human nature: "Everyone desires some things more than life and hates some things more than death because of their 'genuine hearts' of 'constant Virtue,' 'good order and righteousness'" (6A8, 6A6, 6A7).

10.5 Zhu Xi explains, "Everyone has the heart of disdain (2A6, 6A6), but the masses of people are swept up by the desire for profit and forget about it. Only the worthy is able to preserve it without losing it." (The next two verses illustrate the universality of the heart and how it can be forgotten.)

10.6 Just as 2A6 gives an example of how the sprout of benevolence manifests itself, so does this passage provide a vivid illustration of the sprout of righteousness. It might not be true that everyone would act as Mengzi suggests in this particular situation. However, all that is necessary for Mengzi's argument is that, for any human, there are some sensual desires that he or she disdains to satisfy.

10.7 Mengzi is referring to serving a corrupt ruler and pandering to him because he offers a huge salary. Zhu Xi comments, "Above it explains that people all have the heart of disdain. Here it explains how the masses of people lose it."

10.8 Serving a corrupt ruler is as shameful as accepting a handout given with contempt. However, people do not "reflect upon" the similarity, so they do the former even though they would disdain to do the latter. One must "extend" one's disdain to do what is shameful from the one case to the other. (Cf. 6A15 and 7B31.)

15.1 Mengzi claims that we ought to make qualitative distinctions among our motivations (and the aspects of ourselves that are associated with them). So we should consider not only how strong a motivation is (quantitatively), but also how important it is (qualitatively).

This chapter brings together many themes in Mengzi's account of moral failure.   15.2
Sensual desires are not immoral or intrinsically problematic. However, wrongdoing results when we passively follow these desires without also engaging our innate virtuous inclinations. These inclinations motivate altruistic behavior (2A6) or restrain the satisfaction of our sensual desires (6A10). Although the inclinations manifest themselves spontaneously in everyone to a certain degree, cultivation is necessary to fully develop them. Part of this cultivation is using one's heart, whose function (literally, "office") is "reflecting" (see 6A6 and its commentary). What is the "it" the heart will "get" if it reflects? Zhu Xi says it is the Pattern of whatever things or affairs one encounters; to "get it" is to understand how things are and how they should be.

Book 6B

This chapter is an illustration of the need for "discretion" in applying propriety and   1.8
righteousness (4A17). One must be willing to adapt to particular circumstances, as when Shun ignores the ritual of informing his parents when taking a wife (5A2), but one must not compromise what is important, so Mengzi refuses to sacrifice his integrity to take an official position (3B1).

Mengzi's argument in this chapter parallels his argument in 1A1. (For more on Song   4.6
Keng, see Schwartz, *The World of Thought in Ancient China*, 240–42, Graham, *Disputers of the Tao*, 95–100, and John Knoblock, trans., *Xunzi* (Stanford, CA: Stanford University Press, 1988), vol. 1, 59–60. Xunzi critiques Songzi's doctrines at length in *Xunzi* 18, "Rectifying Theses," in Knoblock, *Xunzi*, vol. 3, 45–48.

Zhu Xi compares the first case to Kongzi's relationship with Ji Huanzi of Lu (*Analects*   14.1–4
18.4) and the second case to Kongzi's relationship with Duke Ling of Wei (*Analects* 15.1; cf. 5B4.7).

On Shun, see 5A1 ff. Fu Yue served under King Wu Ding of the Shang. On Jiao Ge,   15.1
see 2A1.8. Sunshu Ao served under the Hegemon Duke Zhuang of Chu. On Boli Xi, contrast 5A9. On Guan Zhong, see 2A1.1–5. Compare this entire passage to 7A18.

Book 7A

This passage links Mengzi's moral psychology to his cosmology. It suggests that the   1.3
heart (the seat of our "feelings") is a manifestation of our nature, which is implanted in us by Heaven (cf. 6A6). Heaven is also responsible for fate (2B13, 5A6.2, 7A2). This suggests a relationship among three distinct entities, but Cheng Yi said, "The heart, the nature, and Heaven are all the one Pattern. However, if one discusses it from the perspective of the Pattern, one calls it 'Heaven.' If one discusses it from the perspective of the endowment that we receive, one calls it our 'nature.' If one discusses it from

the perspective of what is preserved in a person, one calls it the 'heart.'" Similarly, Zhang Zai wrote, "Arising from the Great Vacuity, there comes the name 'Heaven.' Arising from the transformation of the *qi*, there comes the name 'Way.' From the harmony of the Vacuity and the *qi* comes the name 'nature.' From the harmony of the nature and awareness comes the name 'heart.'" The School of the Way interpretation is thus a sort of moderate monism. (See the Introduction, "From Mengzi to Zhu Xi," on the Pattern and *qi*.)

2.4   As Zhu Xi explains, only what is beyond human control is one's "proper fate." Hence, acceptance of fate is not an excuse for giving up or wrongdoing. (See also 2B13.) This passage may be a response to the Mohist accusation that Confucians promote a disabling fatalism.[1]

3.1–2   Zhu Xi comments, "'In oneself' refers to benevolence, righteousness, propriety, and wisdom. These are all things our nature has. . . . 'External' refers to wealth, prestige, profit, and success. These are all external things."

4.1   Many interpreters follow Zhu Xi in translating this, "The ten thousand things are all complete within us." However, this interpretation only makes sense if one accepts the metaphysics of the School of the Way. On Zhu Xi's reading, this chapter "is referring to what the Pattern is fundamentally. . . . There is not a single aspect of the Pattern that is not completely internal to our nature."

4.3   On "Genuineness," see the commentary on 4A12. "Sympathetic understanding" is defined in the *Analects* as "not inflicting on others what you do not desire yourself" (15.24). Kongzi's disciple Zengzi suggests that it is one of the two most important aspects of the Confucian Way (4.15).[2] Zhu Xi thinks verses 7A4.2 and 3 describe two different states of ethical development: "If one turns toward oneself and is Genuine, one is already benevolent. But if one is not Genuine, there are still selfish thoughts interfering, and the Pattern is not pure. Hence, in all activities one should force oneself to extend (one's sympathies) to others. When one is close to the general Pattern, benevolence is not far away."

7.1–3   Zhu Xi comments, "'Shame' is the feeling of disdain that we have inherently" (2A6, 6A6).

11.1   Many contemporary celebrities could learn much from this adage!

15.1   Some have interpreted these phrases as "best capability" and "best knowledge." But here, "genuine" marks the contrast between what is "ingenuous" or "original" as opposed to what is "artificial" or "acquired." (The same term is used in 4A15, 6A8, and 6A17.) In other words, Mengzi is not suggesting that "learning" and "pondering" are bad or inferior methods of understanding. He is simply claiming that we innately understand some things, and have some abilities, without having been taught them.

---

[1] *Mozi* 35, "A Condemnation of Fatalism"; see Burton Watson, trans., *Mo Tzu* (New York: Columbia University Press, 1963), 117–23.

[2] For an argument against Zengzi's view, see Van Norden, *Virtue Ethics and Consequentialism in Early Chinese Philosophy*, 72–82.

This is Mengzi's philosophy of ethical cultivation in a nutshell. We are born with   15.3
incipient tendencies toward benevolence and righteousness, which we must "extend"
so that they reach all other relevantly similar cases. That is, we must feel compassion
not only for our own parents but also for the parents of others. We must revere not only
the elders of our family but also the elders of others. (Cf. 1A7.12, 7A17, and 7B31.)
The later Confucian Wang Yangming emphasized the phrase "genuine knowledge."
However, for him as for other School of the Way philosophers, it does not refer to an
incipient tendency but rather a fully developed faculty of simultaneous ethical insight
and motivation.[3]

The use of quickly flowing water as a metaphor of moral growth is common in Mengzi   16.1
(e.g., 2A2.11–14, 2A6.7).

Li Yu said, "People all have a heart that will not do certain things and does not desire   17.1
certain things. But as soon as a selfish thought sprouts, if one is unable to regulate it
with propriety and righteousness, then one will frequently do what one 'would not do'
and desire what one 'would not desire.' To examine that heart is what is meant by 'ex-
panding and filling out' one's 'feeling of disdain' (2A6). In this case one's righteousness will be inexhaustible. Hence, he says, 'Simply be like this.'" (This chapter should
be read in light of 7A15 and 7B31.)[4]

On Robber Zhi, cf. 3B10.3. See also the dialogue "Robber Zhi" in *Readings*, 369–75.   25.3
Intriguingly, the "Robber Zhi" dialogue is a defense of egoism, and the following passage, 7A26, refers to Yang Zhu, the ethical egoist philosopher.

On the philosophies of Mozi and Yang Zhu, see 3B9.9–10 and the Introduction,   26.1–3
"Mengzi's Philosophy." We don't know anything definite about Zimo.

   There is no simple formula for determining to what extent we should prioritize the   26.4
interests of ourselves, our loved ones, and the world at large. In one context, it might
be appropriate to abandon one's ruler to save one's own life, as Boli Xi did (5A9); in
another context, one should be willing to sacrifice one's life over even a small matter
of principle, like the gamekeeper who would not answer a ritually inappropriate summons (5B7.5–6). In one situation, one must take time away from one's official duties
because of familial responsibilities, as Mengzi did when he returned home for his
mother's funeral (2B7); in another situation, one must sacrifice the well-being of one's
family for the greater good, as when Yu ignored his family for years while trying to save
the Central States from flooding (3A4.7). So we must use "discretion" (4A17) to judge
what is appropriate in each situation.

Zhao Qi explained, "'Treated it as their nature' means that their natures were sponta-   30.1–2
neously fond of benevolence" (*Mengzi zhu*, Commentary on 7A30). Zhu Xi comments, "Tang and Wu cultivated themselves in order to embody the Way." (Cf. 7B33.)
   Zhu Xi suggests that the point of the last verse is that those who feign it long enough
may successfully deceive most people, or even themselves, about whether they are

---

[3]   See Ivanhoe, *Ethics in the Confucian Tradition*, 48–50.
[4]   On this passage, see also David S. Nivison, "Problems in the *Mengzi*: 7A17," in *The Ways of
Confucianism*, 167–73.

virtuous. However, another possible interpretation is that if one acts virtuously long enough, one will become virtuous (cf. 6B4).

35.6   Confucian "differentiated love" requires a special commitment to one's family members (3A5; *Analects* 13.18). This has the potential to create ethical dilemmas like this hypothetical case. Mengzi's solution attempts to preserve both Shun's obligation as a ruler (since he does not interfere with the legitimate actions of his Minister of Crime) and also his obligation to his father (since he resigns and flees to protect him). (Cf. 4B24.)

40.1–6   Zhu Xi suggests that verse 2 describes something like what Kongzi did for Zengzi in *Analects* 4.15. (Zhu Xi interprets this as a case in which Zengzi's long effort left him poised to achieve enlightenment, and Kongzi said precisely the right thing to make him reach the final understanding.)[5] He also says that the methods described in verse 3 "each instruct someone based upon their strong points." "Question and answer" is what Mengzi often does with his disciples Wan Zhang and Gongsun Chou. Finally, "private cultivation" (verse 5) is when one cannot directly study with a gentleman but learns from his teachings and the example he sets. This is how Mengzi says he learned from Kongzi (4B22).

45.1   This is a succinct statement of the Confucian doctrine of "differentiated love" (see the Introduction, "The Confucian Way"). Virtuous people are very compassionate toward all humans, but without the special attachment they feel toward their own kin. They will not indiscriminately harm animals, but their concern for them is significantly less than that for humans. Hence, King Xuan of Qi fails to be a true gentleman, because he shows more compassion to animals than to his own subjects (1A7.4–12). And Mohists fail to be true gentleman, because they are committed to showing equal concern to everyone, regardless of familial relationships (3A5).

Book 7B

1.1–2   On "extension," see also 1A7.12, 7A15, and 7A17.

5.1   This is a criticism of those who, like the Mohists, wish to reduce ethical action to some precise procedure that does not require wisdom. Nonetheless, Mengzi does not completely eschew the use of standards (4A1).

14.4   This verse makes the striking suggestion that human well-being takes precedence over the agency of the spirits associated with the altars to the land and grain.

16.1   According to this passage, the Way is something immanent in this world, not something metaphysical that transcends it (cf. *Analects* 15.29).

---

[5]   See Van Norden, "Unweaving the 'One Thread' of *Analects* 4.15," in *Confucius and the Analects*, ed. Van Norden, 231–32.

What is appropriate for a person to do depends upon his social role. It is not the job   23.2
of a high official to chase tigers. Similarly, Mengzi had once been an official under
the king of Qi, but he resigned and is leaving the state, so he is not in a position to ask
for famine relief.

The term "fate" (or "Mandate") emphasizes what we must simply accept because it   24.2
cannot be changed. The term "nature" emphasizes what we must actively cultivate.
Our sensual desires and our virtuous inclinations are both inevitable aspects of who
we are. However, people do not need to emphasize the cultivation of their sensual desires; they are essentially automatic (6A15). In contrast, people *should* think of their
virtuous inclinations as something that needs cultivation, rather than as simply something one must accept with resignation.[1]

On the philosophies of the Mohists and Yang Zhu, see 3B9.9–10 and the Introduction,   26.1
"Mengzi's Philosophy." Mengzi is suggesting that, because Mohist impartiality makes
demands of people that are psychologically unrealistic, those who fail at fulfilling
those demands will easily lapse into the extreme partiality of egoism (cf. 2A2.9–16).
But since Yang Zhu at least acknowledged the importance of human nature, it is sometimes easier to get his followers to recognize their own "sprouts of virtue" (2A6, 6A10).
  Zhu Xi comments, "In this chapter, we see how sages and worthies oppose other   26.2
positions. They oppose them firmly, but when people are converted, they show sympathy. Because they oppose them firmly, others understand that those positions are
wrong. But because they treat converts with sympathy, people understand that it is alright to turn toward them. This is both the height of benevolence and the fathoming
of righteousness."

The comment is intended as a criticism of how undiscriminating Mengzi is in accept-   30.2
ing students. However, it is recorded here as a testimony to Mengzi's open-mindedness
in accepting students, regardless of their nobility or wealth.

Zhu Xi comments, "People all have the hearts of compassion and disdain (2A6, 6A6).   31.1
Hence, no one fails to have things that he will not bear or will not do. These are the
sprouts of benevolence and righteousness. Nonetheless, because of the partiality of
their *qi* and the obscuration of their material desires, there are sometimes other cases
in which people are unable to have these reactions. But if they extend what they are
able to do so that they reach to what they were unable to do, then there will be nothing
in which they are not benevolent and righteous." (Cf. 1A7.12, 7A15, 7A17, and 7B1.)
  Zhu Xi suggests that "trespassing" is a reference to being a thief, but the phrase   31.2
might also refer to an illicit sexual encounter (3B3.5).
  Cf. 4A27 on "core reaction."   31.3
  Mengzi uses an example familiar to nobles of his era: the temptation to benefit one-   31.4
self by lying or holding back the truth (cf. *Analects* 15.8). Zhu Xi comments, "Whether
someone is being glib or secretive, the intention is to defraud someone. This is in the
category of trespassing, but since it is more subtle, people easily overlook it. Hence,

---

[1] Zhuangzi might be seen as arguing for the opposite position (*Zhuangzi* 4, "The Human
Realm," in *Readings*, especially 229–31).

he particularly holds it up as an example to clarify that one must extend the heart that will not trespass so that it reaches to and avoids this. Only then will one be able to fill out the heart that will not trespass."

37.4 Zhao Qi states that "Qin Zhang" is another name for Kongzi's disciple Zizhang.[2] Comparing him to another disciple, Kongzi said, "Zizhang overshoots the mark, while Zixia falls short of it. . . . Overshooting the mark is just as bad as falling short of it" (*Analects* 11.16). Kongzi chides him for confusing being renowned with being genuinely virtuous (*Analects* 12.20). Zeng Xi was the father of Kongzi's disciple Zengzi. A charming anecdote portrays him as having simple but admirable aspirations (*Analects* 11.26). We don't know anything about Mu Pi.

37.7 Verses 37.1–7 discuss what are technically known as "deformations of virtue," due to exceeding or falling short of the proper mean (cf. 4B7, 4B10; *Analects* 6.29). Liuxia Hui might be an example of someone who is "wild," while Bo Yi is "squeamish" (5B1). Zhu Xi comments, "The wild have resolution. The squeamish preserve something. One can advance on the Way with those who have resolution. Those who preserve something will not lose themselves" (4A19).

37.9 Instead of the high aspirations of the "wild" and the integrity of the "squeamish," the village worthies set low standards for themselves that are easy to meet and adequate to obtain the approval of most people. But genuine Virtue is much more demanding than this, and Kongzi wants nothing to do with those who settle for safe, socially acceptable mediocrity.

37.12 Zhu Xi comments, "Village worthies are neither 'wild' nor 'squeamish,' and everyone regards them as good. They seem to have attained the Way exactly, but that is not actually so. Hence, he fears that they will confuse people about Virtue."

37.13 Verses 37.8–13 discuss what are technically called "semblances of virtue" (cf. 4B6 and 7B11). Yin Tun commented, "Kongzi preferred those who were 'wild' or 'squeamish.' The wild have great resolutions so that one can enter upon the Way with them. The squeamish have some things that they will not do, and so one can act with them (4B8, 7B31). What he hated about the 'village worthies' that made him wish to avoid them completely was that they seem to be right but are wrong. This deeply misleads people. There is no other technique for avoiding them than what he called 'returning to the standard.'"

38.4 The *Mengzi* closes in sadness over the current state of the world, but also with an implicit challenge to pick up where Kongzi left off (cf. 2B13).

---

[2] Zhao Qi, *Mengzi zhu*, Commentary on 7B37.

FINDING LIST

1A

2.3   Mao no. 242.

2.4   See "The Speech of Tang," from *The Documents of Shang* in the *Documents* (Legge, *The Shoo King*, vol. 3 of *The Chinese Classics*, 175).

7.9   Mao no. 198.

7.12   Mao no. 240.

1B

3.3   Mao no. 272.

3.6   Mao no. 241.

3.7   This is from "The Great Announcement," from *The Documents of Zhou* in the *Documents* (Legge, *The Shoo King*, vol. 3 of *The Chinese Classics*, 286), but Mengzi's quotation differs slightly from the received version of the text.

5.3   Mao no. 192.

5.4   Mao no. 250.

5.5   Mao no. 237.

8.1   On Tang, see "The Announcement of Zhong Hui," from *The Documents of Shang* in the *Documents* (Legge, *The Shoo King*, vol. 3 of *The Chinese Classics*, 177 ff.). On Wu, see "The Great Declaration," from *The Documents of Zhou* in the *Documents* (Legge, *The Shoo King*, vol. 3 of *The Chinese Classics*, 281 ff.).

11.2   This is from "The Announcement of Zhong Hui," from *The Documents of Shang* in the *Documents* (Legge, *The Shoo King*, vol. 3 of *The Chinese Classics*, 180–81), but Mengzi's quotation differs slightly from the received version of the text.

2A

2.18   Cf. *Analects* 11.3.

2.19   Cf. *Analects* 7.34. The comment by Zigong that follows in the *Mengzi* is not in the *Analects* passage. Instead, Gong Xihua comments, "This is precisely what we disciples are unable to learn."

3.2   Mao no. 244.

2B

13.1 *Analects* 14.35 (cf. *Mean* 14.3).

3A

1.5   "The Decree to Yue," part 1, from *The Documents of the Shang* in the *Documents* (Legge, *The Shoo King*, vol. 3 of *The Chinese Classics*, 252).

2.2   See *Analects* 2.5, where this saying is attributed to Kongzi, not Zengzi.

2.4   *Analects* 12.19.

4.11   *Analects* 8.18 and 8.19.

4.15   Mao no. 165.

4.16   Mao no. 300.

5.3a   "Announcement of Kang," from *The Documents of Zhou* in the *Documents* (Legge, *The Shoo King*, vol. 3 of *The Chinese Classics*, 389).

3B

1.4   Mao no. 179.

4.3   *Analects* 1.6.

5.2   "The Announcement of Zhong Hui," from *The Documents of Shang* in the *Documents* (Legge, *The Shoo King*, vol. 3 of *The Chinese Classics*, 180).

5.5   Cf. "Completion of the War," from *The Documents of Zhou* in the *Documents* (Legge, *The Shoo King*, vol. 3 of *The Chinese Classics*, 313–14).

5.6   "The Great Announcement," part 2, from *The Documents of Zhou* in the *Documents* (Legge, *The Shoo King*, vol. 3 of *The Chinese Classics*, 293).

9.3   "The Plan of Great Yu," from *The Documents of Tang* in the *Documents* (Legge, *The Shoo King*, vol. 3 of *The Chinese Classics*, 60).

9.6   "Jun Ya," from *The Documents of Zhou* in the *Documents* (Legge, *The Shoo King*, vol. 3 of *The Chinese Classics*, 581).

9.12   Mao no. 300.

4A

1.4   Mao no. 249.

1.10   Mao no. 254.

4.3   Mao no. 235.

7.5   Mao no. 235.

7.6   Mao no. 257.

9.6   Mao no. 257.

14.1   *Analects* 11.17.

4B

29.2   *Analects* 6.11.

5A

1.1   "Counsels of the Great Yu," from *The Documents of Tang* in the *Documents* (Legge, *The Shoo King*, vol. 3 of *The Chinese Classics*, 66).

2.1   Mao no. 101.

3.2   "The Canon of Shun," from *The Documents of Tang* in the *Documents* (Legge, *The Shoo King*, vol. 3 of *The Chinese Classics*, 39–40).

4.1   "The Canon of Shun," from *The Documents of Tang* in the *Documents* (Legge, *The Shoo King*, vol. 3 of *The Chinese Classics*, 40–41).

4.2   Mao no. 205; Mao no. 258.

4.3   Mao no. 243.

4.4   This passage is not in the received *Documents*.

5.8   "The Great Announcement," from *The Documents of Zhou* in the *Documents* (Legge, *The Shoo King*, vol. 3 of *The Chinese Classics*, 292).

7.9   "The Admonitions of Yin," from *The Documents of Shang* in the *Documents* (Legge, *The Shoo King*, vol. 3 of *The Chinese Classics*, 194).

5B

4.4   "The Announcement of Kang," from *The Documents of Zhou* in the *Documents* (Legge, *The Shoo King*, vol. 3 of *The Chinese Classics*, 392).

7.8   Mao no. 203.

7.9   *Analects* 10.20.

6A

6.8   Mao no. 260.

17.3   Mao no. 247.

7B

3.3   "Completion of the War," from *The Documents of Zhou* in the *Documents* (Legge, *The Shoo King*, vol. 3 of *The Chinese Classics*, 315).

4.3   "The Announcement of Kang," from *The Documents of Zhou* in the *Documents* (Legge, *The Shoo King*, vol. 3 of *The Chinese Classics*, 392).

4.5   Contrast "The Great Declaration," from *The Documents of Zhou* in the *Documents* (Legge, *The Shoo King*, vol. 3 of *The Chinese Classics*, 293).

19.3   Mao nos. 26 and 237.

37.1   *Analects* 5.22.

37.2   *Analects* 13.21.

37.8   *Analects* 17.13.

37.12 *Analects* 17.18.

ENGLISH-CHINESE GLOSSARY

ENGLISH	PINYIN	CHARACTER	USAGE
benevolence	*rén*	仁	The virtue that consists in having, and acting on, compassion for others; for Confucians it should extend to everyone but be strongest for close family members (1A7.4–12, 2A3, 2A6 2A7, 3A3, 4A1, 4A4, 4A9, 4A10, 4A27, 4B19, 4B28, 5A3, 6A4, 6A6, 6A8, 6A11, 7A4, 7A14–15, 7A33, 7A45, 7B1, 7B3, 7B16, 7B24, 7B31, etc.). Cf. "humaneness."
Central States	*Zhōng Guó*	中國	The civilized states at the center of the world, as opposed to the barbarian states that surround them (3A4.12, etc.). (This later came to refer to one unified state, the "Middle Kingdom," i.e., China.)
discretion	*quán*	權	Literally meaning to weigh on a balance scale, this refers to the use of judgment to identify exceptions to general rules (4A17, 7A26).
examine	*fǎn*	反	Literally meaning to turn back, this is also used to refer to the act of evaluating oneself or being introspective (see especially 4A4, 4B28; also 1A7.9, 2A2.7).

ENGLISH	PINYIN	CHARACTER	USAGE
extend	*jí, tuī, dá*	及，推，達	To come to recognize and feel appropriately about cases that are relevantly similar to those in which one already has appropriate ethical reactions (1A7.12, 7A15, 7B1, 7B31). Mengzi acknowledges that it is possible to go too far in this process (2A9.1). Cf. "fill out."
fate	*mìng*	命	What "Heaven" decrees will happen in the course of history (5A6.2, 7A2, 7A3, 7B24, etc.). Cf. "Mandate."
feeling	*xīn*	心	Literally meaning "heart," this comes to refer (by synecdoche) to emotions, desires, or attitudes of the "heart." (2A6 illustrates how the senses of "heart" and "feeling" are related.)
fill out	*kuò, chōng*	擴，充	To come to recognize and feel appropriately about cases that are relevantly similar to those in which one already has appropriate ethical reactions (2A6.7, 7B31). Mengzi acknowledges that it is possible to go too far in this process (3B10.6, 5B4.5). Cf. "extend."
gentleman	*jūnzǐ*	君子	Literally "son of a ruler," this was originally a term identifying a social class, but for Confucians it came to refer particularly to a virtuous person, regardless of social class (2B9.4, 3A2.4, 4B14, 4B28, etc.). Cf. "great person" and "noble."

ENGLISH	PINYIN	CHARACTER	USAGE
genuine	*liáng*	良	What is authentic, innate, or ingenuous, as opposed to fake, acquired, or artificial (4A15, 6A8, 6A17, 7A15). (This word can also mean "good"; many translators and commentators think it consistently has this sense for Mengzi.)
Genuine	*Chéng*	誠	The condition of fully realizing one's ethical potential (4A12, 7A4).
great person, great people	*dà rén*	大人	Originally a term referring to those of higher social class, this came to refer to those with virtue, regardless of class (see especially 6A15; also 3A4.6, 4B6, 4B11, 4B12, 7A33). Compare "gentleman" and "noble." Contrast "petty person."
heart	*xīn*	心	Literally referring to the physical organ, this also refers to the faculty of thought and emotion, which has "feelings" (like compassion or disdain) and "reflects." (Hence, some translators render it "mind" or "heart-mind.") (1A7.9, 2A2.1–17, 2A6, 3A4.6, 6A6, 6A7, 6A8, 6A15, 7A1, 7B31, etc.). Cf. "feeling."
Heaven	*Tiān*	天	A semipersonal higher power, responsible for "the Way" and "fate" (1B3, 1B16.3, 2B13, 4A7.1, 5A4.1, 5A5, 5A6.2, 6A7.1, 6A16, 7A1, 7B24, etc.). Cf. "Mandate of Heaven," "Son of Heaven," and "world."

ENGLISH	PINYIN	CHARACTER	USAGE
Hegemon	*Bà*	霸	A ruler who dominates the other states through military power and skillful strategy (see especially 2A3; also 3B1.1, 7A30, etc.). Contrast "King."
human roles	*rén lún*	人倫	The roles that relate humans to one another, especially father and son, ruler and minister, elder and younger, husband and wife, friend and friend (see 3A4.8 and also 4B19).
humaneness	*rén*	仁	For Kongzi, this refers to the summation of human virtue. (Arthur Waley and Edward Slingerland render it "Goodness" in their translations of the *Analects*.) For Mengzi, the term normally means "benevolence," but it sometimes has overtones of this broader meaning (e.g., 7B16).
inherent (traits)	*qíng*	情	What something is like in itself, as opposed to its reputation or appearance (3A4.18, 6A6.5, 6A8.2).
instruct	*jiào*	教	To ethically educate someone: "To cultivate the Way is what is meant by 'instruction'" (*Mean* 1) (see especially 4A18, 6B16; also 1A3.4, 2B2.9, 3A4.8, 3A4.10).
King	*Wáng*	王	In this translation, when capitalized, it refers to someone who has a legitimate right to the title because he rules through

ENGLISH	PINYIN	CHARACTER	USAGE
			Virtue rather than force (2A3). In lowercase, it refers to someone who has usurped the title.
learn	*xué*	學	The emphasis of this term for Mengzi is on acquiring ethical understanding, not just studying to obtain abstract knowledge (6A11.4, 7A15).
Lord on High	*Shàngdì*	上帝	A higher power, functionally equivalent to "Heaven" for Mengzi (1B3.7, 4A7.5, etc.).
Mandate	*Mìng*	命	The decree of "Heaven" by which someone obtains a legitimate right to be "King" (5A5). Cf. "fate."
Mandate of Heaven	*Tiān mìng*	天命	The decree by which someone obtains a legitimate right to be "King" (4A7.5). Cf. "Heaven."
Master	*-zǐ*	子	A respectful title for someone with disciples. Cf. "sir."
nature	*xìng*	性	For Mengzi, this comprises the traits that something will develop if allowed to mature in a healthy environment (3A1, 4B26, 6A1–8, 6B15, 7A1, 7A30, 7B24, 7B33).
noble	*shì*	士	This is originally a class term, referring to those above the common people who occupy or are eligible for government office. But for Confucians this came to connote someone who is ethically worthy (1A7.20, 7A33, etc.).

ENGLISH	PINYIN	CHARACTER	USAGE
			Cf. "great person" and "gentleman."
order, well-ordered, orderliness	*lǐ*	理	For Mengzi, this refers to any aesthetically and ethically pleasing order, including articulate speech (7B19), musical harmony (5B1.6), or social order (6A7.8). Cf. "Pattern."
Pattern	*Lǐ*	理	For Zhu Xi, this is the underlying structure of the universe, fully present in everything that exists. Every entity is a composite of the Pattern and *qi*. Cf. "order."
petty person, petty people	*xiǎo rén*	小人	Originally a term referring to those of lower social class, this came to refer to those of limited virtue, regardless of class (see especially 6A15; also 3A2.4, 3A4.6). Contrast "great person."
propriety	*lǐ*	禮	The virtue manifested in expressing deference or respect via rituals (2A6, 2A7.3, 4A4, 4A10, 4A27, 4B6, 4B28, 6A6, 7A43, 7B24). Cf. "ritual."
qi	*qì*	氣	For Mengzi, a fluid found in the atmosphere and the human body, connected with the kind and intensity of one's emotions (2A2.8–16, 6A8.2, 7A36). For Zhu Xi, this is the fundamental "stuff" out of which all entities condense: every entity

ENGLISH	PINYIN	CHARACTER	USAGE
			is a composite of *qi* and the "Pattern."
reflect	*sī*	思	To engage in the cognitive and mental process by which one "extends" one's innate ethical reactions (see especially 6A6.7 and its commentary; also 4A1.5, 4A12.2, 4B20.5, 6A15, 6A17). Cf. "examine."
righteousness	*yì*	義	Integrity; the virtue that consists in avoiding what is shameful or dishonorable, even when one could acquire wealth or social prestige by doing so (2A2.14–15, 2A6, 3A4.8, 3B10, 4A27, 4B6, 4B11, 4B19, 5B4, 5B7, 6A1, 6A4–8, 6A10, 7A15, 7A33, 7B24, 7B31, etc.).
ritual	*lǐ*	禮	Activities including funerals, musical performances, traditional dances, and matters of etiquette. They are typically social expressions of one's respect for others (see 2B2, 3A2, 4A17, 4A27, 5A2.1, 5B4, 5B7, 6B1, 6B14, 7A43, 7B33, etc.). Cf. "propriety."
role	*wèi*	位	A social position or function (6A5.4). Contrast "human roles."
sir, you sir	*zǐ*	子	A respectful second-person pronoun. Cf. "Master."

ENGLISH	PINYIN	CHARACTER	USAGE
Son of Heaven	*Tiānzǐ*	天子	A ruler with a "Mandate" from "Heaven" to rule the "world"; a legitimate "King" (3A2.2, 3B9.8, 5A3, 5A4, etc.).
sprout	*duān, méng, miáo*	端，萌，苗	Literally a "germinating plant," this refers to our innate but incipient tendencies toward virtue (2A6, 6A8.1, 6A9.2, 1A6.6, 2A2.16, 7B37.12).
various lords	*zhūhòu*	諸侯	All the nobility (including self-proclaimed "kings," dukes counts, etc.) who rule the . assorted states
Virtue	*Dé*	德	The ethical charisma that makes others want to follow one's leadership without the need for coercion (2A3, 3A2.4, 4A7.1, 5A6, etc.).
Way	*Dào*	道	Concretely, this refers to a path or road; by metaphorical extension, it refers to a way of doing something, especially the right Way to live and to organize society (3A1, 4A7.1, 5B4.6, 7B24, etc.).
will	*zhì*	志	This is simply the "heart" when it is focused on a particular aim or goal. We might think of it as one's intention or resolution. (I use this latter term to translate it in 7B37. See also 2A2.9–10 and 7A33.)
wisdom	*zhì*	智	A virtue that consists of understanding the other virtues, being a good judge of the character of others, and skill at means-end delibera-

ENGLISH	PINYIN	CHARACTER	USAGE
			tion (manifested, for example, in a minister's skillful advice and guidance of his ruler; see especially 5A9 and also 2A6, 2B9, 4A4, 4A27, 4B26, 5A2, 5B1.6–7, 6A6, 6A9).
world	*tiān xià*	天下	Literally, "(all) under Heaven" (1B3.6–8, etc.).
worthy	*xián*	賢	A person virtuous enough to be fit for office (4A7.1, etc.).